BRITISH FEMINISM IN THE TWENTIETH CENTURY

British Feminism in the Twentieth Century

Edited by Harold L. Smith

The University of Massachusetts Press

Amherst

Phototypeset by Input Typesetting Ltd, London

Printed in Great Britain

First published in the United States of America in 1990
by the University of Massachusetts Press
Amherst, Ma

ISBN 0–87023–705–5

Library of Congress Cataloging-in-Publication Data

British feminism in the twentieth century/edited by Harold L. Smith.
    p. cm.
  Includes bibliographical references.
  ISBN 0–87023–705–5.
  1. Feminism—Great Britain—History—20th century.
2. Women—Great Britain—Social conditions. I. Smith, Harold L.
II. Title: British feminism in the 20th century.
HQ1597.B78 1990
305.42′0941′0904—dc20
                                  89–20249
                                       CIP

Contents

Contributors

Deborah Gorham (*'Have we really rounded seraglio point?'*: *Vera Brittain and inter-war feminism*) is Professor of History at Carleton University, Ottawa, Ontario. She is the author of *The Victorian Girl and the Feminine Ideal* (Croom Helm and Indiana University Press, 1982), and is now writing a book about Vera Brittain's life and work, to be published by Basil Blackwell.

Sandra Holton (*In sorrowful wrath?: suffrage militancy and the romantic feminism of Emmeline Pankhurst*) is Chief Policy Analyst at the South Australian College of Advanced Education. Her book *Feminism and Democracy* was published in 1986 by Cambridge University Press. She is currently preparing a further study of the suffrage movement for a more general readership, and a book on her current research interests, with the working title *Doctors and Prostitution*.

Susan Kingsley Kent (*Gender reconstruction after the First World War*) is Assistant Professor of History at the University of Florida. She is the author of *Sex and Suffrage in Britain, 1860–1914* (Princeton University Press, 1987), and is currently writing a book on war, feminism and the construction of gender in Britain between 1914 and 1939.

Jan Lambertz (*Feminists and the politics of wife-beating*) is currently at Rutgers University, New Jersey. Her recent publications include an article in *History Workshop Journal* and a chapter in *Labour and Love* edited by Jane Lewis (Blackwell, 1986). Her current research focuses on citizenship and social policy in postwar Germany.

Hilary Land (*Eleanor Rathbone and the economy of the family*) is Professor of Social Policy at Royal Holloway and Bedford New College, University of London. She co-authored *Change Choice* *and Conflict in Social Policy* (1975) and is currently writing a book about State policies and the family for Macmillan.

Jane Lewis (*Myrdal, Klein,* Women's Two Roles *and postwar feminism 1945–1960*) is a reader in the Department of Social Science and Administration at the London School of Economics. She is the author of *Women in England 1870–1950* (Wheatsheaf, 1984). She is currently writing a book on marriage and marriage guidance in the postwar period and a book on women social investigators and social reformers in the late nineteenth and early twentieth centuries.

Elizabeth Meehan (*British feminism from the 1960s to the 1980s*) lectures in politics at the University of Bath. Her book, *Women's Rights at Work*, was published by Macmillan in 1985. Her current research is on equal pay for work of comparable value or equal value and on social policy and citizenship in the EC.

Martin Pugh (*Domesticity and the decline of feminism, 1930–1950*) is Senior Lecturer in History at the University of Newcastle upon Tyne. He is the author of *The Tories and the People 1880–1935* (1985) and is currently working on 'Women and the Women's Movement *c.*1914–1959'.

Harold L Smith (*Introduction* and *British Feminism in the 1920s*) is Professor of History at the University of Houston-Victoria, Texas. He edited *War and Social Change: British Society in the Second World War* (Manchester University Press, 1986), and contributed a chapter on the war's effect on British women. He is preparing a volume on *Women in Britain Since 1850: A Social History* for Longman's 'Themes in Social History' series.

Pat Thane (*The women of the British Labour Party and feminism, 1906–1945*) is Senior Lecturer in Social History at Goldsmith's College, University of London. She is the author of *The Foundations of the Welfare State* (London, 1982). Her current research interests include a study of women in the Labour Party, 1906–64.

Acknowledgements

I would like to thank the contributors to this volume for their co-operation and timely submission of their chapters. Special thanks are due to David Doughan for his enthusiastic assistance during my numerous visits to the Fawcett Library. I would like to express my appreciation to Kathy Wilkinson for reading a draft of my chapter, to Karen Locher and Shirley Parkan for their special efforts on my behalf over the years, and to the members of the UHV Women's Studies Group for their encouragement and stimulating discussions. But the person to whom I am most indebted is my most demanding critic: Judith N. McArthur of the University of Texas.

Jan Lambertz would like to thank Anna Clark, Paul Clemens, Victoria de Grazia, John Gillis, Ellen Ross, Harold Smith and women's history seminars at the Technische Universität Berlin and Rutgers University for comments on earlier versions of her chapter and especially to thank Polly Beals, Judy Walkowitz and the Liverpool Women's History Group for their insights and support.

Elizabeth Meehan would like to thank: Harold Smith for his helpful editing; the Association of University Teachers, the British Federation of University Women, the Equal Opportunities Commission, the Equal Pay and Opportunities Campaign, the European Commission, the European Court of Justice, the European Parliament, the Fawcett Society, the *Guardian* (editors of and contributors to the women's page), the National Council for Civil Liberties, the Political Studies Association Women and Politics Group for access to papers and/or regular information; and the European Commission, the Nuffield Foundation, and the former Social Science Research Council for financial assistance.

Deborah Gorham dedicates her chapter to her friends, Margaret and James Hepburn, with love and thanks. She also gratefully acknowledges the support of the Social Science and Humanities Research Council of Canada.

Susan Kingsley Kent would like to thank Jeffrey Adler, Anne Davidson, Bonnie Smith and Bertram Wyatt-Brown who carefully read various drafts of her chapter and whose criticisms and comments helped her to present her ideas more coherently and persuasively; she also offers profound thanks for her continued generosity to Joan W. Scott who offered invaluable advice and whose suggestions refined and strengthened her interpretation significantly.

1 Introduction
Harold L. Smith

Feminism is both an ideology and a reform movement seeking to
improve the status of women.[1] Feminists share a belief that women
have been, and continue to be, oppressed because of their sex.
But the common use of the singular, 'feminism', obscures one of
its distinctive features: the divergence among feminists as to what
feminist ideology and goals should be. This is so significant that
some feminists use the plural, 'feminisms';[2] others view the history
of feminism as the development of distinct strands which were
only loosely related.[3]

The granting of partial suffrage in 1918 was an important turning-point in revealing the extent of the diversity within feminism.[4]
Prior to then the focus on the vote encouraged the perception of
feminism as a single movement. But once the principle of suffrage
had been conceded, the divisions among feminists became more
apparent: feminists pursued varying objectives, derived from differing analyses of what was oppressing women. While the debate
between new and equality feminists involved charges that the
latter were indifferent to married and to working-class women,
and that they encouraged women to become more like men, the
underlying issue was whether feminism should be based on sexual
difference or the elimination of gender distinctions. Socialist feminists criticized both groups for being excessively preoccupied with
the needs of bourgeois women, and insisted that the class system
was the underlying source of working-class women's oppression.

This tendency to splinter was accelerated by the women's liberation movement in the late 1960s. Three major divisions emerged:
socialist feminism, radical feminism, and liberal or equal rights
feminism. The issues on which they disagreed included: Are men
the oppressors or are they also victims of a sexist system? Are
marriage and family a source of oppression or a natural avenue
for women's self-expression? Are working-class women primarily
oppressed by their class position or by gender distinctions similar

to those which affect women of higher social status? Finally, should feminists use sexual difference as a foundation for feminist reforms or minimize it in an attempt to create a gender-neutral society?[5]

This book contains chapters written especially for it on major developments in feminist thought and action since 1900. It is intended to be sufficiently broad in scope to provide students with a guide to the history of British feminism during the twentieth century while also contributing to the scholarly debate about it. The contributors do not represent a single school of feminist historiography; in selecting them I have consciously chosen authors who reflect the diversity within feminism.

All too often the history of feminism is written through the eyes of present-day feminists, thereby distorting the nature of feminism in earlier periods. The chapters in Part I are useful correctives to this tendency. Rather than viewing the militancy of the Women's Social and Political Union as a precursor of 1970s radical feminism, Sandra Holton presents it as a product of the romantic understanding of the role of heroic individuals in the historical process. While family violence has become a major issue on the agenda of 1980s feminism, Jan Lambertz explores some of the reasons why early twentieth-century feminists remained aloof from the issue.

In Part II the contributors address the question of what happened to feminism once the principle of women's suffrage had been conceded. My chapter provides an overview of 1920s feminism which revises previous accounts on two important points: that equal rights feminism has been misrepresented by claims that it opposed all forms of protective legislation and that it was indifferent to the needs of wives and mothers; 'and that it is misleading to view 1920s legislation on women as a feminist victory since it strengthened women's traditional roles while reducing pressure for the more drastic measures desired by feminists.[7] Susan Kent views the First World War as a decisive turning-point in the history of feminism in that new sexual and gender discourses generated by the war were responsible for the emergence of a more conservative feminism, based on sexual difference, in the postwar years. Although Vera Brittain's support for reforms associated with new feminism has led some to link her with Eleanor Rathbone's group, Deborah Gorham indicates Brittain provides an important example of how equality feminists were able to support motherhood reforms while rejecting sexual difference feminism. Hilary Land concludes that Eleanor Rathbone advocated family allowances chiefly as a means of providing a degree of economic independence for married mothers. While explaining why Labour women should be considered feminists, Pat Thane shows how they used separate spheres ideology to challenge male power rather than allowing it to restrict women to traditional roles. Finally, Martin Pugh notes that the inter-war economic depression is not a sufficient explanation for the decline of feminism after 1930 since it was new feminism, which emphasized birth control and family allowances rather than employment issues, that declined most rapidly in the 1930s. Pugh suggests that the new feminism was rooted in traditional assumptions about a woman's place which left it unable to resist the inter-war revival of the ideology of domesticity.

The contributors to Part III agree that it is misleading to assume that feminism was moribund from the end of the Second World War until revived by the late 1960s·women's liberation movement. Jane Lewis draws our attention to the publication in the 1950s of an important contribution to the development of feminist theory: *Women's Two Roles*, by Alva Myrdal and Viola Klein. While aware of its limitations, Lewis suggests that its analysis of how women can combine marriage and a career anticipates later radical feminist thinking on the issue. Elizabeth Meehan questions the conventional view that feminism flourished in the 1970s only to collapse in the following decade under right-wing political pressure. Although agreeing that Margaret Thatcher's Conservative governments have adversely affected feminism, she concludes that, aided by European Economic Community policies, feminism continued to be a vigorous movement in the 1980s.

Notes

1. The word 'feminism' was imported from France and apparently appeared in print in Britain for the first time in the 1890s. Nancy Cott provides a thoughtful discussion of the origins of the term in *The Grounding of Modern Feminism* (Yale University Press, New Haven, 1987). Also see Karen Offen, 'Defining feminism: a comparative historical approach', *Signs*, vol. 14 (Autumn 1988), pp. 119–57.
2. Rosalind Delmar, 'What is feminism?', in Juliet Mitchell and Ann Oakley (eds), *What is Feminism?* (Blackwell, Oxford, 1986), pp. 8–33.
3. Olive Banks, *Faces of Feminism* (Blackwell, Oxford, 1981).

4.   Although the divisions among feminists became more overt after 1918, recent studies have drawn attention to the tension between equality and sexual difference feminism in the late nineteenth-century women's movement. See Jane Rendall (ed), *Equal or Different: Women's Politics 1800–1914* (Blackwell, Oxford, 1987) and Philippa Levine, *Victorian Feminism 1850–1900* (Hutchinson, London, 1987).

5.   See April Carter, *The Politics of Women's Rights* (Longman, London, 1988), pp. 166–93 and the introduction by Anne Phillips to *Feminism and Equality* (Blackwell, London, 1987). Although many British feminists in the 1980s found sexual difference feminism appealing, the 1986 Sears case in the USA has drawn attention to the dangers of asserting sexual difference. See Alice Kessler-Harris, 'Equal Employment Opportunity Commission v. Sears, Roebuck and Company: a personal account', *Feminist Review*, vol. 25 (March 1987), pp. 46–69.

6.   This is significant not only because it corrects frequently repeated misconceptions about equality feminism, but also because it suggests equality feminists, especially Vera Brittain, were attempting to go beyond the equality versus difference dichotomy by developing a feminism which incorporated difference into the idea of equality. My understanding of the 1920s debate has benefited from reading Joan Scott, 'Deconstructing equality-versus-difference: or, the uses of post-structuralist theory for feminism', *Feminist Studies*, vol. 14 (Spring 1988), pp. 33–50.

7.   Many feminists, especially since 1970, have become sceptical about the efficacy of legislation as an agency for feminist reform. My point is not to belittle the accomplishments of 1920s feminists, but rather to help explain why this legislation did little to alter women's subordinate position in society.

PART I

FEMINISM IN THE EARLY TWENTIETH CENTURY

2 In Sorrowful Wrath: Suffrage Militancy and the Romantic Feminism of Emmeline Pankhurst

Sandra Stanley Holton

During the first half of 1914 Sylvia Pankhurst was imprisoned nine times. It became her practice to go without not only food, but also water and sleep, in order to secure release. Her mother, Emmeline Pankhurst, was similarly constantly in and out of gaol during 1913 and 1914. She also resorted to the combination hunger, thirst and sleep strike, although the authorities failed in their one attempt forcibly to feed her. In Sylvia's case forcible feeding was regularly undertaken, a process which commonly led to the rupturing of the veins in the eyes.[1] A visitor to the nursing home where she was taken to recover after one of these imprisonments recalled:

> . . . The sight of two great gobs of blood in the thin drawn face moving restlessly from side to side on the pillow is a memory which even the horrors of war – and I saw many in France in 1914–15 – have not had the power to dim. Sylvia suffered much. So did the mother who knelt by her bedside . . . The other's face was as the face of one being crucified.[2]

The question this chapter seeks to examine is why it was that members of the militant wing of the suffrage movement lay themselves open to such suffering in pursuit of votes for women. Why did these suffragists feel it necessary to struggle, and suffer even to the point of torture or self-destruction, in a twentieth-century parliamentary democracy, ruled by a Liberal government, in pursuit of a reform which has, arguably, directly affected women's lives very little? What gave such actions their legitimacy among followers of the Women's Social and Political Union? My concern is not so much with the political, ideological, social, cultural and symbolic significance with which feminists at this time imbued the

7

vote.[3] It is rather with the phenomenon of militancy itself, a phenomenon which cannot be explained adequately, in my view, by reference simply to matters of campaign tactics or organization.[4]

At the most obvious level the formation of the Women's Social and Political Union (WSPU) in 1903, and the introduction of a self-styled 'militant' strategy in 1905, can be seen to indicate simply a new temper, a growing impatience among some feminists with the conventional lobby-group tactics of the 'constitutional' wing and the other major suffrage organization, the National Union of Women Suffrage Societies.[5] This body had been formed somewhat earlier, in 1897, in an amalgamation of the several local societies which had grown up since the late 1860s to work for women's enfranchisement. It continued to pursue the well-established methods of parliamentary lobbying: petitioning, the conventional publicity and educational methods of the public meeting, and the production of pamphlet and periodical literature on the subject, alongside campaigning on non-party lines during parliamentary elections. The militants' impatience was expressed, in contrast, in the assertive harassment of leading members of the Liberal Party which was expected to form the government after the forthcoming general election, street demonstrations and street-corner and factory-gate speaking, and a campaign in close alliance with local socialist organizations in north-west England, prior to the 1906 general election.

These early modes of militancy were gradually extended to attempts to provoke public disorder, to attacks on public buildings and art treasures, to arson, bombing and vandalizing pillar boxes, and to the orchestration of large-scale window-smashing raids in London's West End. In the early stages such activities brought fines which, when left unpaid, led to the frequent imposition on militants of short prison sentences. From 1909, WSPU prisoners resorted to the hunger strike to protest against the government's refusal to grant them political prisoner status. The government retaliated initially with the use of forcible feeding, and subsequently with the introduction of the Cat and Mouse Act in 1913, which allowed the repeated rearrest of prisoners released on licence to recover from the hunger strike.

The emergence of a new, impatient temper among feminists would seem, by itself, to offer a quite inadequate explanation for the subsequent developments within the suffrage movement, involving as they did such extreme methods and a readiness to endure such terrible consequences. Writers in this field have continued to bring forward a range of alternative, or additional, explanations for the phenomenon of suffragist militancy. The more sceptical accounts of the militant campaign for votes for women have tended to rest upon suggestions of individual psychological imbalance, or a more generalized pathology within British society and political processes at this time.[6] From this latter viewpoint, militant suffragism was but a symptom of some deeper widespread malaise, with WSPU activists rendered thereby the unconscious transmitters of forces outside themselves.

Among more sympathetic accounts of the WSPU there is to be found an assumption, often implicit, that militancy derived from, and gave expression to, a more radical feminism. Militants are granted a keener perception, a more developed consciousness, of the nature of women's social, political and cultural subordination.[7] In fact, it is difficult to identify much that is specific to the ideology or the intellectual and political heritage of militants, as opposed to constitutionalists. Aside, perhaps, from the growing anti-male stance evident among some of the WSPU leaders from 1912, the ideology of the two wings of the suffrage movement, and the political traditions on which this drew, was largely a shared one. The analysis of, and resisance to, the subordination of women evident in the writings of many constitutional suffragists was at least as sophisticated and committed as that produced by militants.[8] This ideological explanation of militancy, then, proves no more satisfying than the temperamental and pathological explanations first discussed.

More recently, historians have begun to focus on the act of militancy itself, in order to account for the content and the course of WSPU campaigning. In his essay 'The Act of Militancy', Brian Harrison explains the extremity to which militants were brought in terms of the internal logic of the militant act itself, and the nature of organizations committed to promoting such acts.[9] WSPU supporters were, by his account, doomed to engage in ever more dangerous activity once the first challenge to the established order had been offered. The social ostracism and the need for secrecy which increasingly attached to acts of militancy served only further to lock the militant into an automatic progression towards greater and greater risk-taking, and a growing emotional and psychological dependence upon the relatively small cadre of the most committed activists at the centre of an increasingly clandestine operation, among whom intense loyalty was both expected and engendered.

In this analysis we find a convincing account of militancy as a process, moving the individual to ever greater commitment, and readiness to resort to extreme measures. It is a view of militancy which was frequently put forward by the constitutionalists at the time to justify their opposition to WSPU tactics. It is an account of militancy which the WSPU leaders themselves would not have disputed, and of which they would have claimed a full appreciation.[10] They constantly asserted they knew full well that there could be no going back, and that the demands which WSPU policies made of individual militants could only intensify, even to the point of self-destruction.

What is left unexplained by such an account, however, is the initial step upon the path of militancy itself. Whatever the external forces acting upon these women, the commitment to this path was undoubtedly experienced as one of deliberate and conscious choice, and a choice of great moment in an individual life.[11] In committing herself to this path, I want to argue, the militant was more than a victim of her own temper or psychology, more than a vehicle for forces beyond herself, or for processes in which she had become locked. Nor was the militant simply confirming her commitment to the cause of votes for women by expressing her adherence to a particular ideology, or support for a specific set of political tactics. I want to suggest, rather, that the act of militancy must be understood primarily in terms of a cast of mind, a moral philosophy, a way of looking at the world, especially in terms of an understanding of history and the processes of social and political change which had preceded the early twentieth century.

A principal focus for the following discussion will be the world view of Emmeline Pankhurst, mother of Sylvia and Christabel, founder of the WSPU, and perhaps the foremost practitioner of, and apologist for, suffrage militancy.[12] She was renowned in her day for her eloquence in public speaking, for her ability to communicate the authenticity of her convictions. While many thought her wrong-headed, few doubted the sincerity of her actions. Her autobiographical account of the suffrage campaign, published in

1914, expresses with great clarity and open-heartedness the quin-
tessential world view of the militant. It stands as perhaps the most
moving apologia for militancy produced during the campaign,
and reveals a consistency and integrity of outlook which deserve
recognition however distasteful or mistaken the reader finally
adjudges this viewpoint. Three major aspects of Mrs Pankhurst's
cast of mind will be explored here: the historical legacy to which
she often referred, her understanding of social and political
change, and her moral philosophy. These questions will be
reviewed both in regard to the account which she and others close
to her gave of her personal biography, and in regard to the social,
historical and cultural forces with, or against which, she saw herself to be working.

The picture emerging from such an approach is one which
provides the basis for a clear distinction between the outlook of
Mrs Pankhurst, the militant suffragist, and that of her counterpart
in the constitutional wing of the movement, Millicent Garrett
Fawcett.[13] That distinction in outlook is one which, I would argue,
might best be understood in terms of the tensions within modern
European thought between the 'classical' and the 'romantic' world
view.[14] If Mrs Fawcett's pole star was social order, the rule of
law, the exercise of reason, and evolutionary progress within
human affairs through representative parliamentary government,
Mrs Pankhurst's was revolution, social rupture, and the dependence of social regeneration on the exertions of noble individuals
exerting their will upon the world. Perhaps the key issue for
understanding Mrs Pankhurst's world view is the moral imperative
she believed lay upon each individual to be true to herself and
her understanding of human affairs, the dependence of individual
authenticity on a passionate, not merely reasoned, engagement
with society. Only through acting on her instincts and convictions
might the individual achieve both self-realization and service to
humankind. Mrs Pankhurst was a thorough romantic in the weight
she attached to her own being and action, in the high serious-
ness with which she approached the business of living, the inten-
sity with which she responded to events. The grand qualities
within individuals were, for her, those forged in the fire of a great
struggle, ones to be delved out and fostered in each individual.
Through the development of such qualities in *Sturm und Drang*
an individual might change the world, and changing the world

was the highest calling to which an individual might aspire. Mrs Pankhurst's eldest daughter, Christabel, recalled: 'Her ardent nature moved her to desire to do some great thing.'[15] Mrs Pankhurst herself anticipated that future generations of women 'may sometimes wish that they could have lived in the heroic days of stress and struggle and have shared with us the joy of battle, the exultation that comes of sacrifice of self for a great object'.[16]

Mrs Pankhurst did not, of course, discuss her own personal strengths in her autobiographical account of the campaigns, but the qualities which she admired in others provide an indication of those she would have sought to develop in herself, and were indeed the qualities in her remarked upon by others: courage, ardour, vitality. An old family friend, the American suffragist Harriot Stanton Blatch, recalled this picture of her mother for Christabel: 'Your mother was a living flame. As active as a bit of quick silver, as glistening, as enticing . . . she looked like the model of Burne-Jones' pictures – slender, willowy, with the exquisite features of one of the saints of the great impressionists.'[17]

For the militant the value of the campaign derived above all from 'the strenuousness and the desperation of the conflict'.[18] 'Deeds, not words' was a key motto for her, for deeds were 'incontrovertible and immortal', and such testimony would live on 'woven into the fabric of human civilisation'.[19] A fiery and single-minded commitment to the cause was looked for from WSPU members, not simply to wage the suffrage battle, but also to help each realize her potential for individual growth and grandeur.[20] The degree to which militancy helped or hindered the cause of votes for women is a complex and highly contested question. In many ways, however, the question itself misses the point of militancy as it was conceived by Mrs Pankhurst. The struggle was itself at least as important as the ultimate goal in terms of the opportunity it provided each participant for self-realization, for exerting her will, and for securing the regeneration of society.

In leading her 'Women's Revolution' Mrs Pankhurst believed that she was giving expression to the basic human drive to freedom, an instinct which was a prime motor in human history. She saw human progress as having advanced through the tumultuous acts of the oppressed, and identified herself and the WSPU with past revolutionaries and resistance movements. She often rejoiced, for example, that her birthday was also Bastille Day. She counted among her own forebears a grandfather who had narrowly escaped being ridden down at Peterloo. Sylvia Pankhurst later said of her mother: 'Her young mind was early disposed to rebellion and reform by the stories of her paternal grandfather.' Mrs Pankhurst's closest girlhood friend was Noémie de Rochefort, daughter of the republican and *communard*, the Marquis de Rochefort. She herself recalled that this friendship had 'strengthened all the liberal ideas I had previously acquired'.[21]

Among the most influential books Mrs Pankhurst remembered from her childhood were Harriet Beecher Stowe's *Uncle Tom's Cabin* and Carlyle's *The French Revolution*. Of the first she recalled:

> [It] awakened in me the two sets of sensations to which all my life I have most readily responded: first, admiration for that spirit of fighting and heroic sacrifice by which alone the soul of civilisation is saved; and next after that, appreciation of the gentler spirit which is moved to mend and repair the ravages of war.[22]

But of greatest importance for her romantic outlook was Carlyle's work. She insisted it 'had influenced her whole life'.[23] Rebecca West has suggested that Mrs Pankhurst was 'the last popular leader to act on inspiration derived from the principles of the French Revolution'.[24] But it is important also to realize that the militant leader's appreciation of this event drew on Carlyle's powerful interpretation and, in consequence, drew also upon a particular view of how history is made, how social change is wrought.[25] Carlyle saw history neither in terms of cycles nor of organic growth, but rather as a quite unpredictable process, the outcome of which was necessarily always vague and uncertain. There was no destination point or ultimate purpose in human history. History was, rather, a sequence of disruptive actions creating new worlds. Carlyle likened society to the phoenix, continually dying and being reborn in its own ashes, and he defended the 'torching of rotten structures' as a precondition for the building of new foundations. He was the first apologist among historians for the Terror, arguing it to have been at the heart of the French Revolution, and to have borne the hopes of future ages.

Carlyle insisted on the beauty of chaos and conflagration, the importance of the irrational and instinctual in creative human action. He saw humanity itself as a destructive power which was containable only through a collective act of will. The prime duty of the governing classes was to maintain 'the will to order within society'. He was entirely sceptical about government, whose authority might be maintained only through the legitimacy and validity derived from the proper attention to this duty. Once governments denied the existential and material needs of their subjects they were ripe for overthrow.[26]

Individuals, for their part, were confronted with the choice of ensuring a better world in the future, or of allowing society to degenerate into chaos. Carlyle justified, even glorified, revolt when it was occasioned by what one subsequent commentator on his work has termed 'metaphysical provocation'. His conception both of society and of the individual was based on freedom of will. This was why the outcome of history must always be doubtful, unknowable. In subsequent works Carlyle was to stress the importance of the leadership of charismatic individuals in the achievement of society's wish for order. He believed that the full promise of the French Revolution remained yet to be realized, and the issues which it raised yet to be resolved.

In relation to the history of her own country, Mrs Pankhurst saw the militant campaign as continuing a long tradition of popular protest, and struggles for liberty in which she took pride. Hence the WSPU repeatedly appealed, for example, to what it believed to be the established rights of the people to petition the government and the king.[27] The natural enemy of the people was a government which did not maintain its own legitimacy. The Liberal cabinet was portrayed as exhibiting to the full any government's potential for repression and terrorism: 'governments have always tried to crush reform movements, to destroy ideas, to kill the thing that cannot die. Without regard to history, which shows that no government have [sic] ever succeeded in doing this, they go on trying in the old senseless way.'[28]

The militant strategy accepted the analysis of the then Home Secretary, Herbert Gladstone, that it is *force majeure* which activates and arms a Government for effective work'. The WSPU initially took up his challenge that 'power belongs to the masses', by organizing in 1908 one of the largest demonstrations ever seen in Hyde Park.[29] When the government ignored this display of support, the militants' viewpoint was that public opinion had been 'wilfully stifled'.[30] It was only after this reverse that militants turned to stone-throwing, and that violence increasingly character-ized their demonstrations. By 1913 the militant leaders were being arrested on the charge of conspiracy. They argued, however, that any incitement and conspiracy had been on the part of the government, not themselves. Mrs Pankhurst declared every mili-tant act was taken only after some act of repression by govern-ment: 'It is the Government that is our enemy; it is not the MPs, it is not the men in the country; it is the Government in power alone that can give us the vote.'[31]

At her trial for conspiracy Mrs Pankhurst argued: 'Women of intelligence, women of training, women of upright life, have for many years ceased to respect the laws of this country', together with the administration of those laws. Militants acted from the conviction 'that this is the only way in which we can win power to alter what for us are intolerable conditions, absolutely intolerable conditions'.[32] In the militant view disruption of, and resistance to, the government were both a duty and a political necessity. When found guilty at the end of her trial Mrs Pankhurst declared:

> I have no sense of guilt. I feel I have done my duty. I look upon myself as a prisoner of war. I am under no moral obligation to conform to or in any way accept the sentence imposed on me . . . I deliberately broke the law, not hysterically or emotionally, but of set, serious, purpose, because I honestly feel it is the only way.[33]

Her supporters left the court singing the 'Marseillaise'.

The Irish militant, Hanna Sheehy Skeffington, gave voice to a similar view when she supported attacks on pillar boxes. She agreed with those who said such actions suggested:

> Anarchy and the final dissolution of all society . . . It matters little what name it be called . . . Anarchy, Revolution, Upheaval. It is for the public and the Government to recognise that this is not a riot, but a revolution, and that if society attempts to stand much longer in the way, society as at present constituted must go . . . desperate diseases need desperate measures.[34]

Mrs Pankhurst's favourite heroine was Joan of Arc, a figure both she and her followers identified with closely, placing special emphasis on the resoluteness Joan of Arc had demonstrated during her short life. Christabel Pankhurst declared: 'her spiritual descendants, the suffragists, would no more be negotiated into surrender and compromise than would she!' A performance of Raymond Rôze's *Jeanne D'Arc* at Covent Garden was seen as a particularly apposite occasion for a militant demonstration. Three members of the WSPU barricaded themselves into a box with a megaphone, 'calling attention to the impressive scenes on the stage' while declaring that militants were similarly fighting for human liberty only to be 'tortured and done to death, in the name of the King, in the name of the Church, and with the full knowledge and responsibility of the established Government'.[35]

The militant, in being true to her own desire for freedom, was undertaking at the same time, then, the regeneration of a failing society. If a government did not respond to such promptings then social disruption must follow. Sincerity and authenticity, rather than any pragmatic political reckoning, were the only proper measure of militant action. There is an apparent paradox between such emphasis on individual authenticity and the autocratic nature of the WSPU leadership, the quite undemocratic basis of the organization itself. Yet Mrs Pankhurst insisted that the paradox was only apparent. Voluntarism was at the heart of the relationship between the WSPU leaders and the rank and file, and independent initiative was a quality looked for among its followers. No one was ever compelled to participate in militant acts, and, as the modes of militancy became ever more extreme, Mrs Pankhurst was to tell a WSPU audience: 'Be militant each in your own way.'[36]

Brian Harrison has argued that such freedom of choice was, in fact, somewhat illusory and that commitment to the WSPU clearly entailed for many a significant loss of personal autonomy.[37] Self-sacrifice for the cause was, of course, fundamental to the logic of militant campaigning. Christabel Pankhurst exclaimed: 'to lose the personal in a great impersonal is to live!'[38] What mattered for Mrs Pankhurst, however, was that in so doing an individual militant retain her moral integrity and gain the opportunity for a greater knowledge of herself and her own strength. The worst affront which the authorities offered to militant sensibilities was the assault they undertook on the militant's autonomy and her freedom of expression. As Christabel Pankhurst recalled, it was not the physical unpleasantness of prison life, great though this was, which most struck the suffrage prisoner, but the fact of imprisonment itself.[39] The hunger strike became important, not simply as a means of returning to action, but as an assertion of the individual will against the power of the authorities. For the militant Mary Richardson, the worst aspect of forcible feeding was not the pain and brutality involved, but the 'moral humiliation'. When the Bishop of London had suggested that forcible feeding was painful only because suffragists attempted to resist the procedure, Mary Richardson replied: 'To remain passive under it would give one the feeling of sin; the sin of concurrence. One's whole nature is revolted: resistance is therefore inevitable.'[40]

The dual emphasis on individual authenticity alongside unflinching loyalty and committed service to the cause resulted in a further paradox, the tendency to 'type-cast' members. In this way – by being given a role as, for example, an eloquent speaker, a fine strategist, a good manager, and so on – the strengths of an individual could appear to be receiving recognition while the interests of the organization were also being met. Yet despite the autocratic form of WSPU governance, individual members could effectively initiate new directions in militant tactics – window-breaking, hunger-striking, letter-burning and arson were all initiated by the rank and file, and were acknowledged by the leadership as authentic responses to government repression. Where there was disagreement among militants, it was seen as inevitable that each faction go its separate way. Compromise and consensus were simply not compatible with authenticity. The sincerity of dissidents was never questioned by the WSPU leadership, but their dissidence was seen to require a parting of the ways, in order that each viewpoint might be pursued single-mindedly.[41]

By such standards the dealings of politicians, especially those of the Liberal government, could appear only as duplicitous, hypocritical, and cynical. The WSPU leadership never acknowledged the practical difficulties which would have to have been overcome to secure passage of an equal votes for women measure in this period: the scale of the reform programme the government had set itself, the battle with the House of Lords to which this gave rise, the pressing problems of industrial unrest and home rule in Ireland, alongside genuine disagreements within the Liberal Party on the issue, especially in terms of resistance to a measure which would, arguably, given the property basis of the existing franchise, have increased the representation of the more conservative sections of society.[42]

Instead, both as a counterpoint to their own standards of integrity, and as an apologia for the disruptions and inconvenience occasioned to the public by militant activity, the WSPU leadership constantly argued the lack of principle and the moral and political bankruptcy of their parliamentary opponents, especially those in the Liberal Party. How could a truly liberal government deny a fundamentally liberal demand; attempt to suppress the time-honoured right to question politicians at election meetings, and to speak publicly at Hyde Park; use mounted police against peaceable demonstrators; refuse the right to petition the king and prime minister; inflict forcible feeding upon hunger-striking prisoners while calling it 'medical treatment'; cynically single out working-class demonstrators for arrest while sparing influential and well-connected prisoners from forcible feeding; attack basic civil rights in the passage of the Cat and Mouse Act; censor a supposedly free press?

In their numerous court appearances, the WSPU leadership constantly argued that the government, not they, was responsible for the social disorder occasioned by militant acts.[43] In refusing a just demand the Liberal government provoked rightful resistance, while its party organizers and their leading spokesmen themselves engaged in or promoted violence against suffragists, and incited the suffragists themselves to ever greater violence by their references to past riots for parliamentary reform. To attempt to play the political game in such circumstances was, in the militant view, to offer an endorsement of that game and its rules and thus to deny the values on which militancy was based. It was impossible to compromise with such men without oneself being compromised, and almost certainly duped. In the militant view, then, the only way to succeed was through the assertion of the rightful will of those superior spirits engaged in the militant campaign for votes for women.[44]

The final years of the suffrage campaign appeared in the eyes of Mrs Pankhurst and her followers to offer repeated proof of the correctness of such an assessment of male politicians and all their works. As a result, the maintenance of the complete integrity of the WSPU and the militant position became a priority over securing the vote itself. In the summer of 1914 Sylvia Pankhurst (who by this time had been expelled from the WSPU) and the Labour politician George Lansbury secured a promise from Lloyd George to refuse to join the next Liberal government unless comprehensive franchise reform, including women's suffrage, were undertaken. Lloyd George's price was a cessation of militancy, particularly in the form of the clandestine destruction of property, by this time a central mode of WSPU campaigning. Christabel Pankhurst refused to embark on any negotiations with the government, or even to meet her sister to discuss the possibility. If the WSPU campaign had become a holy war, Lloyd George was now cast in the role of the devil incarnate. An honourable agreement between the two sides simply was not possible. The complete vanquishing of such an enemy could be the only acceptable outcome for the militant leadership.

If such severe moral probity was at the heart of the WSPU rejection of a very real opportunity to secure its supposed prime goal, it also served to limit the effectiveness of militancy as a political strategy. Militancy had begun as civil disobedience, and then proceeded by passive or token resistance during imprisonment. The authorities had shown no scruples about using the full force of the state's power to parry such pinpricks. But the moral stance of the militant made it impossible for her, in most cases at least, to reply in kind. The WSPU leadership slowly and sadly came to realize that the government of men was not to be moved by the suffering of women, indeed that it sometimes seemed to relish the power it had legally to inflict torture and suffering on women prisoners. Nonetheless, militants refused to be provoked into using physical violence against the persons of their opponents, other than purely token acts, or to wage an all-out campaign of terror within the community. Though Mrs Pankhurst might talk of women's revolution, and of the guerilla warfare in which her followers were engaged, in both instances her usage confused metaphor with actuality. The WSPU never offered any serious threat to human life (except that of its own followers) or to social order. Brian Harrison has suggested that such a stance was especially precarious, and that if war had not intervened, it is at least possible that an individual militant would at last, on her own initiative, have attempted the assassination of a leading opponent.[45] Certainly there were continual rumours of plans for such an act.

Militancy only ever entailed, in fact, a severely limited threat to the social order. The restrictions placed by militant suffragists on their own revolution reflected, as well as a moral stance, an analysis of the ills of society against which they were acting. This was an analysis which required the rejection of the male-dominated social order and masculine modes of political activity. Their opponents, the anti-suffragists, argued the need for physical force in the maintenance of social order and the government of empire. They opposed votes for women both as threatening to undermine the necessary power of the state by introducing the feminine element in politics, and 'unsexing' women by involving them in what they believed, by its very nature, must be men's work.[46] Underlying the constitutional suffragists' position can be seen a similar association between the male and the operation of physical force in human affairs. For the constitutionalists the destructive power of men was very real, and one of the chief errors of militancy from such a viewpoint was the occasion it provided for the unleashing of such forces within society, the legitimacy it appeared to offer for the expression of male brutality during demonstrations and through the justice system. Constitutionalists sought the women's vote in large part to strengthen the operation of reason, stability and order in human affairs, against that of physical force.

The militant standpoint, in contrast, reflected an appeal to an essentially chivalrous conception of male–female relations. Though Mrs Pankhurst spoke often of the wrongs of women and children at the hands of men, she also continued to rely on men's capacity to rise above their lower natures when confronted with the 'sorrowful wrath' of women.[47] Mrs Pankhurst's autobiography contains frequent references to the courtesies shown her by a variety of male oppressors: judges, prison authorities, American immigration officials charged with investigating her supposed moral obloquy. On more than one occasion of great personal danger or stress, Mrs Pankhurst appealed to the manhood of those within call. In remembering a visit to one of the western states in America where women had already won the right to vote, she asserted that she 'never had seen greater respect, courtesy, and chivalry shown to women than in that one suffrage state it has been my privilege to visit'.[48]

If the militant appeal to male chivalry was to be effective, it demanded that Mrs Pankhurst and her followers themselves demonstrate their own conformity to an idealized notion of womanhood. The nicest standards of feminine dress were set by the leaders themselves, and the militant always attempted to behave like a lady, even when forced to assault a policeman to ensure a quick arrest and rescue from the crowd. Above all, as we have seen, it was essential that suffrage violence be presented in terms of moral force rather than any attempt to take on aggressive roles, or the resort to physical force, upon which male supremacy was argued to rest. Hence, the frequent emphasis on merely symbolic violence within militant acts – policemen were lightly tapped on the cheek, charred paper was fed into pillar boxes. The brute strength of male authority was to be defeated by the ingenuity of women, not by meeting like with like.[49] Hence, Mrs Pankhurst's explanation of why militant violence was restrained in the ways it was concerned the reverence among women for the sanctity of human life, for 'we know what life costs'. Mrs Pankhurst always insisted that her militants were never 'reckless with human life . . . we leave that to the enemy. We leave that to the men in their warfare. It is not the method of women.'[50]

The blackguardly character of the Liberal government could only be confirmed by its failure to respond to what was, at its heart, an appeal to male chivalry. What was worse, the government further dramatized its despicable want of feeling and honour by saving its most brutal and repressive acts for female rebels alone. Syndicalist strike leaders and Ulstermen were left free or given comparatively negligible punishments for incitement to mutiny and threats of real riot and disorder. Mrs Pankhurst asked the reader of her autobiography:

> Why is it that men's blood-shedding militancy is applauded and women's symbolic militancy punished with a prison cell and the forcible feeding horror! It means simply this, that men's double standards of sex morals . . . really apply to morals in all departments of life. Men make the moral code and they expect women to accept it.[51]

Militancy represented essentially a moral critique of male-ordered society. It sought to advance that society by appealing to the best that was in men, mistakenly and tragically believing that this was to be brought about by the dramatization of female oppression and distress through militant confrontation with the brute power of that male order. It was the wit, the fervour, the integrity, the sincerity of individual heroic women asserting their authentic will against a morally corrupt and politically bankrupt government which would bring about a new order, and the next main advance in human affairs, an honourable and just relationship between the two sexes. According to such a viewpoint the progress of civilization occurred not in a steady stream but in moments of fire and tempest, not in the pursuit of reason but in the assertion of spiritual grandeur, not through the workings of established social institutions but by the actions of heroic individuals. This is where militancy differed fundamentally from constitutionalism. This is why, by the end, the vote had become of secondary importance to the engagement in struggle itself.

Notes

1. E. Sylvia Pankhurst, *The Suffragette Movement. An Intimate Account of Persons and Ideals* (Virago, London, 1977 reprint), pp. 441, 473–7; Patricia W. Romero, *E. Sylvia Pankhurst. Portrait of a Radical* (Yale University Press, New Haven and London, 1987), p. 80; Emmeline Pankhurst, *My Own Story* (Source Book Press, New York, 1970 reprint), pp. 329–31.
2. Geraldine Lennox, quoted in Romero, *idem*, pp. 79–80.
3. For discussion of these questions see Les Garner, *Stepping Stones to Women's Liberty: Feminist Ideas in the Women's Suffrage Movement 1900–1918* (Hutchinson, London, 1984); Sandra Stanley Holton, *Feminism and Democracy. Women's Suffrage and Reform Politics in Britain 1900–1918* (Cambridge University Press, Cambridge, 1986), especially chaps. 1 and 2; Susan Kingsley Kent, *Sex and Suffrage in Britain 1860–1914* (Princeton University Press, Princeton, 1987), especially chaps. 6 and 7. This last study is primarily concerned with establishing as a common and continuous theme within first-wave feminism the sexual subordination of women. It does suggest the particular contribution of the WSPU to suffrage ideas in terms both of a more assertive anti-male stance and a more explicit exposition of women's sexual wrongs, see e.g. pp. 84, 171. It does not, however, address the question of militancy as such, so that, once again, WSPU activity is taken to represent simply a more intense commitment to the cause, rather than a distinctive, alternative perspective on achieving social and political change.
4. Studies of militant suffragism include George Dangerfield, *The Strange Death of Liberal England* (Paladin, London, 1970 paperback edn); Roger Fulford, *Votes for Women* (Faber and Faber, London, 1957); Andrew Rosen, *Rise Up Women* (Routledge and Kegan Paul, London, 1974).
5. For accounts of the NUWSS see Leslie Parker Hume, *The National Union of Women's Suffrage Societies 1897–1914* (Garland, New York, 1982); Holton, *op. cit.* note 3.
6. See e.g. David Mitchell, *Queen Christabel* (MacDonald and Jane, London, 1977); Dangerfield, *op. cit.* note 4, especially pp. 132–95; Fulford, *op. cit.* note 4, p. 302.

7. Elizabeth Sarah, 'Christabel Pankhurst: reclaiming her power', in Dale Spender (ed), *Feminist Theorists. Three Centuries of Women's Intellectual Traditions* (Women's Press, London, 1983), pp. 259–83, especially 263–7; Jane Marcus, 'Transatlantic sisterhood', *Signs*, vol. 3 (1978), pp. 744–55.

8. I am not here intending to question the radicalism of the WSPU, only suggesting that the ideological basis of such radicalism was evident throughout the movement, and that, therefore, such radicalism cannot, in itself, explain militancy. See Holton, *op. cit.* note 3, pp. 9–28, especially p. 28, and Brian Harrison, 'The act of militancy', in his *Peaceable Kingdom. Stability and Change in Modern Britain* (Clarendon Press, Oxford, 1982), pp. 26–81, especially pp. 36–9 for the relative ideological homogeneity of the movement.

9. Harrison, *ibid.* For a further insightful discussion of this topic see Martha Vicinus, *Independent Women: Work and Community for Single Women 1850–1920* (Chicago University Press, Chicago, 1985), pp. 247–80. Once again, however, the analysis is also pertinent to many aspects of constitution-alist campaigning, and cannot, therefore, explain militancy as such.

10. The several accounts of WSPU campaigning left by the three Pankhursts identify different dates and events as marking the onset of militancy. See E. Pankhurst, *op. cit.* note 1, p. 43; Dame Christabel Pankhurst, *Unshackled. The Story of How We Won the Vote* (Hutchinson, London, 1959), p. 46; E. Sylvia Pankhurst, *The Life of Emmeline Pankhurst. The Suffragette Struggle for Women's Citizenship* (T. Werner Laurie, London, 1935), p. 52.

11. See e.g. Evelyn Sharp, *Unfinished Adventure* (John Lane, London, 1933) especially pp. 127–51. This chapter was written before I had the opportunity to read Ann Morley and Liz Stanley, *The Life and Death of Emily Wilding Davison* (The Women's Press, London, 1988), which explores this issue fully and effectively.

12. The following discussion will draw especially on E. Pankhurst, *op. cit.* note 1. This autobiographical account is sometimes described as ghost-written, see e.g. Romero, *op. cit.* note 1, p. 23, but this is not indicated in Pankhurst's acknowledgement to the American journalist Rheta Childe Dorr at the begin-ning of the book. Nor is it borne out by a reading of the text, where the authentic sound of Pankhurst's voice is fully evident throughout. Christabel Pankhurst appears to have accepted it as her mother's personal account of events, and quoted it at length in her own book, see C. Pankhurst, *op. cit.* note 10, pp. 259–62.

13. Ann Oakley, 'Millicent Fawcett and her 73 reasons', in her *Telling the Truth about Jerusalem* (Basil Blackwell, Oxford, 1986), pp. 18–36 provides an especially stimulating account of the life and work of the leading constitution-alist suffragist. It is one which this account of Mrs Pankhurst, in part, seeks to counterpoint.

14. In suggesting this distinction I draw upon the discussion of the romantic and the classic in Jacques Barzun, *Classic, Romantic and Modern* (Secker and Warburg, London, 1962), especially pp. 2–16, 36–49. Lionel Trilling, *Sincerity and Authenticity* (Harvard University Press, Cambridge, Mass., 1972), especially pp. 2–11, was also helpful to my understanding of this and related issues.

15. C. Pankhurst, *op. cit.* note 10, p. 18.

16. Emmeline Pankhurst, Preface to E. S. Pankhurst, *op. cit.* note 1, n.p.

17. C. Pankhurst, *op. cit.* note 10, p. 27.

18. E. Pankhurst, *op. cit.* note 1, p. 324.

19. Frederick Pethick-Lawrence, Introduction to C. Pankhurst, *op. cit.* note 10, pp. 13–14.

20. C. Pankhurst, *idem*, pp. 67, 77. Not surprisingly, therefore, the militant leaders placed considerable emphasis on attracting a younger generation to the movement, *idem*, pp. 12, 77, and E. Pankhurst, *op. cit.* note 1, p. 36.
21. C. Pankhurst, *idem*, p. 16; E. S. Pankhurst, *op. cit.* note 10, p. 7; E. Pankhurst, *idem*, p. 11.
22. E. Pankhurst, *idem*, p. 3.
23. E. S. Pankhurst, *op. cit.* note 10, p. 7.
24. Quoted in Harrison, *op. cit.* note 8, p. 37.
25. Thomas Carlyle, *The French Revolution: a History*, 3 vols. (James Fraser, London, 1837). The account of his work in the following paragraphs draws heavily on Kenneth Marc Harris, *Carlyle and Emerson. Their Long Debate* (Harvard University Press, Cambridge, Mass., 1978), and Albert J. La Valley, *Carlyle and the Idea of the Modern* (Yale University Press, New Haven, 1968).
26. Harris, *idem*, pp. 114, 116, 117; La Valley, *idem*, pp. 123, 132.
27. E. Pankhurst, *op. cit.* note 1, pp. 337, 138, 140.
28. *Idem*, p. 221.
29. *Idem*, p. 111.
30. *Idem*, p. 242.
31. *Idem*, p. 234.
32. *Idem*, pp. 290, 292.
33. *Idem*, pp. 297, 299.
34. Quoted in Leah Levenson and Jerry H. Natterstad, *Hanna Sheehy Skeffington, Irish Feminist* (Syracuse University Press, Syracuse, 1986), p. 45.
35. E. Pankhurst, *op. cit.* note 1, p. 335, and C. Pankhurst, *op. cit.* note 10, p. 282.
36. E. Pankhurst, *idem*, pp. 59, 265; C. Pankhurst, *idem*, p. 83; E. S. Pankhurst, *op. cit.* note 10, pp. 70–1.
37. Harrison, *op. cit.* note 8, pp. 43, 65–6.
38. C. Pankhurst, *op. cit.* note 10, p. 78.
39. *idem*, p. 53.
40. Quoted in E. Pankhurst, *op. cit.* note 1, p. 334.
41. E.g. the account of the split with the Pethick-Lawrences in *idem*, p. 265.
42. See David Morgan, *Suffragists and Liberals* (Basil Blackwell, Oxford, 1975) for a detailed account of this question.
43. E. Pankhurst, *op. cit.* note 1, pp. 232–4.
44. See e.g. C. Pankhurst, *op. cit.* note 10, pp. 54, 76.
45. Harrison, *op. cit.* note 8, p. 56.
46. I have discussed this in more detail in my *Feminism and Democracy*, p. 13.
47. This phrase was coined by Sylvia Pankhurst in E. S. Pankhurst, *op. cit.* note 10, p. 36, with reference to broader aspects of her mother's career in social reform, but it encapsulates very well the tenor of militant suffragism.
48. E. Pankhurst, *op. cit.* note 1, pp. 182, 207, 286, 325, 327.
49. *Idem*, p. 14 and C. Pankhurst, *op. cit.* note 10, pp. 40, 126.
50. E. Pankhurst, *idem*, pp. 241, 264–5.
51. *Idem*, p. 268, and see also pp. 251, 346.

3 Feminists and the Politics of Wife-Beating

Jan Lambertz

If domestic violence is a new story, it has also been a series of older stories emerging at very particular moments in the more distant past. The labels, recognition and meanings given to particular kinds of abuse and exploitation of women or children obviously differed somewhat from those prevailing today. Then, as now, communities, political movements and individuals contested definitions of abuse or violation. Family violence has ruled the consciousness of a great many women and young people day in day out, but its ability to propel political bodies into action or to evoke public outrage more generally remains, as before, highly uneven. This chapter will trace the political fortunes of the wife-abuse issue – above all, wife-beating – in early twentieth-century England. With a few fleeting exceptions, neither Victorian feminist agitators nor the generations of activists immediately succeeding them demonstrated a commitment to sustaining wife-beating as a centrepiece of their politics. Scrutinizing and publicizing such abuse as a major social problem was, strikingly, one of those roads not taken in the feminisms of the early twentieth century, even if its presence lingered on alongside several related major issues, such as family income or male sexuality. This chapter will explore the changing faces of both women's vulnerability and the abusive husband in the context of earlier feminist initiatives. It will seek to explain why feminists addressed wife-beating only obliquely and never developed a stable, highly visible prototype of the cruel husband, even as they waged war on a whole range of male prerogatives.

In the mid to late Victorian years some limited political space existed for talking about a 'battered wife' problem and physically abusive husbands in England. This space intersected with concurrent discussions of cruelty to children and sexual abuse of females;

like her children, the beaten wife and mother could be drawn as highly vulnerable. However, she and this abusive partner essentially disappeared from the stage of public discussions in the first decades of this century. The abusive husband at most entered later depictions of marital conflict as one who did not provide financial support. Concurrently, the abused child, in its various incarnations, came to occupy a new and somewhat different place in the public eye. One of the unavoidable questions raised here will be, when did women's and children's perceived interests share political space and when did they compete for it?

Twentieth-century feminists left wife-beating off their political agendas for complicated reasons. In part this silence was a strategic decision, bound up with fostering cross-class alliances with men. This entailed abandoning pejorative if convenient class stereotypes of family violence. Highlighting wife-battering would also have conflicted with emerging feminist visions of how best to strengthen the position of women and particularly mothers in marriage; above all, these visions came to centre on wives' economic claims on husbands and fathers. There were both political and personal limits on the extent to which these British feminist activists could implicate more than a few men in physical abuse of wives.[1] To move from a claim that marital financial 'partnerships' were fragile to an exposure of the home as a *dangerous* place for many wives was too radical and unpalatable for these activists, given the political world in which they operated. Thus, feminists never undertook a social investigation of the prevalence and causes of marital violence that may have pushed them to this conclusion about domestic life. Few mothers, for instance, could have contemplated living independently of men throughout this period in anything short of dire poverty. Finally, consciously or not, feminists could displace wife abuse onto other issues such as child prostitution and child sexual abuse only to a very limited degree. Wife-beating and even marital rape were not easily captured under the rubric of male vice and violence towards children. Nor could feminists discuss such violence very directly, given their investments in the family as a social unit.

Victorian violence

From the late 1840s through the turn of the century in England a range of feminists, social reformers and law enforcement officials sporadically featured wife-beating as a serious problem. Through their varied efforts Parliament enacted limited legislation: an 1853 Act, for instance, laid down stiffer punishments for assaults on women and children (up to six months in gaol, a fine and an order to keep the peace). While divorce remained inaccessible into the twentieth century for both the middle and working classes, Acts in 1878 and 1886 made it possible for wives to obtain separations with financial maintenance orders, and laws passed in 1895 and 1902 further aided wives seeking separations.[2] There were clearly severe limitations on the effective help such legal provisions could either materially or symbolically offer to wives. While these defects are in themselves telling, we also need to speculate on how and to what extent wife-abuse – or domestic disputes of the working class in particular – became politicized at all during this period (and here the focus will remain on feminist agitators).

For at least a few women's rights advocates from the late 1840s onwards, such as John Stuart Mill and Harriet Taylor Mill, beaten wives poignantly came to symbolize women's political and legal disabilities, particularly in marriage.[3] Furthermore, through several decades the feminist press in particular drew attention to many law enforcement agencies' indifference to wives' victimization and revealed their incompetence in ending assaults on wives; reprinting court decisions, they exposed the hypocrisy of a male-controlled judicial system in which women had no direct representation and only minimal protection from 'male' interests.[4] This wife-abuse discussion revolved largely around a working-class cast of characters and working-class marriage. A few dramatic exceptions, such as the earlier Caroline Norton case in the late 1830s, the *R v Jackson* case in 1891, and perhaps others threading through the campaign of the Married Women's Property Committees (1850s–1880s) featured middle- or upper-class couples.[5] Most reform initiatives, however, set the problem in the broader context of working-class urban manhood, a contextualization aided by mass press accounts of court decisions. These generated a stereotype of the culprit in 'wife-torture' as a 'lower' type of working-class man, an insensitive, drink-crazed brute, a primitive. Frances

Power Cobbe and others – be they slumming writers seeking cultural colour or more sober-minded social reformers – usually cast his counterpart as a one-dimensional image of a cowering and passive wife, deserving of sympathy to the extent that she conformed to middle-class ideas of femininity and domesticity.[6]

What, then, might this abused wife figure have resonated metaphorically and symbolically for her occasional middle-class feminist champions? At least some of the middle-class women involved may have taken up the issue to 'speak out' about their own feelings of physical violation and abuse at the hands of male marital partners; but by fixing on a stereotype of an outsized rough hovering over a highly vulnerable working-class wife, they could avoid a volatile, frontal attack on men of their own class, fatal in the least for netting influential male political friends. Initiatives against wife-beating may at some levels and for a limited time have offered a veiled way of talking about sexual violation as well. Or middle-class women appropriating such a loaded and negative image of working-class (perhaps often Irish) men may have found a feminized version of expressing anxiety about the so-called urban residuum or the 'dangerous sex' in the 'dangerous classes'.

Despite these multiple possibilities for using wife-beating to voice women's cultural and personal apprehensions, explicitly *sexual* violation of the female body in fact claimed much more symbolic space in mid to late Victorian political campaigns, particularly women's campaigns. Male *sexual* abuse became a clearer feminist paradigm of female victimization than wife-beating ever did. Sexuality tipped the anxiety scales of the late Victorians, as perhaps few other clusters of conflict, confusion, danger and pleasure could. While at one level also a confrontation over bodily integrity, the feminist politicization of wife-beating in the late nineteenth century was at best episodic and fragmentary. Wife-beating was and remained part of the repertoire of 'crimes against women' trotted out in the columns of the feminist press up to the First World War, but there is little evidence that a sustained political pressure group centring on the issue ever emerged.

Feminist historians today have made much of the 1878 pamphlet, *Wife-Torture in England,* by Frances Power Cobbe, a prolific writer and highly visible social reformer, but it actually constituted an anomaly. That same year, in singularly rapid legislative response and owing much to Cobbe (rather than any drawn-out mass campaign), Parliament passed the Matrimonial Causes Act.[7] Perhaps the very existence of the Act pre-empted a massive, sustained women's campaign and public debate around wife-beating. In contrast, however, the campaign for the repeal of the Contagious Diseases Acts drew thousands of women into the political arena for the first time from late 1869 onwards. The sexual abuse issue continued to be a potent organizing focus for many women, with later efforts turning to the 'Maiden Tribute', the question of child prostitution in London,[8] and to promoting laws against incest and to raise the age of consent for sex.[9] Women also publicly broached abusive male sexual practices in marriage in both the nineteenth and twentieth centuries, above all in feminist rhetoric decrying the sexual or moral 'double standard' (which primarily counterposed prostitution and VD with marital fidelity).[10]

Paradoxically, the large-scale mobilization and collection of voices around sexual violation may have precluded campaigns about other kinds of violence against women or wives, rather than offered a coded space in which middle-class women could talk about wife-beating. For instance, husbands giving wives 'the clap' arguably bore quite different cultural consequences than those furnishing wives with black eyes and bruises. Furthermore, Judith Walkowitz's recent work on the representations and political constellations around the 'Maiden Tribute' story of the 1880s in fact suggests that alongside upper-class male clients, working-class mothers were also in part indicted as villains, as accessories to their daughters' launch into prostitution. The presence of this mother-blaming element in the campaign against child prostitution suggests distinct differences from the few political discussions of wife-beating available in the period; in the latter, commentators painted most working-class wife-mothers as being as vulnerable to male brutality as their children. As already suggested here, wife-beating publicizers had assigned men a different script, one earmarking working-class men for villainy. By contrast, the iconic enemy of the child prostitute remained most often explicitly upper class and this made it possible, too, to pull working-class male activists into various incarnations of the anti-vice campaign. Finally, returning to the complicated issue of what middle-class feminists articulated when they chose to take up working-class-centred campaigns for women and girls, it seems that working against *child* prostitution (so central to late Victorian 'social purity' campaigns) was perhaps at best a highly indirect vehicle for decrying the abuse of *adult* women. Walkowitz has likewise shown that middle-class women's relationship to the prostitutes they championed was by no means an unambiguous form of identification with them.[11]

My questions about the meanings invested in the sexually exploited child by women and for women could be expanded in several ways. The same questions need to be posed about feminist or women's contributions to the whole range of child rescue and protection campaigns outside child prostitution and social purity work. While it appears that many battered wives in fact sought intervention from the major child-protection societies, the Societies for the Prevention of Cruelty to Children,[12] the degree to which *feminist* groups saw these societies – with their predominantly male inspectorate – as either a champion of or a threat to working-class mothers remains unclear. More work needs to be done on where socially active women gravitated or did not gravitate in the expanse of child welfare work.[13]

Male justice in twentieth-century England

If feminist voices of the nineteenth century resorted only episodically or very indirectly to marital violence as a symbol of women's victimization, and their political and legal 'slavery', conjugal violence became ever more deeply submerged in both legal and feminist discussions in the first few decades of the twentieth century. Physical abuse still appeared as the occasional spectre in feminist journals' chronicle of male crimes treated leniently by 'male justice'. But its cultural purchase as a potential feminist rallying point diminished even further. If some suffrage pamphleteers put wife-beating on their grievance lists, it never became a staple of the visual iconography of the suffrage movements, for instance.[14] A range of factors underlay this transformation and also hesitatingly created space for another type of husbandly culprit.

The appearance of legal redress may have diffused some alarm over marital violence. Thanks to the 1878 Act, battered wives in England gained a hypothetical legal escape hatch from abusive husbands. But feminists who had cut their teeth on suffrage and social purity battles were never content to linger long over half-loaf concessions. It was unusual for them to be satisfied with legislation that fell short of their initial reform proposals or that worked badly in practice. The courts and their social service affiliates probably blocked much public consciousness about marital violence; by working extensively for 'reconciliations' of estranged couples, these services played down the full implications of battering for many women. However, feminists remained well aware that the court system did not serve women seeking help in marital disputes well.

The feminist critique of the operation of the justice system occurred on a number of fronts, initiated before the First World War and continuing into the 1920s. It was also a critique played out across northern Europe, focused not only on the double standard embedded in anti-prostitution measures, but also on a battery of discriminatory statutes and inadequate provisions for women in a whole range of legal capacities and as policewomen.[15] Beginning in the mid-1890s in Dresden, for instance, German women organized legal advice and aid bureaux for women, in many cases counselling them on their rights in marital disputes and separations. By 1917 their umbrella group, the *Rechtsschutzverband für Frauen,* claimed 103 member organizations in Germany and Vienna, many continuing into the 1920s.[16] An equivalent movement never materialized in Britain (although perhaps much similar ground came to be covered by the Poor Man's Lawyer centres of the inter-war years).[17] Nevertheless, watchful feminists gave harsh reviews to women's and girls' treatment in British courtrooms and at the hands of the police in the first decades of the twentieth century, and they initiated small-scale confrontations with the courts handling women's cases.

Before the First World War, for instance, the Women's Freedom League (WFL) journal, *The Vote*, began running the acidly titled column, 'The "Protected Sex"'. Various WFL members and women's groups elsewhere started 'Watch the Courts' campaigns to keep an eye on various court proceedings involving women and girls, publicizing instances of justice to women being 'maladministered'.[18] If these were courageous steps in asserting the legitimacy of a public female moral presence, it remains unclear how effective such 'interventions' could ever hope to be.[19] While eager to alleviate the 'loneliness' of women and girls in courts, the court rota of women in Cambridge, for instance, attempted to provide more direct help than a mere judgemental presence, working to offer 'practical helpfulness' in individual cases and 'to smooth the way to putting [presumably female and juvenile] first offender[s] on probation' as *ad hoc* 'Police Court Visitors'.[20] During the war and after, the Association for Moral and Social Hygiene likewise formed police court rotas in London and elsewhere, and held lectures on women under the law for rota members (including one on recent cases of wife murder by soldiers). The Association initiated these rotas mainly for collecting evidence about use of the increasingly repressive laws levied against alleged 'prostitutes', but they also became the springboard from which to argue for better, more supportive treatment of child plaintiffs testifying in sex assault cases.[21]

In the postwar period, most feminist groups also very explicitly promoted women's right to serve as magistrates and jurors in the face of ongoing hostility from the male legal establishment.[22] The courts' discretionary right to exclude women categorically from juries (typically for trials concerning sexual assault) remained intact well into the 1920s, despite the 1919 Sex Disqualification (Removal) Act.[23] The advent of women police patrols in the First World War proved a mixed blessing; not surprisingly, authorities often used them to police rather than protect other women. In some places these patrols did much family counselling, and clearly worked to stage marital reconciliations rather than to shield wives from, for instance, physically abusive husbands.[24] This notwithstanding, feminist and women's organizations across a wide political spectrum vigorously promoted the hiring of women police with full and official powers from the war years onward. It would remain an uphill battle all over Britain, lasting well into midcentury.

These campaigns used the dearth of women engaged in administering justice as a wide-reaching emblem of their ongoing second-class social status. Wife-abuse cases were not, however, at the heart of these women's critiques of the justice system; such cases remained a rare reference point indeed. Nor, arguably, were wrongful arrests of women on solicitation charges central concerns. Much more typically, they pointed towards a growing preoccupation with sexual assaults on children.[25]

If in the nineteenth century sexual abuse – even child sexual exploitation – could in part serve as a paradigm of adult women's victimization, the terms of the public discussion on sexual abuse by the inter-war years (perhaps even *by* the First World War) no longer really allowed this. The discussion of sexual abuse in a variety of national and local committees and conferences from the 1910s to the 1930s appears to have greatly narrowed the idea of sexual victimization, moving it away from references to male sexual prerogatives in general to the crimes of individual perverts; this process strongly parallels United States developments recently noted by Linda Gordon.[26] With the rise of the 'amateur' prostitute during the First World War, even adolescent girls in some communities could no longer count on much sympathy if molested. Only very young children tended to be seen as the victims of indecent assault.[27] Feminist groups remained somewhat impervious to this narrowing lens, still in the 1920s pushing for a higher age of consent (to at least sixteen for both sexes) and vigorously attacking the age of marriage permitted under the law, which anachronistically remained at twelve for girls and fourteen for boys until 1929. On the one hand, as in the United States, the discussion of sexual abuse moved out of the home: a pathologized, stray sex offender became the favoured culprit in most analyses, while father–daughter incest was consigned to the outer periphery of all debates, including those among feminists.[28] On the other hand, to the extent that the discussion suggested a problem *in* the home, parents (implicitly mothers) were the ones often blamed for not providing enough supervision or moral training of daughters.[29]

The idea of sex offenders who preyed on children may have served as a vehicle for 're-domesticizing' families in the wake of the war's upheavals. If mothers ironically drew some fire for not protecting their daughters, feminists and women's organizations could nonetheless feature child assault to assert the importance of mothers (and women) in protecting their children. Other things were arguably also at stake in discussions on these assaults, for a number of feminists even took their concern for child sexual abuse abroad. The keen, even obsessive interest displayed by a number of 1920s and 1930s feminist activists (such as the leader of the National Union of Societies for Equal Citizenship (NUSEC), Eleanor Rathbone, or WFL affiliate, C. Nina Boyle) over the age of consent and child marriage in India, child marriage in Palestine, or 'wife slavery' in Africa and the 'South Seas' awaits further historical analysis.[30] However, if these reference points resembled the domestic sexual abuse problem, their origins probably lay elsewhere, perhaps in women's anxieties about national and racial boundaries, and how newly enfranchised women came to grips with their new public, imperial 'responsibilities'. These discussions were, in any event, far removed from a confrontation with violence towards adult women on the domestic hearth.

Visions of class and family

The option for confronting wife abuse closed down for other reasons as well. Old stereotypes of working-class men were gradually altered in the first decades of the twentieth century. Old-style labels and slights about working-class 'brutes' were difficult to maintain in the face of a growing recognition of structural unemployment, a hedging disaggregation of the inhabitants of the Victorian slum 'residuum', a recognition of working-class male contributions to the nation as veterans of the First World War and as serious bargaining partners through the parliamentary Labour Party and the TUC.[31] And in the light of alliances built up between suffrage activists in the National Union of Women's Suffrage Societies (NUWSS) and the growing Labour movement,[32] it became ever more politically problematic to cast working-class men in the rough terms of the nineteenth-century wife-beater. More clearly, as turn-of-the-century social investigators began to cast their gaze on working-class women's lives, the already fragile stereotypes of the (usually) passive, helpless battered wife which had been generated by the late nineteenth-century discourse about working-class marriage lost their holding power. If investigators from organizations such as the Fabian Women's Group found squalor and victimization, many also discovered women who were resourceful, driven, resilient and tough.[33]

One of the consequences of seeing working-class women as capable and resourceful was that they could then be cast as responsible and, indeed, culpable adults. In tandem with social investigation, the language and imagery of different strands of twentieth-century child- and infant-welfare initiatives also played a significant role in dissolving the attribution of inordinate passivity to working-class mothers (along with their claims for a blameless victim status). By the turn of the century, rhetoric around child health and deprivation increasingly suggested that mothers, through their alleged ignorance, played some significant role in contributing to this deprivation or even 'neglect'. Both Anna Davin and Jane Lewis have forcefully argued that twentieth-century child-welfare work as a whole came to operate with an intense, increasing pressure and reliance on working-class mothers.[34] Both private and state welfare initiatives often did so instead of directly pressuring fathers to become more responsible breadwinners or making greater material provisions available to destitute households. This did not happen all at once. But it did represent a near reversal of male and female roles in 'marital abuse' imagery: women moved from playing passive victims to active agents. And men, in turn, were no longer rendered so aggressively abusive; rather, they became either passively abusive (as non-supporters) or almost neutral (as inadequate earners).

Women's organizations entered the discourse on family poverty on a number of fronts, and forcefully if not always effectively attempted to counter the mother-blaming message lurking in nascent health and welfare bureaucracies. In concert with working-class groups such as the Women's Co-operative Guild, many middle-class feminists tied the welfare of married women more and more explicitly to their vulnerable position as mothers, their limited access to material resources and the deeply flawed premises of the wage system, rather than male brutality and selfishness or female incompetence. The previous emphasis on how individual men's demands or temperament contributed to wives' vulnerability was also being undercut by campaigns demanding expanded state and local authority provisions for families. Thus, for instance, in 1914 a commentator asserted in the NUWSS journal:

> Where the husband – in any class, or earning any income – is a brutal or intemperate man, the life of a dependent wife is likely to be far from pleasant . . . There is no need, however, to suppose an intemperate or even unkind husband in order to show that the wife of the working man lives a life full of grinding responsibility, of sordid and unceasing toil, of wearing anxiety, combined with utter powerlessness – a life cruel enough to crush the vitality of any human being.[35]

Feminists were inevitably divided on how to raise the status of the wife or mother and to give recognition to her unwaged household contribution. A commentator writing in *The Woman's Leader* in 1923 echoed the ambivalence of her contemporaries when she wrote:

> Everyone knows of hundreds of cases in which husbands do not, in fact, support their wives: both cases where they cannot – through incapacity or ill-health or bad luck – and cases where they will not . . .
>
>   From the feminist point of view there is much to be said about the law of maintenance, and much to be said against it, and all the pernicious consequences of the economic dependence of women not attributed to it. But there is also this to be said for it, that it is the only form in which any financial recognition whatever is given for the life-work of the normal woman.[36]

This tension around married women's financial dependence represented a subtle change in feminism emerging in the twentieth century, certainly evident by the 1920s in groups such as the NUSEC. Increasingly feminists began to look to a dual system of family maintenance for a solution. On the one hand, they called for better state enforcement of a husband's obligation to share his income (where one existed) with wife and children – even after partnerships dissolved or husbands died; on the other hand, they pushed for increased state benefits to family units – but under the control of mothers and channelled through alternatives to the humiliating Poor Law machinery.[37] The renegotiation of the obligations of state and married man to the family provided the context for new representations of the abusive husband.

Some historians have recently argued that an emphasis on happy heterosexual togetherness became a dominant discourse on gender relations in the wake of the First World War.[38] Nonetheless, feminist groups never questioned the legitimacy of a woman's decision to seek a separation order, and they could voice ready scepticism over the basis of reconciliation work in many courts.[39] Groups such as the NUSEC drafted bills and lobbied MPs to make legal separations work better financially, although these efforts are not always apparent, as many progressive feminist schemes were swallowed up in postwar corporatist politics.[40] The NUSEC was instrumental in pushing through a Summary Jurisdiction (Separation and Maintenance) Bill, which came into force in October 1925, slightly extending the grounds for separation orders. Yet many of the problems pinpointed by Rathbone and others before the Act went unresolved.[41] The problems of an equitable division of furniture between man and wife, allocation of a tenancy, of 'finding lodgings that will take children, or furnishing them with the necessary bedding and equipment when found', and even enforcing inadequate maintenance orders were battles still being fought by feminists in Parliament and with trade unions in the years after the Second World War.[42] Curiously, the reasons women by the thousands continued to seek separations each year were never rigorously analysed in the context of these campaigns. Yet the trickle of references to brutal men or their 'ill conduct'[43] suggests that marital violence continued to play a role in many women's journey to the courts that processed separation orders, and that feminist efforts were thus intrinsically bound up with securing protection and rights for battered wives.

The Married Women's Association, founded in mid-1938 as an offshoot of the 'equalitarian' feminist Six Point Group, was the national organization which most clearly highlighted the practical problems of separation orders in the inter-war period and after.[44] Paradoxically, it did so in great detail, while professing to be primarily interested in making marriage a legal financial partnership and raising the status of married women.[45] The Association aimed to make marriage a 'financial partnership' under marital law, with the pooling of incomes and earnings, and 'equal responsibility' for the upkeep of home and family, but its literature and campaigns sometimes remained rather vague about how this ideal might ever be enforced where partners cohabited.[46] Of course the continuing political struggles waged by this group and its local branches around the conditions and social cost of separation orders necessarily spoke to the needs of battered wives. However, despite this scrutiny of broken marriages, the Association's journal, *Wife and Citizen*, did not invoke the battered wife as a particular symbol of married women's disabilities in its pages. Only a few instances of violence by husbands or lovers ever appeared.[47]

With this in mind, the image of the 'abusive' husband in the inter-war years increasingly became that of a man who did not provide for his wife and family, particularly *after* marriages broke apart – rather than a physically aggressive, violent, drunken brute. On the one hand, this new abusive husband (the non-supporter) was at least a more democratic image in that it relied less on reference to working-class men only; less class-based, he could implicate all men as potentially abusive, including those of the middle class. On the other hand, the individual husband also became far less culpable for abuse and 'neglect' of mothers (and children) in the contemporary feminist programme for welfare and, in some senses, in child welfare politics as a whole. The range of 'culprits' had expanded: the husband was but one. And in the context of other feminist struggles, he remained by necessity a nebulous figure.

The large sectors of feminists committed to campaigns for family allowances, as well as married women's rights in the realm of employment and state insurance, had much to lose by insisting that husbands and fathers *could* adequately support wives and families, if only the state agencies, the courts and even employers applied a little more pressure, organized pay day a little differently and changed their definitions of property. At stake here was the feminist challenge to the state's and Labour's romance with the male family provider, the provider who could adequately support his dependent wife and children on a wage or, more remotely, insurance allotments. For many feminists this radical challenge always restrained the creation of a clear-cut 'wife abuser' (be he a wilful non-supporter or not). In this context, a full-blown image of the abusive husband would have been a political liability for many of their other campaigns.

Conclusion

Cumulatively, these various factors – ranging from class politics to political tactics to the family economy – closed off any real discussion of wife-beating in virtually all the positions orbiting around that sometimes rather diffuse axis, twentieth-century feminism. Many different histories of domestic violence and of family struggles remain to be written; these are no less important than the story told here, the place of wife abuse in the political campaigns of past British feminists. There is little evidence for sustained, late Victorian political campaigns making wife-beating their centrepiece, even if the stories of wife mutilation drifted as an undercurrent through both the feminist and mass circulation press into the twentieth century. Nor was wife abuse very obviously subsumed under the rubric of either sexual exploitation or cruelty to children, both of which were important political rallying points in the period confronted in this chapter.

In the twentieth century more than the nineteenth, marital violence competed for political space with child welfare in Britain. Both the expansion of all women's political and legal rights after the First World War and the strong recasting of the working-class wife-mother in particular as a responsible, indeed powerful figure, truncated a social exploration and recognition of their vulnerability to wife-beating. But in a feminist movement which stressed women's poverty – both as wage workers and as mother-dependents in an incongruous wage system – women were again linked to the vulnerability of their children. Vulnerable wives existed politically to both a greater and lesser extent than before. Feminist eyes remained trained on women's disabilities in the Englishman's proverbial 'castle'. By the end of this period, the politics of family maintenance spun out by women's activists came very close to talking about marital violence and abuse, but never gave it a name. The non-supporting or poorly supporting father-husand was also to remain an 'abuser' in a limited way only. Neither the structure of social work, the welfare and state bureaucracies nor the rising feminist vision of welfare itself allowed for a very sustained pursuit of him. Because early twentieth-century feminists never chose to analyse the prevalence and causes of marital violence, they could never reveal the full extent of unequal power relations between husbands and wives, nor the obstacles to marital reform.

Notes

1. Cf. Linda Gordon, *Heroes of Their Own Lives: The Politics and History of Family Violence* (Viking, N.Y., 1988), pp. 254–7.
2. O. R. McGregor, *Divorce in England: A Centenary Study* (Heinemann, London, 1957), p. 23n.
3. See Carol Bauer and Lawrence Ritt, ' "A husband is a beating animal": Frances Power Cobbe confronts the wife-abuse problem in Victorian England', *International Journal of Women's Studies*, vol. 6, no. 2 (March/April, 1983); and Bauer and Ritt, 'Wife-abuse, late-Victorian English feminists, and the legacy of Frances Power Cobbe', *International Journal of Women's Studies*, vol. 6, no. 3 (May/June, 1983); J. R. Lambertz, 'The politics and economics of family violence in Liverpool, from the late nineteenth century to 1948', M.Phil. thesis, University of Manchester, 1984.
4. E.g., *The Women's Suffrage Journal* or the *Englishwoman's Review* of the 1870s and 1880s.
5. See Caroline Norton, *Caroline Norton's Defense: English Laws for Women in the Nineteenth Century*, Intro. by Joan Huddleston (Academy Chicago, 1982, orig. 1854); David Rubinstein, *Before the Suffragettes: Women's Eman-*

cipation in the 1890s (St Martin's Press, N.Y., 1986), pp. 51–66; Lee Holcombe, *Wives and Property: Reform of the Married Women's Property Law in Nineteenth-Century England* (University of Toronto Press, 1983); and cf. Julia Brophy and Carol Smart, *Women-In-Law: Explorations in Law, Family and Sexuality* (Routledge and Kegan Paul, London, 1985).

6. See Ellen Ross, '"Fierce questions and taunts": married life in working-class London, 1870–1914', *Feminist Studies*, vol. 8 (Fall, 1982), pp. 575–602; Nancy Tomes, ' "A torrent of abuse": crimes of violence between working-class men and women in London, 1840–1875', *Journal of Social History*, vol. 11 (1978), pp. 328–45; and Elizabeth Pleck, *Domestic Tyranny: The Making of American Social Policy against Family Violence from Colonial Times to the Present* (Oxford University Press, 1987). For earlier periods, papers by Margaret Hunt and Anna Clark, Session on 'Gender, Class, and Family Violence in Britain', American Historical Association conference (Dec. 1988).

7. F. P. Cobbe, *Life of Frances Power Cobbe, By Herself*, Vol. 2 (Richard Bentley and Son, London, 3rd edn, 1894), pp. 218–25.

8. Judith Walkowitz, 'Male vice and feminist virtue: feminism and the politics of prostitution in nineteenth-century Britain', *History Workshop Journal*, no. 13 (Spring, 1982), p. 80; and Judith Walkowitz, 'Maiden Tribute of Modern Babylon,' typescript (1987).

9. Victor Bailey and Sheila Blackburn, 'The Punishment of Incest Act 1908: a case study of law creation', *Criminal Law Review* (1979), pp. 708–18; Sheila Jeffreys, *The Spinster and Her Enemies: Feminism and Sexuality 1880–1930* (Pandora, London, 1985), esp. Chaps. 3 and 4; Jeffrey Weeks, *Sex, Politics and Society* (Longman, London, 1981), pp. 31, 36 n.34. Cf. Frank Mort, *Dangerous Sexualities: Medico-moral Politics in England since 1830* (Routledge and Kegan Paul, London, 1987).

10. Lucy Bland, 'The married woman, the "New woman" and the feminist sexual politics of the 1890s', in Jane Rendall (ed), *Equal or Different: Women's Politics 1880–1914* (Basil Blackwell, Oxford, 1987); and Bland, 'Marriage laid bare: middle-class women and marital sex *c.*1880–1914', in Jane Lewis (ed), *Labour and Love: Women's Experience of Home and Family, 1850–1940* (Basil Blackwell, Oxford, 1986); cf. Susan Kent, *Sex and Suffrage in Britain, 1860–1914* (Princeton University Press, 1987). The extent to which marital rape was invoked in 'Equal Moral Standard' campaigns of different stripes remains unclear.

11. Walkowitz, *op. cit.* note 8.

12. E.g. testimony of the long-time solicitor to the Liverpool S.P.C.C. before the Royal Commission on Divorce and Matrimonial Causes: *Brit. Parl. Papers*, 20 (1912–13), 13 Dec. 1910, pp. 429–33.

13. See e.g. Patricia Hollis, 'Women in council: separate spheres, public space', in Rendall, *op. cit.* note 10. The NSPCC did on occasion explicitly assert that it was also a champion of women: NSPCC *Annual Reports* (1913–14, 1920–1); and the *Child's Guardian*, vol. 33 (Oct. 1923), p. 79.

14. Lisa Tickner, *The Spectacle of Women: Imagery of the Suffrage Movement, 1907–1914* (Chicago University Press, 1988). For contemporary pamphleteers, see Anna Martin, 'Mothers in mean streets; or, the toad under the harrow' (The United Suffragists, London, n.d.), and Lady [Laura Aberconway] McLaren, 'The Women's Charter of Rights and Liberties' (Grant Richards, London, 5th edn, 1910), which proposed a novel solution to the wife abuse problem (cited in R. E. Dobash and R. Dobash, *Violence against Wives: A Case against Patriarchy* (Free Press, N.Y., 1979)).

15. Ample evidence is recorded in *Jus Suffragii: The International Woman Suffrage News*, organ of the International Woman Suffrage Alliance in the 1920s.
16. Elisabeth Altmann-Gottheiner (ed), *Jahrbuch des Bundes Deutscher Frauenvereine*, 1912–21 (B. G. Teubner, Leipzig/Berlin); *Die Frau*, vol. 8 (1900–1901), pp. 55, 185, 697–8, vol. 11 (1904), p. 375. I am grateful to the historian Nancy Reagan for alerting me to these.
17. At least one women citizens' association set up such a service, in Richmond in 1928. *Women in Council. 'N.C.W. News'* (Jan. 1932), pp. 18–19.
18. *Jus Suffragii*, vol. 12 (1 June 1918), p. 138; *The Vote*, vol. 10 (20 Nov. 1914), p. 397; E. D. Hutchinson, 'The law at work: police court visiting', *The Woman's Leader*, vol. 15 (23 Feb. 1923), p. 29; and cf. Jeffreys, *op. cit.* note 9, pp. 58–9. On early court protests (1907–8), see the pamphlet by Stella Newsome, 'Women's Freedom League, 1907–1957' (London, *c.*1960).
19. AMSH Rota members, for instance, were confused about the legal procedures at work when women were accused of solicitation: *Fifth Report* (1/1919–3/1920), p. 12.
20. Hutchinson, *op. cit.* note 18.
21. AMSH, *Third [Annual] Report* (1917), p. 11; *Fourth Report* (1918), pp. 18–19; *Fifth Report* (1/1919–3/1920), pp. 12–14.
22. See, e.g., 'Solicitor' [pseud. Conway Loveridge Hodgkinson], *English Justice* (Geo. Routledge and Sons Ltd, London, 1932), who complained of the harsh conditions placed on men by maintenance orders, and that (p. 65): 'Women magistrates are like women motor drivers, either very good or very bad, but usually the latter.' By contrast, a London police court magistrate, Claud Mullins, *Wife v. Husband in the Courts* (Allen and Unwin, London, 1935), thought (married) women magistrates were particularly good at sniffing out instances of wives using 'an unjustified pose of injured innocence in court' (pp. 75–6 and cf. p. 72).
23. E.g. *Jus Suffragii*, vol. 19 (March 1925), p. 89; *Jus Suffragii*, vol. 24 (Nov. 1929), p. 16.
24. Lucy Bland, 'In the name of protection: the policing of women in the First World War', in Brophy and Smart, *op. cit.* note 5; Liverpool Women Police Patrols, *A.R.*s (1933, 1935). Cf. Mort, *op. cit.* note 9, pp. 149–50, on increasing investments made in justice through the law.
25. In this instance I think that Jeffreys, *op. cit.* note 9, has read the feminist pulse of the 1920s more accurately than Mort, *idem.*
26. Gordon, *op. cit.* note 1, pp. 222–6. For a slightly later period, cf. Estelle B. Freedman ' "Uncontrolled desires": the response to the sexual psychopath, 1920–1960', *Journal of American History*, vol. 74 (June 1987), pp. 83–106.
27. In Liverpool, for instance, representatives of the Women Citizens' Association joined the women police patrols, various religious and moral welfare workers, and child protection societies (but *not* the LSPCC) in the 1930s to form a 'Sexual Offences Against Young Children Sub-Committee'. One group belonging to the committee concluded in its 1934–5 report, 'a differentiation ought to be made between assaults against really young children and cases of misconduct in which older girls are involved'. Cf. *The Shield*'s 'Sexual offences against young children', Series 4, vol. 1 (April 1932), pp. 12–23, and (October 1932), p. 101.
28. See, e.g., Jeffreys, *op. cit.* note 9, pp. 67–70, 85; Weeks, *op. cit.*, note 9, pp. 200, 221; *Time and Tide*, vol. 1 (1920), p. 520; AMSH, *A.R.* (1934), p. 14; and somewhat typically, 'Hampstead Heath and policewomen', *Policewoman's Review*, vol. 3 (June 1929). For a voice from the medical profession, 'The work of the woman police surgeon' *[Manchester and Salford] Woman*

Citizen, no. 148 (1930), pp. 4–5; Nesta Wells, 'Ten years as a woman police surgeon', *The Shield*, Series 5, vol. 5, no. 3 (Dec. 1937), p. 120; and Wells, 'Sexual offences as seen by a woman police surgeon'. *British Medical Journal* (6 Dec. 1958), pp. 1404–8. For government concern, report of the Departmental Committee on Sexual Offences against Young Persons (HMSO, London, 1926) and Report of the Departmental Committee on Sexual Offences against Children and Young Persons in Scotland (HMSO, Edinburgh, 1926).

29. E.g. for Liverpool, [Liverpool] Catholic Children's Protection Society, *A.R.*s (1928/29–1945/46); and Liverpool Women Police Patrols, *A.R.* (1942), pp. 3–4. Cf. the Report on the Departmental Committee for Scotland, *idem*, pp. 39, 53.

30. Correspondence, *Jus Suffragii* (June 1922), pp. 132–3, and (Jan.-Feb., April 1928); *Jus Suffragii* (Dec. 1927), p. 45; (Jan. 1928), p. 61; (July 1928), pp. 158–9; (March 1930), p. 85; 'Notes and news: child marriage in India', *The Woman's Leader*, vol. 21 (8 Feb. 1929), p. 2, and 'Women slaves in the British Empire', *The Woman's Leader*, vol. 22 (21 Feb. 1930), p. 22; 'What is slavery? An appeal to women', *The Shield*, Series 3, vol. 7 (July 1931), pp. 136–45 and 'The status of women of native African races', Series 4, vol. 1 (Oct. 1932), pp. 115–20; Mary D. Stocks, *Eleanor Rathbone: A Biography* (Victor Gollancz, London, 1949); 'Tribal customs and the status of women', AMSH, *A.R.* (London, 1933), pp. 16–17; *The Townswoman*, vol. 2, no. 3 (June 1934), p. 55.

31. On disaggregation of the labouring poor, see discussion in Stuart Hall and Bill Schwarz, 'State and society, 1880–1930', in Mary Langan and Bill Schwarz (eds), *Crises in the British State 1880–1930* (Hutchinson, London, 1985), especially, pp. 19–20. On Labour men, Labour women and women's issues, see Harold Smith, 'Sex vs. Class: British Feminists and the Labour Movement, 1919–1929', *The Historian*, vol. 47 (Nov. 1984), pp. 19–37; and Susan Pedersen, 'The failure of feminism in the making of the British welfare state', *Radical History Review*, no. 43 (Winter, 1989), pp. 86–110.

32. See Sandra Stanley Holton, *Feminism and Democracy: Women's Suffrage and Reform Politics in Britain, 1900–1918* (Cambridge University Press, 1986).

33. On the Group's politics, see Polly Beals, 'State endowment of motherhood: perspectives on the case of Britain', Gender and the Welfare State conference paper, Harvard University (Nov. 1987).

34. Anna Davin, 'Imperialism and motherhood', *History Workshop Journal*, no. 5 (1978), pp. 9–65; Jane Lewis, *The Politics of Motherhood: Child and Maternal Welfare in England, 1900–1939* (Croom Helm, London, 1980). On US parallels, cf. Gordon, *op. cit.* note 1, Chap. 5.

35. M. S. Reeves, 'The wife of the working man', *The Common Cause*, vol. 5 (6 Feb. 1914), p. 833. O. R. McGregor, L. Blom-Cooper, and C. Gibson, *Separated Spouses* (Gerald Duckworth and Co., London, 1970), p. 16, also suggest that by the 1920s the emphasis in activism shifted away from securing physical protection of wives in favour of providing them with financial security.

36. 'The obligation to support a wife', *The Woman's Leader*, vol. 14 (5 Jan. 1923), p. 387. For similar ambivalence about the privileges and disabilities that marriage offered women, see 'Married v. single', *The Woman's Leader*, vol. 14 (24 March 1922), p. 59.

37. On women's control of welfare benefits, see e.g. A. Martin, *The Common Cause*, vol. 3 (1911), pp. 206–7 and (6 July 1911).

38. See e.g. Jeffreys, *op. cit.* note 9; Mort, *op. cit.* note 9.

39. 'When mercy seasons justice', *The Woman's Leader*, vol. 15 (1923), p. 238. Similarly, 'The police court and its work', *The Woman's Leader*, vol. 17 (1925), p. 180, but less sceptically for the pre-war period, V. M. Shillington, 'Maintenance grants under separation orders', *Women's Industrial News*, vol. 16, *New Series*, no. 60 (1913), pp. 106–10.

40. Cf. Pedersen, *op. cit.* note 31; John Macnicol, *The Movement for Family Allowances, 1918–45: A Study in Social Policy Development* (Heinemann, London, 1980).

41. Eva M. Hubback, 'The Summary Jurisdiction (Separation and Maintenance) Bill', *The Woman's Leader*, vol. 17 (6 March 1925), pp. 43–4; Eleanor F. Rathbone, *The Disinherited Family: A Plea for the Endowment of the Family* (Edward Arnold, London, 1924), pp. 95–7; E. Rathbone, *[Manchester and Salford] Woman Citizen*, no. 118 (1927), pp. 12–13.

42. See Edith Summerskill, *A Woman's World* (Heinemann, London, 1967), pp. 143–59; and regarding 'reduction at source' (attaching wages to pay for orders), the Married Women's Association, and the TUC, see *Wife and Citizen*, vol. 9, no. 13 (May 1949), p. 51.

43. *Jus Suffragii*, vol. 16 (Aug. 1922), p. 167, and vol. 19 (July 1925), p. 154.

44. During the war years the group counted some 2000 members and its journal had 6000 subscribers: *Wife and Citizen*, vol. 6, New Series, no. 1 (Jan. 1945), p. 3.

45. Cf. Ambrose Appelbe, 'Should a woman leave her husband?', *Wife and Citizen* vol. 8, New Series, no. 12 (Dec. 1947), p. 66; 'The Liverpool memorandum', vol. 8, New Series, no. 5 (May 1947), p. 16, and 'Liverpool investigates', in vol. 8, New Series, no. 11 (Nov. 1947), pp. 63–4.

46. See e.g. *Wife and Citizen*, vol. 6 (1945), p. 17; vol. 7 (1946), p. 42; vol. 8 (1947), p. 51.

47. E.g. *Wife and Citizen*, vol. 6 (1945), pp. 31, 37, 47, and vol. 8 (1947), p. 5.

PART II

FEMINISM IN THE INTER-WAR YEARS

4 British Feminism in the 1920s

Harold L. Smith

With the principle of women's suffrage secured in 1918, British feminists appeared poised for a significant reformation of society during the 1920s. New feminist groups were created, an important feminist journal was established, an intense debate over the nature of feminism clarified some of the assumptions underlying feminist ideology, and significant legislation was enacted improving the status of wives and mothers. But by 1930 feminism seemed much less of a threat to traditional structures. Postwar social and cultural patterns help explain why this was so.

The First World War unleashed a powerful current of cultural conservatism which helped shape the direction of postwar feminism.[1] Alarm over the perceived wartime changes in sex roles strengthened the forces seeking to restore traditional roles. As Elizabeth Roberts has suggested, the 'full flowering' of the Victorian domestic ideology occurred in the inter-war years.[2] Public concern over the declining rate of population growth also contributed to changes intended to encourage women to become mothers.[3] The increased preoccupation with marriage and motherhood helped ensure that those who wished to make this central to feminism would find a receptive audience, while increasing the resistance to feminists wishing to improve women's employment opportunities.

The internal divisions that were to plague the National Union of Women's Suffrage Societies' (NUWSS) successor organization, the National Union of Societies for Equal Citizenship (NUSEC), throughout the 1920s emerged even before women aged thirty and over gained the vote in 1918. NUWSS members engaged in heated debates during 1917 over what the Union should do once women's suffrage had been achieved. Two main alternatives were proposed. Ray Strachey spoke for equality feminists when she urged the Union to concentrate on equal opportunities for women.[4]

Eleanor Rathbone led a group known as the new feminists, who opposed this, urging instead that the NUWSS seek 'real equality' for women. By this she meant that because of sexual difference women's needs were different from men's; feminists should seek reforms related to women's special concerns, especially those involving motherhood, rather than seeking what men had. Family allowances paid to the mother, for example, were more important than equal pay for women. Although the term 'new feminism' came into general use only after the First World War, it did not originate in this period; many of its central ideas can be found in the writings of pre-war feminists, including those by Rathbone.[5]

While some equality feminists supported specific reforms Rathbone advocated, they found her vision of feminism disturbing. When equality feminists presented the case for granting women workers equal pay for equal work, for example, Rathbone endorsed the common anti-feminist argument that men deserved higher pay than women because they had families to support.[6] Even though she concluded that women would be entitled to equal pay once family allowances had been introduced, equality feminists considered her assumption that unequal pay was not based on sex discrimination both mistaken and an illogical feminist stance.[7]

Although they differed as to which reforms should have the highest priority, new and equality feminists are not easily distinguished by their reform programmes; some equality feminists advocated family allowances, for example, while new feminists maintained equal educational and employment opportunities were desirable. The fundamental distinction between new and equality feminism arises from the assumptions underlying those reforms. New feminists accused equality feminists of seeking to become like men, of adopting male values and priorities. Equality feminists warned that new feminists placed a 'dangerous insistence on women's natures', which encouraged traditional notions of femaleness, thereby making it harder for women to escape from traditional roles.[8] Whereas new feminists referred to maternity as the 'most important of women's occupations',[9] equality feminists stressed the 'common humanity of men and women, not their differences' in order to move toward what would now be called a gender-neutral society.[10]

Although Rathbone was elected NUSEC president in 1919, replacing Millicent Fawcett, the new NUSEC programme included many reforms urged by equality feminists: equal suffrage (and an increased number of women in Parliament), equal pay for equal work, equal employment opportunities, an equal moral standard (including equal grounds for divorce), equal parental rights of guardianship over children and state pensions for widows with dependent children. But new feminists were successful in having the NUSEC objective defined as 'all such reforms as are necessary to secure a real equality of liberties, status and opportunity' for women, which provided the basis for adding reforms later which more explicitly reflected new feminist thinking.[11]

Due in no small part to the leadership of Ray and Pippa Strachey, the London and National Society for Women's Service (LSWS) became one of the most influential equality feminist organizations in the years immediately following the First World War. Previously called the London Society for Women's Suffrage, it had been the NUWSS's London branch prior to 1919. New and equality feminists also struggled for control of the LSWS, but in this instance Ray Strachey guided the equality feminists to victory.[12] While the LSWS pledged to continue working for equal suffrage, its new programme identified women's economic equality as its immediate priority.[13]

Another suffrage organization, the Women's Freedom League (WFL), provided additional support for equality feminism in the 1920s. Founded in 1907 by dissident WSPU members, it also adopted a new programme at the end of the war. While it focused on equal suffrage, equal pay and equal opportunities, the programme also included new feminist proposals such as better housing and child care.[14] With Charlotte Despard, a socialist and Labour Party activist, as its president until 1926, the WFL made special efforts to link feminism with the Labour movement; promoting trade unionism among women workers was part of its immediate programme.

Vera Brittain's 1922 claim that hopes for female liberation were pinned chiefly on the Six Point Group (SPG) reflects an equality feminist's perspective, but it does suggest the SPG's importance.[15] Established by Lady Rhondda in February 1921, many of its prominent members, including Rhondda, had been suffragettes. Although non-militant, it viewed itself as a descendant of the

WSPU and in 1925 urged Mrs Pankhurst to assume the leadership of the equal suffrage campaign.[16] Its membership included some of the most talented young feminists: Vera Brittain and Winifred Holtby were prominent examples of the new generation of feminists that emerged after the war. It also attracted women whose politics were on the left: Brittain and Holtby were Labour Party members, while Dorothy E. Evans and Monica Whately contested parliamentary seats for Labour in the 1920s.

Although the SPG was an equality feminist organization, its programme was not limited to equality reforms. In addition to standard equality proposals such as equal pay for women teachers and equal opportunities for women civil servants, the SPG advocated legislation for widowed mothers, for the unmarried mother and her child, and on child assault. Its first major campaign was for the 1921 Criminal Law Amendment Bill, which proposed to strengthen the legal protection for young females against male sexuality.[17]

Lady Rhondda also established *Time and Tide*, a weekly feminist journal, in 1920. Staffed and directed entirely by women, *Time and Tide* continued the WSPU principle that women should organize independently of men. It employed some of the most distinguished inter-war feminist writers: Elizabeth Robins, Rebecca West, Cecily Hamilton and Winifred Holtby. Although Rhondda was no socialist, she included left-wing women among the circle around her at *Time and Tide*: Helen Archdale, the editor until 1926, was a socialist, Holtby became a director in 1926, and other Labour women, including Mary A. Hamilton and Vera Brittain, wrote frequently for the journal in the 1920s.[18]

From its first issue *Time and Tide* maintained that women comprised a distinct sex-class, and that the function of the journal was to teach women to view issues from a woman's point of view. Rhondda believed the vote would not bring equality for women unless accompanied by drastic changes in their consciousness. Traits which had been ingrained in women for generations, such as docility and timidity, would have to be replaced by a new assertiveness, especially in relations with men. She urged women to repudiate the notion that they could define their identity only through the men in their lives: the belief that women's 'main business is not to help build the world but only to build the people (men) who build the world' was a major obstacle to equality. In focusing on child rearing as their primary function, women were accepting men's view of their role; doing this would ensure that new legislation would alter women's lives very little even when it provided the opportunity for change.[19]

With feminists splintering into numerous groups, the Consultative Committee of Women's Organizations (CCWO) attempted to provide a single voice for feminism. It was established in March 1921 by Lady Astor to co-ordinate efforts by women's groups to pressure Parliament for legislation that would improve women's status.[20] Especially during the early 1920s the Committee added credibility to Lady Astor's claim that she was the women's parliamentary spokesperson. Astor was the Committee's president until 1928; her political secretary, Hilda Matheson, was its secretary during its early years. Although parliamentary lobbying was a major concern, the CCWO also intervened during parliamentary elections, circulating lists of desired reforms to the leading political parties and publishing their responses so that women voters could reward their friends and punish their enemies.[21]

Feminists made special efforts during the 1920s to secure the election of women to Parliament. A non-party Women's Election Committee was established in 1920 to help women seeking parliamentary seats. It provided assistance to twelve female candidates in the 1922 general election; only two, Lady Astor and Margaret Wintringham, won seats, but several others, including Ray Strachey, did well.[22] But by the mid-1920s the conflict between new and equality feminists on two issues had virtually paralysed the Committee: Should it support all female candidates or only those who stood for feminist equalitarianism? and should women be encouraged to run as independents or seek selection by a party (which meant accepting party discipline and perhaps abandoning feminist positions)?[23]

In the mid-1930s Rathbone claimed that the legislative results achieved by feminists in the postwar decade had exceeded expectations. She stated that in the nine years following 1918 twenty laws especially pertaining to women were passed which improved women's status.[24] Subsequent studies of this period have referred to the 'impressive programme of legislation' which feminists achieved in the 1920s, and identified 'the ease with which these successes were achieved' as the 'most striking' aspect of this legislation.[25]

While feminist achievements were considerable, this view overstates feminist responsibility for this legislation; it also ignores the extent to which it was a substitute for the changes feminists desired. Some of the legislation which appeared to be an important victory for feminism was phrased in such a way as to give the appearance of substantial reform while actually impeding change. Most of the legislation enhanced the status of mothers, thus encouraging women to view motherhood as a woman's primary function, rather than facilitating new roles. What seems most striking about this burst of legislative activity is the extent to which non-feminist forces guided the pressure for reform into channels which preserved women's traditional place in society.

The 1919 Sex Disqualification (Removal) Act illustrates this point; the belief that it 'removed the last legal disabilities faced by professional women' suggests how far some historians have misconstrued its significance.[26] Ostensibly it prohibited disqualifying a person from the exercise of any public function or appointment because of sex or marital status. It thus appeared to fulfil the feminist demand that women be granted equal access to political and professional positions. But its effect on women's legal status demonstrates that the Act's title was misleading.

The government hastily introduced the bill after the Labour Party's Women's Emancipation Bill had passed through the House of Commons against the government's wishes.[27] The Sex Disqualification Bill was intended to satisfy the pressure for reform, but it was carefully drafted to avoid the more sweeping changes proposed in the Women's Emancipation Bill.[28] Ray Strachey warned feminists that the Sex Disqualification Bill was a trap, but her efforts to have it amended were not successful.

While the Sex Disqualification (Removal) Act did enable women to enter certain previously forbidden professions, such as law and accounting, and to become justices of the peace and jury members, its deficiencies as an instrument for change are suggested by the unsuccessful efforts to use it to remove sex-based barriers. Lady Rhondda's attempt to enter the House of Lords was one of the most publicized cases. Her father, Lord Rhondda, drafted his will so that she would inherit his title and be eligible to sit in the House of Lords. In 1922 she petitioned the House of Lords to be allowed to take her seat, citing the Sex Disqualification (Removal) Act in support of her appeal. But the Lord

Chancellor, Lord Birkenhead, organized a successful campaign to reject her petition and continue the practice of excluding women from the House of Lords.[29]

Married women desiring employment also found the Act did not protect them against sex discrimination. The use of the marriage bar to exclude married women from the labour force increased substantially in the 1920s even though the Act ostensibly made it illegal to deny employment to a person on the ground of marital status. In the early 1920s the marriage bar for the first time became a standard practice in teaching, resulting in the dismissal of many married women teachers solely because of their sex (the bar did not apply to married men) and marital status.[30] In 1923 some of these women sued the Rhondda Urban District Council on the ground that the Sex Disqualification (Removal) Act made such dismissals illegal. But in *Price v Rhondda UDC* the court upheld the dismissals, ruling that the Act merely provided that marriage did not disqualify women from employment; it did not mean married women were necessarily entitled to employment.[31]

The perception that women's status was substantially improved in the years immediately following the partial extension of suffrage to women in 1918 is especially misleading with respect to female employment. Equality feminists considered the removal of barriers to employment opportunities a top priority, but they met with much stronger resistance than when they urged improvements in the status of motherhood. When the 1919 reorganization of the civil service excluded women from positions above the clerical level, the LSWS organized a campaign to ensure that women would be allowed into higher positions.[32] It succeeded in obtaining a parliamentary resolution directing the Treasury Department to grant women equal opportunities, but, while appearing to implement this new policy, Treasury officials ensured that few women were successful. The publicity devoted to the handful of females appointed helped obscure the extent to which the postwar decade brought a restoration of pre-war patterns of sex segregation in employment in the civil service and elsewhere.[33]

Although some local authorities had a marriage bar before the war, it was only in the 1920s that it became the general practice in the civil service and in local government as well as in teaching. In 1927 a NUSEC-sponsored bill which would have eliminated the marriage bar for public employees was easily defeated in the House of Commons despite intensive feminist lobbying. Public alarm over the declining rate of population growth contributed to the defeat of the bill; some MPs opposed to the bill thought it would accelerate the decline in the birth rate as married women workers tended to have fewer children than women who were not employed.[34]

Unemployment policies also promoted gender differentiation and discouraged mothers from working for pay. Under the 1920 Unemployment Insurance Act unemployed women were allowed only a twelve-shilling weekly benefit, while men received fifteen. The 1922 Unemployment Insurance Act attempted to reduce the cost of the programme by establishing that benefits were payable only to those 'genuinely seeking whole-time employment'. The main effect of this clause was to exclude many married women from eligibility for benefits.[35]

While Parliament was strengthening sex differentiation in employment, it also enacted new legislation to enhance the status of mothers, thereby encouraging women to continue in traditional roles. Both equality and new feminists urged reform in this area, but their lobbying efforts were noticeably more successful when seeking legislation promoting motherhood than that which increased sex equality. Equality feminist involvement in the campaigns to improve the position of wives and mothers provides further evidence that it is misleading to assume they were concerned solely with single-women and equality issues.

The 1923 Matrimonial Causes Act is an important example of this type of legislation. Drafted by the NUSEC, it enabled wives to sue for divorce on the same basis that husbands could: adultery. Feminists supported the Act for a variety of reasons which suggest the diversity within feminism: while some endorsed it as a step toward equality between the sexes, others thought it desirable because it strengthened the position of wives, and a third group saw it as progress toward an equal moral standard between the sexes. Because feminists disagreed as to whether divorce should be easier to obtain, the NUSEC lobbied against including this change in the bill.[36]

New and equality feminists also agreed that mothers should have equal guardianship rights over their children. On the eve of the 1923 general election *Time and Tide* even gave it priority over equal franchise in the list of items it wished the next government to implement. But Rathbone and Rhondda clashed over the content of what eventually became the 1925 Guardianship of Infants Act. Mrs Wintringham introduced a NUSEC-drafted Equal Guardianship Bill in Parliament, but the government substituted its own bill which deleted the provision for equal guardianship rights.[37] Equality feminists considered the government's bill an 'insult' to the women's societies because it did not provide equal guardianship rights for mothers, but Rathbone supported it because it did improve the position of mothers.[38] A NUSEC resolution welcoming the government's bill while regretting it did not provide for equal guardianship was defeated at the 1925 Consultative Committee meeting by equality feminists, who replaced it with a resolution expressing regret that the bill did not make mothers equal guardians.[39]

Although the government did not claim the Act provided equal guardianship for mothers, historians continue to state that it did, thereby obscuring the degree to which it was a conservative measure intended to prevent the more drastic change urged by feminists.[40] While the Act established equal parental rights to their children once a dispute went to court, it left the mother in a subordinate legal position prior to that point. Mothers did not achieve full equality until the 1973 Guardianship Act was passed, nearly fifty years later.

Both new and equality feminists actively sought passage of two non-equality measures, the 1922 Criminal Law Amendment Act and the 1925 Widows', Orphans' and Old Age Contributory Pensions Act. The first raised the age of consent from thirteen to sixteen, thereby providing young females with greater legal protection against unwanted sexual advances. Widows' pensions had been urged by women's groups since the end of the war. The delay in passage suggests that reform was not easily accomplished; it also indicates that pressure from feminists tended to be successful when other groups, for non-feminist reasons, joined in the demand for reform.[41] Finally, the continuing commitment to both measures by the SPG and equality feminists in other groups indicates equality feminists were not narrowly concerned with careers for single women as their opponents, and some historians, have claimed.

Even Rathbone admitted that after the mid-1920s feminists

were less successful in influencing Parliament. The increasing conflict between feminists, culminating in the 1927 NUSEC executive committee split, contributed to this. Three issues proved especially divisive for feminists: birth control, family allowances and protective legislation.

In her 1925 NUSEC presidential address Rathbone urged a significant shift in the NUSEC programme. She claimed that if feminists continued to emphasize efforts to achieve what men already had, they would have difficulty recruiting young women. What feminists should do was to accept woman's special sphere and work for reform 'not because it is what men have got, but because it is what women need to fulfil the potentialities of their own natures'.[42] This meant focusing on women's special contributions as mothers rather than seeking to eliminate sex role differences. Her address provided a theoretical basis for two new reforms she wished to be included in the NUSEC immediate programme: birth control and family allowances.

During the 1920s the government would not allow public clinics to provide birth control information even to married women. The immediate issue was whether the NUSEC should join in the campaign being conducted by other organizations, such as the Workers' Birth Control Group, to reverse this policy. This became a contentious issue when equality feminists objected to including it in the NUSEC programme. Equality feminists were not necessarily opposed to birth control; some, like Cicely Hamilton and Emmeline Pethick-Lawrence, were prominent birth control advocates. Within the NUSEC at least two main groups of equality feminists resisted adding it to the Union's programme: those like Florence M. Beaumont, who thought it morally wrong, and others, such as Lady Dorothy Balfour of Burleigh and Helen Fraser, who endorsed birth control but considered it a 'human' question rather than a feminist issue, and thus likely to divert energy away from the equality reforms that were central to feminism.[43]

Despite the internal divisions on the issue, birth control was added to the NUSEC programme in 1925. The NUSEC lobbied the Ministry of Health later that year to allow the provision of birth control information at public clinics; during the 1929 election campaign it and the Workers' Birth Control Group formed a joint committee chaired by the NUSEC parliamentary secretary, Eva

Hubback, which sought from parliamentary candidates commitments to birth control reform. Hubback's group were regarded as a 'difficult lot' by Ministry of Health officials subjected to their lobbying efforts, but it was only after Labour-controlled city councils joined in the campaign that the government agreed in 1930 to allow public clinics to provide birth control information.[44]

While Rathbone's NUSEC colleagues, Mary Stocks and Eva Hubback, spearheaded the feminist birth control efforts, the unmarried and childless Rathbone personally directed the family allowances campaign. She formed the Family Endowment Committee in 1917, and in 1924 engineered its expansion into the broader Family Endowment Society. With the assistance of Stocks and Hubback, she in effect ran both organizations. Her 1924 book, *The Disinherited Family*, was the most important new feminist text published in the 1920s.

Family allowances became a cornerstone of the new feminism. New feminists viewed state payments to mothers as recognition that motherhood was as valuable a service to society as the various forms of gainful employment outside the home. Some new feminists saw it as a means of shifting the balance of power within marriages: allowances paid to the mother would lessen a woman's financial dependence on her husband. Some assumed it would liberate wives by removing the economic necessity of working outside the home; family allowances would permit married women to remain at home, thus avoiding the double burden of housework and gainful employment.[45]

Although Rathbone is famous for her scathing remarks about the male 'Turk complex', she used a variety of arguments for reform, not all of which were feminist. By 1925 her proposal to endow motherhood in order to grant wives greater independence from their husbands had become a scheme to provide family allowances to alleviate child poverty.[46] Also, while feminism is ordinarily associated with restricting family size, Rathbone thought family allowances desirable in part because they would encourage middle-class women to have more children.[47] While she may have shifted grounds in the hope of appealing to a wider audience, it left equality feminists wondering whether her proposal would not bind women more firmly to traditional roles.

Rathbone claimed family allowances would make feminism more relevant to working-class women. But working-class women were divided on the issue. The Standing Joint Committee of Industrial Women's Organizations chose not to support it partly due to concern that employers would claim that family allowances made wage increases unnecessary.[48] Even in the Women's Co-operative Guild, an important base of support, family allowances remained a controversial issue.[49] Married working-class women employed in the northern textile mills also expressed reservations about the scheme's implications. Some, like Ada Nield Chew, valued the independence they derived from paid employment and feared that behind family allowances lurked 'the ideal of the domestic tabby-cat-woman as that to which all womanhood should aspire'.[50]

Although the 1925 NUSEC annual council voted by a large margin (111 to 42) to include birth control and family allowances in its immediate programme, this step hastened the widening rift between new and equality feminists. But it would be wrong to infer that equality feminists necessarily opposed family allowances. Both Lord Balfour of Burleigh and Lady Astor, who sided with the equality feminists during the 1927 crisis, were Family Endowment Society officers in the 1920s; others, such as Ray Strachey, had endorsed family allowances.[51] But even the equality feminists who supported family allowances were alarmed by the inclusion of that reform in the NUSEC immediate programme; they believed it was replacing equality reforms, such as equal pay for equal work, as the union's top priority. Equality feminists perceived the two reforms as symbols of contrasting conceptions of feminism. Equal pay did not mean just higher wages for women; it was an attack on the system of gender differentiation. Family allowances seemed, in contrast, to imply accepting gender distinctions and striving to improve women's status within the existing system.

It was the issue of protective legislation more than any other, however, which precipitated the break between new and equality feminists in 1927. Following the war the NUSEC had adopted the equality position on this matter: 'regulations concerning wages, hours of labour, night work, etc. should be based upon the type of work and not upon the sex of the workers'.[52] Conflict over the issue within the NUSEC intensified in 1924 when the Labour Government introduced a Factories Bill proposing additional protective legislation exclusively for women. Equality feminists suspected that, especially for Labour proponents, the reduction of female employment opportunities was the intent of sex-based protective legislation, and not merely an incidental result.

Alarmed at the increasing pressure within the NUSEC to alter its policy, and at the possibility that the government's Lead Paint Bill might be passed, in May 1926 a group of equality feminists led by Lady Rhondda formed the Open Door Council (ODC) to campaign exclusively for equal pay, equal status and equal opportunity for women workers.[53] Its original members included Elizabeth Abbott and Miss Clegg, respectively members of the NUSEC and the LSWS executive committees, and the presidents of three other feminist societies: Emmeline Pethick-Lawrence (WFL), Virginia Crawford (St Joan's Social and Political Alliance), and Lady Rhondda (SPG).[54] By June 1927 seven of the eleven NUSEC executive committee members who resigned in March of that year had joined the ODC executive.[55]

Equality feminists were accused by their opponents of opposing all protective legislation; unfortunately, historians continue to reiterate this misconception.[56] Equality feminists supported protective legislation based on the nature of the work rather than on the sex of the worker, but their opponents ignored this and portrayed them as *laissez-faire* opponents of all state intervention. Equality feminists objected only to protective legislation that applied solely to women, not to all protective legislation. One of the first ODC publications explicitly urged protective legislation that applied equally to both sexes.[57] Equality feminists reiterated this position in public and in private meetings with cabinet ministers in the following years.[58]

Misperceptions of the equality feminist position on protective legislation may explain why they have been erroneously portrayed as opposing special maternity provisions for working mothers. Under the 1901 Factory Act it was illegal to employ a woman in a factory within four weeks after giving birth. Equality feminists joined with other women's groups in seeking to change this, not because it conflicted with a theoretical principle of equality or a commitment to *laissez-faire*, but for the practical reason that many working-class mothers could not do without an income for four weeks and illegally returned to work early, without regard for the effect on their health. When in 1929 a feminist delegation met with the Home Secretary, J. R. Clynes, to present its views on what should be included in the government's proposed Factories

Bill, the ODC representative urged that instead of banning women from their jobs for a specified period after giving birth, they should be paid maternity benefit so that the pressure to restore their income would not force them into returning to work prematurely.[59] Equality feminists, such as Vera Brittain, who opposed sex-differentiated protective legislation, defended paid maternity leave on the ground that it enabled women to perform their normal activities, including childbirth, and that this was implied in the concept of equality.[60]

At the March 1927 NUSEC annual council meeting two votes were crucial in demonstrating that the balance of power within the Union had shifted to the new feminists. When a resolution reaffirming the Union's traditional position on protective legislation was under consideration,[61] Rathbone moved an amendment which would have allowed the NUSEC to support such legislation under certain conditions, even when it applied solely to women. After 'prolonged' debate her amendment carried by an 81 to 80 vote. Later, Lord Balfour of Burleigh proposed an amendment stating that family allowances and birth control should have a lower priority in the NUSEC immediate programme than those reforms, such as equal pay, which were more directly concerned with sex equality. The discussion of this amendment was 'even longer and more heated' than that on protective legislation; it was defeated by a large majority.[62]

Following these votes the NUSEC secretary, Lady Balfour of Burleigh, and ten other newly elected members of the twenty-three-person executive committee resigned their positions, claiming the annual council had introduced changes in the NUSEC's 'fundamental principles' which entailed a 'betrayal' of the women's movement. Those resigning included Winifred Soddy, the NUSEC treasurer for the previous six years, and several of the most experienced executive committee members: one, Chrystal Macmillan, had been on the executive since 1910.

It is misleading to view this split as simply a disagreement over specific reforms. Helen Ward and Mrs James Taylor, for example, remained on the executive even though they agreed with those resigning on the protective legislation issue.[63] Edith Picton-Turberville continued on the executive even though she agreed with those resigning that the sex equality items on the NUSEC programme were of greater importance than those, like family allowances, which did not involve sex equality.[64] Some of those who resigned, including their leader, Lady Balfour of Burleigh, endorsed new feminist reforms such as birth control and family allowances. But the resigners did not consider these reforms central to feminism; by focusing on sexual difference they reinforced traditional notions of femaleness, thus undercutting feminist efforts to change those conceptions. Jane Lewis has noted that some inter-war feminists relied upon the same analytical framework as anti-feminists; this seems precisely what equality feminists found alarming about new feminism.[65]

The clash between NUSEC new and equality feminists was replayed in other feminist societies and may have contributed to the demise of the Consultative Committee of Women's Organizations in 1928. Following a debate on protective legislation at its January 1927 meeting, Lady Astor expressed support for the equality feminist position and agreed to try to amend the government's Factories Bill to make it apply to persons rather than just to women.[66] But conflict on the issue continued; in 1928 the NUSEC resigned from the committee, Lady Astor declined to run for re-election as its president, and in October it was dissolved.[67]

The equal suffrage campaign also divided feminists. Impatient with Rathbone's strategy of quiet backstage lobbying, in 1926 Lady Rhondda founded the Equal Political Rights Campaign Committee. She intended to bring Mrs Pankhurst into the campaign, and to revive the pre-war suffrage tactic of protest demonstrations. Lady Astor, among others, cautioned her against this but Rhondda thought it important for women to take an active public role in pressuring the government to grant equal suffrage.[68]

A crucial factor in the passage of the 1928 Representation of the People (Equal Franchise) Act granting women aged twenty-one and over the suffrage on the same basis as men was Baldwin's belief that the Conservative Party would not be harmed by the additional female voters.[69] Equal suffrage weakened feminist pressure for drastic change by removing what was, in the eyes of British women, the last great symbol of women's inequality. By the 1930s NUSEC membership had declined substantially; the majority of its members had chosen to join the non-feminist towns-women's guilds, which sought to teach women how to perform their traditional roles better, rather than continue in NUSEC's feminist branches. What seemed in 1928 to be an important victory for feminist reformers now appears to be one of a series of successful steps by Conservative-controlled governments which strengthened women's loyalty to traditional institutions and roles.[70]

At the end of the 1920s feminists could look back on a decade of intense activity and significant improvements in the status of women. But in spite of these accomplishments they seemed a beleaguered band very much on the defensive: they were bitterly divided over fundamental feminist principles, membership and income of the largest feminist society, the NUSEC, was declining rapidly,[71] and the very word feminist had strong pejorative connotations. Vera Brittain acknowledged that feminists were perceived as 'spectacled, embittered women, disappointed, childless, dowdy, and generally unloved'.[72]

While the granting of equal suffrage in 1928 contributed to the declining support for feminism by removing an obvious symbol of legal inequality, other factors were involved. Both new and equality feminists agreed that feminism had little support among the younger generation of women, but divided as to the reason for this. Rathbone claimed equality feminism had little appeal to younger women because the latter had 'never known the harsher forms of inequality' experienced by those who had grown up before the First World War.[73] Equality feminists attributed the limited feminist appeal to the difficulty in presenting the idea of the eradication of gender differences in a popular slogan which could be easily understood.[74] Others claim that feminism was associated with a sexual prudery and high-mindedness repellent to a younger generation seeking pleasure and sexual expression.[75] While the postwar backlash against alterations in women's roles was a powerful barrier to change, some aspects of feminist ideology may also have hampered efforts to recruit women. Equality feminists needed to stimulate women's awareness of gender inequality in order to mobilize them to work for equality, but in emphasizing what women lacked in comparison to men they seemed to be encouraging a negative image of women's self-worth. Part of the new feminist appeal stemmed from its avoidance of this pitfall. By stressing the positive feminine qualities men lacked, new feminists encouraged women to take pride in their femaleness but in so doing they weakened women's sense of acute injustice, something which had been an important driving force propelling women into reform efforts in other periods. But 1920s feminists were hardly unique in finding it difficult to reconcile the demand for equality with the assertion of sexual difference.

Notes

1. Susan K. Kent, 'The politics of sexual difference: World War I and the demise of British feminism', *Journal of British Studies*, vol. 27 (July 1988), p. 239.
2. Elizabeth Roberts, *Women's Work 1840–1940* (Macmillan, London, 1988), p. 72.
3. Anna Davin, 'Imperialism and motherhood', *History Workshop Journal*, vol. 5 (Spring 1978), pp. 13–14.
4. NUWSS Executive Committee minutes, 22 November 1917, Fawcett Library.
5. Eleanor Rathbone, 'The economic position of married women', *Common Cause*, 4 January 1912. In *Victorian Feminism 1850–1900* (Hutchinson, London, 1987), Philippa Levine traces new feminism back to the Victorian period.
6. Eleanor Rathbone, 'The endowment of motherhood in its bearing on the doctrine of equal wages for equal work', *Common Cause*, vol. 9 (1 March 1918), p. 601.
7. Ray Strachey, 'Equal pay for equal work', *Common Cause*, vol. 9 (8 March 1918), pp. 620–1.
8. *Time and Tide*, 12 March 1926.
9. Eva Hubback in *Time and Tide*, 20 August 1926.
10. *Time and Tide*, 12 March 1926.
11. *Common Cause*, vol. 10 (21 February 1919), pp. 546–7.
12. *LSWS Annual Report 1919*, p. 7.
13. *Common Cause*, vol. 11 (25 April 1919), p. 17.
14. WFL, *Report of the 12th Annual Conference 1919*, p. 16.
15. Vera Brittain, *Testament of Youth* (Macmillan, London, 1933), p. 583.
16. Lady Rhondda to E. Pankhurst, November 1925. Cited in David Mitchell, *The Fighting Pankhursts* (Jonathan Cape, London, 1967), p. 156.
17. *Time and Tide*, 19 January 1923. Cited in Dale Spender, *Time and Tide Wait for No Man* (Pandora, London, 1984), p. 178.
18. *Idem*, pp. 37–8.
19. *Time and Tide*, 14 May 1920, in *idem*, pp. 6–7. *Time and Tide*, 5 July 1930, p. 856 and Muriel Mellown, 'Lady Rhondda and the changing faces of British feminism', *Frontiers*, vol. 9, no. 2 (1987), p. 10.
20. Consultative Committee of Women's Organizations minutes, 1 March 1921. Box 342, CCWO Papers, Fawcett Library.
21. CCWO, *Second Annual Report 1922–23*, p. 4.
22. Brian Harrison, 'Women in a men's house: the women MPs, 1919–1945', *Historical Journal*, vol. 29, no. 3 (1986), p. 625.
23. *The Vote*, vol. 29 (23 March 1928), p. 91.
24. Eleanor Rathbone, *The Harvest of the Women's Movement* (NUSEC, London, 1935), p. 6.
25. Olive Banks, *Faces of Feminism* (Blackwell, Oxford, 1981), p. 164.
26. Suzie Fleming, 'Introduction', in Eleanor Rathbone, *The Disinherited Family* (Falling Wall Press, London, 1986), p. 58.

27. Harold L. Smith, 'Sex vs. class: British feminists and the Labour movement, 1919–1928', *The Historian*, vol. 47 (November 1984), p. 19.

28. Home Affairs Committee minutes, 16 May 1919. CAB 26/1 HAC 28 (19) 6, Public Record Office.

29. Shirley M. Eoff, *The Life of Margaret Haig Thomas Mackworth, Second Viscountess Rhondda* (Ph.D. diss., Texas Tech, 1985), pp. 164–75.

30. Alison Oram, 'Serving two masters? The introduction of a marriage bar in teaching in the 1920s, in *The Sexual Dynamics of History* (Pluto Press, 1983), p. 135.

31. Susan Atkins and Brenda Hoggett, *Women and the Law* (Blackwell, Oxford, 1984), p. 17.

32. See the minutes of the Joint Committee on Women in the Civil Service beginning 1 March 1920, Fawcett Library.

33. Meta Zimmeck, 'Strategies and stratagems for the employment of women in the British civil service, 1919–1939', *Historical Journal*, vol. 27 (December 1984), pp. 901–24.

34. *Parliamentary Debates*, 205 H.C. Deb. 5 s., 29 April 1927, cols. 1204 and 1209.

35. Pat Thane, *The Foundations of the Welfare State* (Longman, London, 1982), p. 174.

36. Dorothy Stetson, *A Woman's Issue: The Politics of Family Law Reform in England* (Greenwood Press, Westport, Conn., 1982), p. 97.

37. The government's bill was explicitly intended to avoid introducing equal guardianship rights. See the Home Affairs Committee minutes, 4 April 1924. CAB 26/6 HAC 9 (24) 2.

38. At the request of feminists Lady Astor moved an equality clause be added to the bill, but when this was opposed by the government she withdrew her amendment rather than endanger the bill. See *Time and Tide*, 27 March 1925.

39. *Time and Tide*, 6 March 1925.

40. See Jane Lewis, *Women in England 1870–1950* (Wheatsheaf Books, Brighton, 1984), p. 119. After this was written I discovered that Julia Brophy presented an argument similar to mine, but based on different sources, in 'Parental rights and children's welfare: some problems of feminists' strategy in the 1920s', *International Journal of the Sociology of Law*, vol. 10 (1982), pp. 149–68.

41. The Act's provisions were substantially different from those urged by feminists. See *Time and Tide*, 8 May and 3 July 1925.

42. Eleanor Rathbone, *Milestones: Presidential Addresses at the Annual Council Meetings of the NUSEC* (Lee and Nightingale, Liverpool, 1929), p. 29.

43. See *The Woman's Leader*, vol. 18 (26 March 1926), p. 75 and vol. 18 (16 April 1926), p. 99 and Lady Balfour of Burleigh's letter to the editor in *Time and Tide*, 26 March 1926.

44. Richard Soloway, *Birth Control and the Population Question in England, 1877–1930* (University of North Carolina Press, Chapel Hill, 1982), pp. 309–10.

45. Fleming, *op. cit.* note 26, pp. 10–11.

46. Jane Lewis, *The Politics of Motherhood* (Croom Helm, London, 1980), p. 172.

47. Eleanor Rathbone, *The Disinherited Family* (E. Arnold, London, 1924), p. 247.

48. *Report of the 11th National Conference of Labour Women* 3–5 June 1930, p. 54.

49. Introductory note by Margaret Llewelyn Davies in *Life As We Have Known It* (W. W. Norton, New York, 1975), p. xiii.
50. Cited in Jill Liddington and Jill Norris, *One Hand Tied Behind Us: The Rise of the Women's Suffrage Movement* (Virago, London, 1978), p. 260.
51. John Macnicol, *The Movement for Family Allowances 1918–45* (Hutchinson, London, 1980), p. 25.
52. NUSEC Executive Committee minutes, 22 January 1920, Fawcett Library.
53. Open Door Council, *First Annual Report, 1926–27* (London, 1927).
54. *Equal Rights*, vol. 14 (19 February 1927), 15.
55. *Equal Rights*, vol. 14 (4 June 1927), 131.
56. See Brian Harrison, *Prudent Revolutionaries: Portraits of British Feminists between the Wars* (Clarendon, Oxford, 1987), p. 148.
57. ODC, *The Real Protection of the Woman Worker* (London, 1926).
58. See the letter to the editor by Elizabeth Abbott and other equality feminists in *The Times*, 11 February 1929, and the minutes of the Equal Political Rights Campaign Committee's deputation to the Prime Minister, 19 April 1929, Box 335, EPRCC Papers, Fawcett Library.
59. Minutes of the EPRCC's deputation to the Home Secretary, 4 November 1929. Box 335, EPRCC papers, Fawcett Library.
60. Vera Brittain, 'Women in industry', *Manchester Guardian*, 8 December 1927. Reprinted in Paul Berry and A. Bishop (eds), *Testament of a Generation* (Virago, London, 1985), p. 111.
61. This resolution, moved by an equality feminist (Monica Whately), endorsed protective legislation which was not sex differentiated.
62. Report (minutes) of the March 1927 Annual Council meeting. Box 342, NUSEC papers, Fawcett Library.
63. *The Woman's Leader*, vol. 19 (18 March 1927), p. 50, and *Time and Tide*, vol. 8 (1 April 1927), p. 316.
64. *The Woman's Leader*, vol. 19 (25 March 1927), p. 59.
65. Lewis, *op. cit.* note 40, p. 103.
66. *Equal Rights*, vol. 14 (5 March 1927), p. 32.
67. Consultative Committee of Women's Organizations, *Seventh Annual Report 1927–28* (1928).
68. Lady Rhondda to Lady Astor, 5 November 1925 and Astor's marginal notes in reply. Ms 1416/1/1/261, Lady Astor Papers, University of Reading.
69. Martin Pugh, *The Evolution of the British Electoral System 1832–1987* (Historical Association, London, 1988), p. 9.
70. Harrison, *op. cit.* note 56, p. 305.
71. Brian Harrison, 'Women's suffrage at Westminster, 1866–1928', in Michael Bentley and John Stevenson (eds), *High and Low Politics in Modern Britain* (Clarendon, Oxford, 1983), p. 88.
72. *Manchester Guardian*, 13 December 1928, p. 8.
73. *The Woman's Leader*, vol. 18 (26 February 1926), p. 36.
74. Vera Brittain, *op cit.* note 60, p. 101.
75. Harrison, *op. cit.* note 56, p. 320.

5 Gender Reconstruction After the First World War

Susan Kingsley Kent

The conservative nature of feminism after the Great War and the significant shift in the ideologies and attitudes of postwar feminists cry out for analysis and explanation. Pre-war feminists vigorously attacked the notion of separate spheres and the medical and scientific discourses about gender and sexuality upon which those spheres rested.[1] Many feminists after the First World War, by contrast, pursued a programme that championed rather than challenged the prevailing ideas about masculinity and femininity that appeared in the literature of psychoanalysis and sexology. In embracing radically new – and seemingly liberating – views of women as human beings with sexual identities, many feminists ironically accepted theories of sexual difference that helped to advance notions of separate spheres for men and women. By the end of the 1920s, new feminists found themselves in a conceptual bind that trapped women in 'traditional' domestic and maternal roles, and limited their ability to advocate equality and justice for women.[2]

Historians have interpreted the nature of postwar feminism in a variety of ways. Brian Harrison attributes the reticence and discretion of inter-war feminists to the requirements of political opportunity, to the sensible decision of feminist leaders to accommodate themselves to the prevailing political culture. His 'prudent revolutionaries', moreover, have not lost any of their radicalism; they have simply switched tactics. 'Their prudence does not signify mildness of feminist commitment; on the contrary, they envisaged a new society very different from the old – transformed not just in its political system, but in the details of family life.' Jane Lewis concurs, arguing that 'New Feminism had the potential to develop a radical analysis of women's position . . . new feminists were asking fundamental questions about the position of women in the family.' In their efforts, however, to attract working-class women and feminists in the labour movement who, since the turn of the century, had focused much of their attention on women's demands as mothers, middle-class feminists 'failed to make strong enough analytical connections with the position of women in relation to other structures, especially in respect to the workplace and to educational institutions'. In an entirely different approach, Sheila Jeffreys lays the blame for the demise of feminism at the feet of sexologists, whose sexual ideology 'undermine[d] feminism and women's independence . . . The promotion of the ideology of motherhood and marriage together with the stigmatising of lesbianism helped to reinforce women's dependence upon men.' Sexual reform had the effect of sapping women's rage and blunting their criticisms of male behaviour. [3]

Harrison, Lewis and Jeffreys have identified the political, socio-economic, and ideological difficulties feminists faced in the crucial period following the First World War. Their accounts, however, do not fully explain why the ideology of motherhood and constraining ideas about gender found so ready an acceptance among women who had before the war rejected them so decisively. The key lies in the postwar discourses about sexuality and gender. In simultaneously promising sexual 'liberation' and a new identity for women, and continually referring to the threat of discord and, ultimately, war, these discourses led feminists to compromise their earlier egalitarianism.

A linking of eroticism and war and the use of sexual imagery to evoke wartime experience appear in much of the writing of the postwar period. In 'Recalling War', for instance, Robert Graves described the outbreak of the conflict in August 1914 in terms of erections and ejaculations: 'we . . . thrust out/Boastful tongue, clenched fist and valiant yard./Natural infirmities were out of mode,/For Death was young again: patron alone/Of healthy dying, premature fate-spasm.' Siegfried Sassoon's *Memoirs of an Infantry Officer*, whose hero repeatedly enters and exits from the trenches, is organized around 'the dynamics of . . . penetration and withdrawal'.[4] Many Britons held as 'a deeply rooted cultural assumption' the view of war as a release from long-suppressed libidinal energies.[5] Magnus Hirschfeld, a sexologist and sex reformer, articulated these attitudes in *The Sexual History of the World War*.

'The war', he wrote, 'was . . . a sudden unchaining of atavistic impulses which for five years stormed through the world unimpeded and constituted the terrible forms in which the historical necessity of a moral transformation came to expression.' While repressed eroticism did not bring about the war, he noted, 'war is an opportunity for throwing off, for a while, all the irksome repressions which culture imposes and for satisfying temporarily all the repressed desires'.[6]

The association of sex and war carried potentially explosive implications for society when it became clear that this war would require the participation of all segments of the population. Very early on press warnings proliferated about threats to the chastity of respectable women, war nymphomania and the sexual attraction that men in uniform held for women.[7] Hirschfeld asserted that 'the great experience of the outbreak of the war, the tremendous emotional excitement that it brought, exercised a stimulating effect upon the women of every land and appears to have raised their need of love considerably . . . woman reacted to the war with an increase of her libido'.[8] Before they even reached France, members of the Women's Auxiliary Army Corps (WAAC) were accused of loose living and of corrupting the morals of 'our poor lads'. 'Within a year of the arrival of the first WAACs on the Continent,' Trevor Wilson writes, 'allegations of "immoral conduct" and unwanted pregnancies were so rife that it became necessary to appoint a commission of inquiry.' Though the commission found the charges of widespread immorality to be unjustified, 'the presumed sexual aspirations of WAACs towards British soldiers' continued to excite the public imagination.[9]

The linking of sex and war made it possible for some to conceive of the First World War as a war between the sexes. Hirschfeld, extrapolating from Freud's *Beyond the Pleasure Principle* and *Group Psychology and the Analysis of the Ego*, argued that 'in the depths of the human soul, eroticism, cruelty and the mad desire to destroy, are all intimately connected'. Sadistic impulses that had been repressed in peacetime found legitimate expression in the atrocities perpetrated in the war. 'Without the sexual background,' Hirschfeld asserted, 'the numerous, meaningless acts of cruelty of the World War are incomprehensible'.[10] Eric Leed, Paul Fussell and Sandra Gilbert highlight the hostility and anger directed towards the home – symbolized and epitomized by

women – by the soldiers at the front. In 'Glory of Women',
Sassoon seethed,

> You love us when we're heroes, home on leave,
> Or wounded in a mentionable place.
> You worship decorations; you believe
> That chivalry redeems the war's disgrace.
> You make us shells. You listen with delight,
> By tales of dirt and danger fondly thrilled.
> You crown our distant ardours while we fight,
> And mourn our laurelled memories when we're killed.
> You can't believe that British troops 'retire'
> When hell's last horror breaks them, and they run,
> Trampling the terrible corpses – blind with blood.
> O German mother dreaming by the fire,
> While you are knitting socks to send your son
> His face is trodden deeper in the mud.[11]

'The visiting of violent and if possible painful death upon the
complacent, uncomprehending, fatuous civilians at home was a
favourite fantasy indulged by the troops', Fussell argues.[12] Hirschfeld recounted that with the outbreak of war 'women demonstrated the most incredible readiness to part with, nay to send
away their beloved ones, husbands and sons', offering up the
scenario of a 'given man, who had been virtually pushed into the
war by his wife or mother'.[13] 'Women of Britain Say "Go!"' urged
one War Office poster,[14] while hyperpatriotic women bestowed
white feathers – a symbol of cowardice – upon able-bodied men
in civilian clothes. Slogans such as 'Shells Made By a Wife May
Save a Husband's Life', recruiting women for the munitions factories,[15] could scarcely conceal the reality that shells made by
women also took men's lives. These discrete impressions, Gilbert
suggests, in the light of the dramatic gains in employment and
freedom women achieved precisely because of the war, coalesced
into a perception that the persistent horrors of the war were,
somehow, women's fault. D. H. Lawrence's wartime poem, 'Eloi,
Eloi, Lama Sabacthani', conveys this sense of being preyed upon
by women: 'Why do the women follow us, satisfied,/Feed on our
wounds like bread, receive our blood/Like glittering seed upon
them for fulfilment?'[16]

Misgivings about the return of soldiers following the Armistice
stemmed from an appreciation of the implications of the war for
sexual and gender relationships. 'With the conclusion of conflict,'

Leed asserts, 'the notion that war had been the playing field of insubordinate libido was a crucial feature in the anxieties which surrounded the figure of the returning veteran.'[17] Demobilized soldiers were certainly violent when they returned to England, and accounts of sexual attacks upon women filled the columns of newspapers.[18] Contemporaries could readily believe, on the basis of immediate past experience, that aggression, destructiveness, and violence were inherent characteristics of masculinity, and that social peace and order would depend upon minimizing the provocations of men to anger. Removing women from their wartime jobs so as to eliminate competition with men for work was regarded as one way to assure, as Ray Strachey put it, 'that everything could be as it had been before'.[19]

Everything could not be as it had been before, however. Many contemporaries remarked upon the persistence of the war long after the Armistice had brought an end to actual combat. Fussell reminds us that during the war 'one did not have to be a lunatic or a particularly despondent visionary to conceive quite seriously that the war would literally never end and would become the permanent condition of mankind'. With the cessation of hostilities in November 1918, front soldiers continued to experience in nightmares the anxieties of the trenches: Sassoon dreamed that the war was still going on 'every two or three months' until 1936 at least. In 1926 Carl Jung's dreaming about the war led him to conclude that 'the war, which in the outer world had taken place some years before, was not yet over, but was continuing to be fought within the psyche'.[20] Conflict became the model through which political, social, literary, artistic, sexual and psychological experience was lived.[21] Much of the conservatism of 'new' feminism can be attributed to the fear of renewed conflict that women competing with men in public and private arenas seemed to suggest. As Cicely Hamilton, a committed feminist both before and after the war, observed in 1927, 'the peace in our time for which we all crave will mean a reaction, more or less strong, against the independence of women'.[22]

Sexual conflict and polarization between the sexes, or sex war, provided one of the few adequate means by which the political, economic, and social upheaval occasioned by the First World War could be represented.[23] This development would have a significant impact upon the thinking of those involved in theorizing about the relations between men and women, particularly physicians, psychiatrists and sexologists, and feminists. Pre-war feminists consistently refused to accept the dominant discourses on sexuality,[24] which in the nineteenth century defined women as 'the Sex' and men as sexual aggressors. Feminists' challenges contained an often explicit assertion that gender and sexuality were culturally or socially constructed; their goal was the establishment of a society in which the 'natural' equality and freedom of women and men could be realized. By the end of the 1920s 'new' feminist positions on such issues as marriage, motherhood, birth control and sexual pleasure underscored not fundamental equality but the primacy of sexual difference in determining the relations between men and women. Many feminists embraced the conservative images of femininity and masculinity that arose as British society sought in the establishment of harmonious marital relationships a resolution to the anxieties and political turmoil caused by the First World War.[25] Britons, including feminists, looked to create peace and order in the public sphere of social, economic and political relations by imposing peace and order on the private sphere of sexual relations. Because the theories offered by the 'experts' on women's sexuality seemed, in their advocacy of sexual pleasure and satisfaction, so liberating, many feminists, lacking any other language of sex, hailed them as advanced.

The inscription of large societal anxieties and conflicts on to marital relationships operated on at least two levels. On the one hand, gender, sexuality and the relationship between the sexes served as metaphors through which issues of power might be resolved by referring to notions of sexual difference. As Joan Scott has observed, 'war is represented as a sexual disorder; peace thus implies a return to "traditional" gender relationships, the familiar and natural order of families, men in public roles, women at home, and so on'.[26] On the other hand, sexuality and war were understood by the culture – consciously or unconsciously – to be inextricably intertwined. Thus, the resolution of conflict through mutual, pleasurable sexual experiences within marriage was regarded by many sexologists and sex reformers as a means of reducing the threat of war by removing the sexual repressions and tensions that, they sometimes implied, helped to bring it about. 'There are certain inter-relationships between the negative forces of destruction and the positive might of Eros', Hirschfeld asserted.

For every repression and violation of Eros can, under certain conditions, produce an emergence of the destructive sadistic powers. The
sexual misery of peace time, the hypocritical morality of the ruling
social classes, pervert the natural impulses and finally bursts [*sic*] out
in aberrant reactions. The liberation of violated impulses through the
war, the tremendous expression which they had never been able to
achieve in peace time, produced a tremendous intoxication which carried men with it beyond all reason. The primeval combat of the powers
of life and death, which is forever being fought anew, came to an
armistice.

'How will the primeval enmity of both these powers end up?'
Hirschfeld asked. Professing his faith in the perseverance of the
positive might of Eros, he replied by quoting Freud: 'we must
hope that the second of the two divine forces, namely, the eternal
Eros will make a great effort to maintain itself in the struggle with
its equally immortal enemy'.[27]

The discourses on sexuality that predominated in the postwar
years appropriated the language and imagery of war as psychoan-
alysts, sexologists and sex reformers sought in the study of sexuality the solutions to the maintenance and salvation of civilization
itself. As Havelock Ellis, the most influential sexologist in inter-
war Britain, wrote in *The Psychology of Sex*, his popular textbook,
sex 'is not merely the channel along which the race is maintained
and built up, it is the foundation on which all dreams of the future
world must be erected'.[28] For Ellis, as for all 'scientists of sex' in
the 1920s and 1930s, sexual activity was firmly located within
marriage,[29] and its chief and central aim, after the carnage wrought
by the First World War, was procreation. A more insistent ideology of motherhood[30] demanded that women leave their wartime
jobs, give up their independence, and return to home and family,
where their primary occupation – their obligation in fact – would
be the bearing and rearing of children.

If the sexual disorder of war was to be followed by peace,
the metaphor required sexual peace, a model of marital accord
achieved through mutual sexual enjoyment. Discourses about
female sexuality which before the war had emphasized women's
lack of sexual impulse, and even distaste for sexual intercourse,
underwent modification to accommodate the political, social and
economic requirements of the postwar period. The new accent
on motherhood was accompanied by a growing emphasis on the
importance of sexual activity, sexual pleasure, sexual compatibility

between husband and wife.[31] As marriage and marital sex bore the brunt of restoring social harmony in postwar Britain, sex manuals – how-to guides to conjugal fulfilment – became best-sellers. Marie Stopes's *Married Love*, published in 1918, sold more than 2000 copies in the first two weeks, and 400 000 by 1923. Theodore Van de Velde's *Ideal Marriage, Its Physiology and Technique* went through forty-three printings.[32] Such books as Isabel Emslie Hutton's *The Sex Technique in Marriage*, Helena Wright's *The Sex Factor in Marriage* and Van de Velde's *Sexual Tensions in Marriage* attest to the broadly perceived need to establish sexual peace through sexual pleasure.[33]

Domestic harmony, and thus social peace, appeared to Britons to depend upon a return to 'traditional' sex roles – to separate spheres of public and private. With the popularization of Freudian theory in the 1920s, separate sphere ideology based on constructions of masculinity and femininity and male and female sexuality received additional scientific justification. Psychoanalysis filtered into Britain through the lens of biology. Whereas Freud had posited a psychological bisexuality in males and females, and asserted that masculinity and femininity and sexuality were cultural phenomena that required explanation, British psychiatrists and sexologists put forward theories of sexuality and sexual difference that stemmed from biology. Femininity, argued Ernest Jones, 'develops progressively from the promptings of an instinctual constitution'.[34]

While undermining the belief in the passionlessness of the female – a development that had considerable appeal for many feminists and contributed to the conceptual dilemma within which they trapped themselves – Freud's British followers thus gave credence to the belief that biological factors determined the differences between masculinity and femininity and male and female sexuality. Freud had argued that the personality development of the female centered upon her discovery in early childhood that she lacked a penis; penis envy created in the female child a lifelong dissatisfaction with her identity as a woman. Her discomfiture could be overcome only through the substitution of the penis with a child.[35] Happiness and health for women, in other words, depended upon motherhood. Those women who refused motherhood, who continued in their work or study, brought down upon their heads the wrath of many psychiatrists and sexologists, who found in their presumptions a sexual pathology. Diagnoses of a 'female castration complex' or of frigidity were applied to women who ventured out of their assigned domestic, sexual sphere. Karl Abraham, a close colleague of Freud, described feminists as women who 'are unable to carry out a full psychical adaptation to the female sexual role', women who, quite mistakenly, 'consider that the sex of a person has nothing to do with his or her capacities, especially in the mental field'.[36]

Using terminology and imagery evocative of war, sexologist Walter Gallichan wrote in *The Poison of Prudery*: 'These degenerate women are a menace to civilisation. They provoke sex misunderstanding and antagonism; they wreck conjugal happiness.' Wilhelm Stekel, a Freudian analyst, agreed, insisting that 'we shall never understand the problem of the frigid woman unless we take into consideration the fact that the two sexes are engaged in a lasting conflict'.[37] Weith Knudsen, a Norwegian professor of jurisprudence and economics who had a large British audience, argued that this 'sexual anaesthesia . . . so prevalent among civilised women . . . actually reinforces the threats to our civilisation'.[38] Gallichan blamed frigid women for producing spinsters, attributing to women what was, in fact, a consequence of the great losses of life on the battlefield. 'Many daughters of cold mothers die spinsters. They imbibe the maternal prejudices and ideas at the school age or earlier, and they grow up with a smouldering antipathy towards men'.[39] Janet Chance, a prominent sex reformer, stated that 'non-orgasmic' women should be kept out of politics. 'The effect of your spinster politicians, whether married or single,' she wrote – conflating, significantly, frigidity and spinsterhood – 'has yet to be analysed and made plain to the women they represent. I consider the lack of orgasm by women a fundamental question which deserves serious consideration'.[40]

The description of feminists as abnormal, sexually maladjusted women who hated men and the equating of feminism with sex war were not, of course, new, but the context in which such charges were levelled was entirely different. The existence of large numbers of unmarried women produced a great deal of anxiety. The diatribes directed at them reflected society's longing to return to the familiar, 'traditional' ways of life before August 1914, a nostalgic projection that failed to recall the way life 'really' was in Edwardian times. Denied husbands, many of them, by the destruction of the First World War, single women were visible reminders of the war that had only recently ended. Feminism soon became linked in the public mind not merely with sex war, a somewhat familiar concept, but with armed conflict, death and destruction. In 1925 Anthony M. Ludovici, in *Lysistrata, or Woman's Future and Future Woman*, maintained that the 'body-despising values' of feminists would lead ultimately to an 'evanescence of sexual love', and thus the disappearance of the one thing that offered 'our most effective protection against the instinctive hostility of the sexes'. He envisaged a world organized according to feminist ideals and principles as one that would reproduce itself through parthenogenesis, and finally 'proceed to a systematic slaughter of males'.[41]

Feminists participated in the linking of sexual disharmony and the threat of war, and in seeing in sex the salvation of civilization. Marie Stopes hinted at this in recounting the evolution of her work. 'I had written "Married Love,"' she said, 'some years before it was published, but early in 1918, while the war was still raging, I felt that psychologically the time was ripe to give the public what appeared to me a sounder, more wholesome, and more complete knowledge of the intimate sex requirements of *normal* and healthy people than was anywhere available.'[42] Dora Russell's *Hypatia* (1925), a response to Ludovici's *Lysistrata*, opened with a statement that equated marital discord with war. 'Matrimonial quarrels, like modern war,' she asserted, 'are carried on on a large scale, involving not individuals, nor even small groups of individuals, but both sexes and whole classes of society.'[43] Russell was one of the few feminists in the postwar period willing to speak about hostility between women and men;[44] she saw in sexual reform the 'way out of the intolerable tangle in which their quarrelling has landed us'. 'To understand sex,' she promised, 'to bring to it dignity and beauty and knowledge born of science, in place of brute instinct and squalor – that is the bridge that will span the breach between' the sexes.[45]

And not just the sexes. In many of her writings Russell articulated some of the misgivings about equal rights feminism that haunted the proponents of 'new' feminism: that by insisting upon equality with men, by competing with men in the marketplace, equal rights feminists threatened to undo the international peace.[46] In chapter 1 of *Hypatia*, subtitled 'Is there a Sex War?', Russell conceded that, owing to women's rebellion against 'a system of masculine repression', there had indeed been one. 'It was a disgraceful exhibition', she observed, slipping into an equation of feminism and the First World War, 'and would not have come to a truce so soon, but that it was eclipsed by the still more disgraceful exhibition of the European war.' Completing the metonymy, she concluded: 'In 1918 they bestowed the vote . . . as a reward for our services in helping the destruction of our offspring.' Wholly sympathetic to the cause, Russell nevertheless gave voice to a widespread understanding of feminism as war. Mutual sexual pleasure, she believed, offered a solution not only to antagonism between men and women, but to conflict between nations as well. 'I think that through sex and through parenthood we might get people away from admiration of a social system built on war', she told a Guildhouse audience. More explicitly, she argued in *The Right to Be Happy* that:

> in sex-love, through physical sympathy and intimate union, we draw into ourselves as in no other way the understanding of another human personality, and the knowledge that two very different creatures can live together in exquisite harmony. Such an experience alone, widespread, would be worth ten million platforms blaring pacifism.[47]

Peace 'through sex and through parenthood' depended upon the availability of reliable contraceptives. Russell regarded birth control as the 'keystone' of motherhood. In demanding that birth control information and contraceptive devices be made available to working-class women through maternity centres, she again enlisted the language and imagery of war. She charged that the government, by refusing to provide birth control information, forced working-class women to produce a yearly baby in intolerable circumstances. 'The crime of war is bad enough', she lamented, but 'this butchery of hope and promise and human lives is one so black that the heart and mind of every woman who has borne a child should revolt against it until it is tolerated no more.' Working-class women, she claimed, 'know . . . contraceptives are better than infanticide and war'.[48]

Moreover, women could not participate unreservedly in the joys of sexual activity if they had to worry about conception and pregnancy. Russell saw birth control as the means by which sexual freedom could be realized. Few feminists, however, shared her view. Unlike Russell, Cicely Hamilton, Vera Brittain or Winifred Holtby, who, with Stella Browne, insisted that 'the fundamental importance and value of birth control lies [*sic*] in its widening of the scope of human freedom and choice, its *self-determining* significance for women',[49] most women affiliated with feminist organizations such as the National Union of Societies for Equal Citizenship (NUSEC) held ambiguous and ambivalent opinions about contraceptives. Even Stopes, who regarded contraceptives as vital ingredients of women's marital happiness because they removed the fear of pregnancy, often diluted her feminist message with eugenic arguments and paeans to motherhood.[50]

In 1923 *The Woman's Leader*, the organ of the NUSEC, opened its letters columns to a discussion of the pros and cons of birth control, observing that while it was not 'part of our policy to express any opinion as to the rights and wrongs of birth control', it was 'plain that the conditions under which the greatest of all occupations open to women – motherhood and the rearing of children – is carried on is a question of first-class importance, not only to all who care for woman's status, but for the race'.[51] In March 1925 the NUSEC overwhelmingly passed a resolution calling on the Minister of Health to allow maternity and infant welfare centres to give birth control information to mothers who asked for it or whose health recommended such an action. As *The Woman's Leader* put it, the NUSEC was 'not calling for general indiscriminate propaganda in favour of birth control'. Its demand had 'the strength of extreme moderation', and could be defended on the grounds that it would eliminate other sources of birth control information which did not 'discriminate in terms of clientele' and sold 'to unmarried people'. Furthermore, contraceptive advice in the hands of the right people would help put abortionists out of business. Only belatedly did the paper refer to 'the intolerable burden of undesired parenthood'.[52]

Pressed to defend its stance that birth control was a feminist reform, *The Women's Leader* announced in October 1925 that it would not make a case for birth control *per se*, but a 'case for regarding birth control, when once its justifiability is established, as a *feminist reform*'. In other words, declared the editors:

> we are not advocating birth control as good in itself. There are individual circumstances in which we too would regard it as ethically wrong.

We are advocating it as admissible in certain forms, and under certain circumstances, and we think that the person best fitted to decide under what circumstances it is admissible is the individual mother; that the person best fitted to decide what form it shall take is the responsible medical officer of an infant welfare centre.

In a formulation that put the rights of women last, *The Woman's Leader* asserted that its position grew out of 'a reverence which revolts at the thought that the seeds of life may be sown thoughtlessly and on unprepared ground; at the thought that its fruit may be unwanted and inadequately tended; at the thought that its increase may destroy instead of fulfilling the life from which it comes'.[53]

This position on contraceptives derived from the new feminist direction in which the NUSEC was heading under the leadership of Eleanor Rathbone. 'New' feminism started from the premise that women's needs and interests were not identical to those of men, and that demands for equality with men, or 'old' feminism, failed to address those areas specific to women. Harrison and Lewis are right to point out the potential radicalism of the 'new' feminist agenda. The rhetoric marshalled to support 'new' feminist claims, however, justified them on the basis of women's special needs and special functions. The *needs* of women *as mothers* rather than the *rights* of women backed 'new' feminist appeals. Sexual difference rather than equality characterized the relationship between men and women as 'new' feminists understood it. Thus birth control was not advocated as a means of enlarging a woman's freedom in general, but as a reform that would provide 'maximum freedom to determine under what conditions she will or will not *perform her function*, and how far by reasonable "limitation of output" she may improve the standard of her "product"'.[54]

The insistence upon maternity as virtually the only conceivable occupation for the overwhelming majority of women drew upon the current psychoanalytic and sexological literature on sexual difference. As Rathbone put it, 'there is scarcely a department of human activity in which the physiological differences between men and women and the ensuing differences in their activities have not some effect, though in many departments it may be only slight, upon the outlook of the two sexes'.[55]

This position was a new development, and did not characterize feminist thinking prior to the war.[56] In February 1914, for instance, Maude Royden, editor of *Common Cause*, the newspaper of the National Union of Women's Suffrage Societies (NUWSS), stated in an editorial entitled 'Our Common Humanity': 'the "difference of function" which Anti-Suffragists urge as a reason for denying women the vote without insisting on their inferiority, has no reality in the facts of life. The "functions" of men and women are not divided into political and domestic.'[57] By 1917 Royden had markedly altered her stance. Believing 'that most women desire to have children, and that motherhood is to them an absorbing duty and not merely an episode', she concluded that 'the average woman will generally be in other walks of life but an amateur'. While men might be expert in the arts and the professions women could only be dilettantes; their expertise lay in 'human life'. This new feminist version of separate spheres for men and women derived from what Royden described as 'a permanent difference between the average woman and the average man, due to their natural qualities and vocations'.[58]

Royden's ideological shift stemmed from the postwar discourses that represented war and peace in sexual terms. In 1923 she lamented 'that the world is too great for us, that the passions created by the war are uncontrollable, that you cannot master your own civilisation'. Respite from 'the wounds of war [that] are so terrible and so recent' would come once those 'differences of function' Royden had repudiated in 1914 were acknowledged. The values, outlook and behavior inherent in women's 'actual experience', 'the fact that to be a woman gives one a rather different angle of vision to certain things in life', offered the best prospects for peace, the greatest chance of convincing men 'to cease thinking of the world as a battlefield and to begin thinking of it as a home'.[59]

The insistence on sexual difference received its impetus from two contradictory and paradoxical developments of the war. On the one hand, the vastly different experiences of the front and of the home created an almost insurmountable barrier between the individuals – men and women – who inhabited those realms. We see this expressed in Royden's demand for the endowment of motherhood. 'No one says a man must depend on his wife for maintenance because he is a soldier', she argued. 'No man, though he be a millionaire, refuses his soldier's pay. So should it be with women . . . You cannot, indeed, pay for all that motherhood means, but neither can you pay for a man to die. Yet soldiers are "endowed" by the State.'[60] Men are by nature soldiers, whose business is war, women by nature mothers, whose business is peace.

On the other hand, the apparent blurring of gender lines brought about by the requirements of total war compelled society to establish dichotomies based on sexual difference as a way to recreate a semblance of order and peace. Egalitarian feminism threatened to renew the conflict so recently ended, as Royden intimated in a letter to the NUSEC. 'When I reflect that the legalistic interpretation of equality must lead us to abandon our work for the League of Nations . . . and concentrate on agitation in favour of women being admitted on equal terms to all ranks of the Army, Navy, and Air Force,' she wrote, unwittingly caricaturing the positions of 'new' and 'old' feminism respectively, 'it seems to me that it was time that the Union should clear its mind on what it meant by "equality".'[61]

The 'new' feminist emphases upon women as mothers and sexual difference caused a great deal of concern among many 'old' feminists, who argued a more strictly egalitarian agenda.[62] The NUSEC ultimately split over these issues. But more fundamentally, new feminism failed to challenge, and in fact contributed to, a reconstruction of gender that circumscribed the roles, activities and possibilities of women. Just as nineteenth-century physicians and scientists had created sexual discourses that upheld a particular social and gender system by establishing the political identity of individuals on the basis of their sexuality,[63] twentieth-century psychiatrists, sexologists and sex reformers built up a vast literature about masculinity and femininity and male and female sexuality that served to restore order in the face of dramatic upheavals in the political, economic, social and gender structures of Britain. A gender system of separate spheres for men and women based upon scientific theories of sexual difference, a new emphasis upon motherhood, and an urgent insistence upon mutual sexual pleasure within marriage provided parameters within which 'normal' activity was to be carried out and a return to normalcy effected. Many feminists, no less interested in the establishment of peace and order, adopted these discourses as they articulated their demands. In so doing, they abandoned the radical critiques of gender and sexuality that marked their pre-war ideologies, and undermined their ability to advocate equality and justice for women. We must ask why feminists in the pre-war period were able to dissent from and challenge the dominant scientific and medical discourses about gender and sexuality when in the postwar years they more readily accepted prevalent ideologies. What alternative discourses permitted dissent earlier? Why were they no longer available in the 1920s?

Notes

1. Not all historians will agree with this interpretation, but see Susan Kingsley Kent, *Sex and Suffrage in Britain, 1860–1914* (Princeton University Press, N.J., 1987), *passim*; and Lisa Tickner, *The Spectacle of Women: Imagery of the Suffrage Campaign, 1907–14* (Chicago University Press, 1988), pp. 162, 167.
2. See Susan Kingsley Kent, 'The politics of sexual difference: World War I and the demise of British feminism', *Journal of British Studies*, vol. 27 (1988).
3. Brian Harrison, *Prudent Revolutionaries: Portraits of British Feminists between the Wars* (Clarendon Press, Oxford, 1987), pp. 323, 322; Jane Lewis, 'Feminism and welfare', in Juliet Mitchell and Ann Oakley (eds), *What is Feminism?* (Pantheon, New York, 1986), pp. 88, 94; Sheila Jeffreys, *The Spinster and Her Enemies: Feminism and Sexuality, 1880–1930* (Pandora, London, 1985), pp. 155–6.
4. Quoted in Paul Fussell, *The Great War and Modern Memory*, (Oxford, New York, 1975), pp. 272, 96.
5. Eric Leed, *No Man's Land: Combat and Identity in World War I* (Cambridge University Press, Cambridge, 1979), p. 6.
6. Magnus Hirschfeld, *The Sexual History of the World War* (Falstaff, New York, 1937), pp. 22, 32.
7. Leed, *op. cit.* note 5, p. 45.
8. Hirschfeld, *op. cit.* note 6, p. 29.
9. Trevor Wilson, *The Myriad Faces of War: Britian and the Great War, 1914–1918* (Polity Press, Cambridge, 1986), pp. 724, 725.
10. Hirschfeld, *op. cit.* note 6, p. 34.
11. Siegfried Sassoon, 'Glory of Women', in Jon Silken (ed), *The Penguin Book of First World War Poetry*, 2nd edn (Penguin Books, Harmondsworth, 1981), p. 132.
12. Leed, *op. cit.* note 5, pp. 109–10; Fussell, *op. cit.* note 4, p. 86.
13. Hirschfeld, *op. cit.* note 6, p. 37.
14. Quoted in Sandra Gilbert, 'Soldier's heart: literary men, literary women, and the great war', *Signs*, vol. 8 (Spring 1983), p. 433.
15. Quoted in Bonnie G. Smith, *Changing Lives: European Women in History Since 1700* (D. C. Heath, Lexington, Mass., 1989), p. 363.
16. Gilbert, *op. cit.* note 14, p. 424.
17. Leed, *op. cit.* note 5, p. 8.
18. *Idem*, p. 201; see Philip Gibbs, *Now It Can Be Told* (Harper, London, 1920), p. 551.
19. Ray Strachey, *The Cause: A Short History of the Women's Movement* (Virago, London, 1978 reprint), pp. 370–1.

20. Quoted in Fussell, *op. cit.* note 4, pp. 71, 73, 113.
21. *Idem*, p. 76. Leed, *op. cit.* note 5, p. xi: 'the cessation of hostilities did not mean the end of the war experience but rather the beginning of a process in which that experience was framed, institutionalized, given ideological content, and relived in political action as well as fiction'.
22. Cicely Hamilton, 'The return to femininity', *Time and Tide* (12 August, 1927), in Dale Spender, *Time and Tide Wait for No Man* (Pandora, London, 1984), p. 79.
23. Fussell, *op. cit.* note 4, p. 334, has claimed that until it became acceptable, in the 1960s and 1970s, to publish works that contained sexually explicit, often brutally obscene scenes between men and women, the war could not be fully portrayed: ' . . . it is the virtual disappearance during the sixties and seventies of the concept of prohibitive obscenity, a concept which has acted as a censor on earlier memories of "war", that has given the ritual of military memory a new dimension. And that new dimension is capable of revealing for the first time the full obscenity of the Great War . . . it is only now . . . that the literary means for adequate remembering and interpreting are finally publicly accessible.'
24. See Michel Foucault, *The History of Sexuality, Volume I: An Introduction* (Random House, New York, 1978).
25. I am indebted to Bonnie G. Smith for this insight.
26. Joan W. Scott, 'Rewriting history', in Margaret Randolph Higonnet, Jane Jenson, Sonya Michel, and Margaret Collins Weitz (eds), *Behind the Lines: Gender and the Two World Wars* (Yale University Press, New Haven, Ct, 1987), p. 27.
27. Hirschfeld, *op. cit.* note 6, pp. 34–5.
28. Havelock Ellis, *Psychology of Sex* (Heinemann, London, 1948), p. 124. Quoted in Jeffrey Weeks, *Sex, Politics and Society, The Regulation of Sexuality since 1800* (Longman, London, 1981), p. 149.
29. Weeks, *idem*, p. 206.
30. See Lewis, *The Politics of Motherhood* (Croom Helm, London, 1983), *passim*; Weeks, *idem*, pp. 127, 128.
31. Weeks, *idem*, pp. 200, 207.
32. *Idem*, pp. 188, 206.
33. See Isabel Emslie Hutton, *The Sex Technique in Marriage* (Emerson Books, New York, 1932); Helena Wright, *The Sex Factor in Marriage* (Vanguard Press, New York); Theodore H. Van de Velde, *Sexual Tensions in Marriage* (Random House, New York).
34. See Weeks, *op. cit.* note 28, pp. 154–5.
35. Sigmund Freud, 'Some psychical consequences of the anatomical distinction between the sexes', in Jean Strouse (ed), *Women and Analysis* (Dell, New York, 1925), pp. 27–38.
36. Karl Abraham, 'Manifestations of the female castration complex' (1920), in Strouse, *idem*, p. 139.
37. Quoted in Sheila Jeffreys, 'Sex reform and anti-feminism in the 1920s', in London Feminist History Group, *The Sexual Dynamics of History* (Pluto Press, London, 1983), pp. 185, 190.
38. Quoted in Jeffreys, *op. cit.* note 3, p. 176.
39. Quoted in Jeffreys, *op. cit.* note 37, p. 12.
40. Quoted in *idem*, p. 199.
41. Anthony M. Ludovici, *Lysistrata, or Woman's Future and Future Woman* (E. P. Dutton, New York, 1925), pp. 92, 87.

42. Quoted in Irene Clephane, *Toward Sex Freedom* (John Lane, London, 1935), p. 204.
43. Dora Russell, *Hypatia, or Woman and Knowledge* (Kegan Paul, London, 1925), p. 1.
44. See Kent, *op. cit.* note 2, p. 244.
45. Russell, *op. cit.* note 43, pp. 12, 24–5.
46. See Kent, *op. cit.* note 2, p. 252.
47. Dora Russell, 'Marriage', delivered at the Guildhouse, 30 October, 1927; in *The Guildhouse Monthly*, vol. 13, no. 2, February 1928, p. 53; Dora Russell, *The Right to Be Happy* (George Routledge, London, 1927), pp. 131–2.
48. Russell, *op. cit.* note 43, pp. 58, 63, 64.
49. F. W. Stella Browne, 'The feminine aspect of birth control', in Raymond Pierpoint (ed), *Report of the Fifth International Neo-Malthusian and Birth Control Conference* (London, 1922), p. 40. See Cicely Hamilton, *Life Errant* (J. M. Dent & Sons Ltd, London, 1935), pp. 249, 251; Vera Brittain, *Lady Into Woman* (Andrew Dakers, London, 1953), p. 163; Winifred Holtby, *Women and a Changing Civilization* (Academy Press, Chicago, 1978, reprint from 1935), pp. 68, 169.
50. Marie Carmichael Stopes, *Wise Parenthood. The Treatise on Birth Control for Married People. A Practical Sequel to 'Married Love'* (G. P. Putnam, London, 1933, first published 1918); *Queen's Hall Meeting on Constructive Birth Control* (G. P. Putnam, London, 1921). See Richard Allen Soloway, *Birth Control and the Population Question in England, 1877–1930* (University of North Carolina Press, Chapel Hill, N.C., 1982).
51. 'The Stopes libel action', *The Woman's Leader*, 9 March 1923, p. 42.
52. 'A word with the Minister of Health', *The Woman's Leader*, 20 March 1925, p. 59.
53. 'Is birth control a feminist reform?', *The Woman's Leader*, 2 October 1925, p. 283.
54. *Ibid.* Italics added.
55. Eleanor Rathbone, 'What is equality?', *The Woman's Leader*, 11 February 1927, p. 3.
56. See Kent, *op. cit.* notes 1 and 2.
57. 'Our common humanity', *The Common Cause*, 20 February 1914, p. 884.
58. Maude Royden, 'The women's movement of the future', in Victor Gollancz (ed), *The Making of Women* (Allen and Unwin, London, 1917), p. 143.
59. A. Maude Royden, *Women at the World's Crossroads* (The Woman's Press, New York, 1923), pp. 116, 43, 79–80, 95.
60. Royden, *op. cit.* note 58, p. 140.
61. Letter to *The Woman's Leader*, 18 March 1927, p. 50.
62. See Kent, *op. cit.* note 2.
63. Foucault, *The History of Sexuality*, p. 123; Kent, *op. cit.* note 1, pp. 15, 16.

6 'Have We Really Rounded Seraglio Point?': Vera Brittain and Inter-War Feminism

Deborah Gorham

The writer Vera Brittain, born in 1893, was a feminist from her girlhood until her death in 1970. An educated upper-middle-class woman who achieved success in her profession, Brittain combined her professional career with marriage and motherhood. As a woman who benefited from and contributed to the cause of feminism, she is representative of one important type of twentieth-century British feminist.

For Vera Brittain, feminism was more than a cause she espoused. It was the central organizing principle of her personality, the belief that gave direction to her energies, that enabled her to make the best use possible of her talents as a writer, and through which she defined her personal relationships and her own sense of self. An analysis of what feminism meant in her life underlines its importance as inspiration and as validating principle in the experience of twentieth-century women.

Brittain was most actively involved with feminism as a movement in the 1920s, when she was a young and relatively obscure aspiring writer attempting to establish herself in the literary milieu of London after receiving her degree from Oxford in 1921. By the latter years of the decade, she had become a prolific feminist journalist. After the publication of her most successful book, *Testament of Youth*, in 1933, her primary public contribution to feminism was as a successful serious writer of autobiography, biography and fiction. Finally, not least among her contributions to feminism was her commitment to living a feminist life.

By the time Vera Brittain had earned her degree from Oxford, the two most important feminist organizations of the inter-war decades, the National Union of Societies for Equal Citizenship (NUSEC) and the Six Point Group, had been established. Eleanor

Rathbone, the leader of the NUSEC, was the leading exponent of new feminism, a position challenging what its supporters claimed was the traditional feminist preoccupation with equal political rights, in favour of a greater concern with the special needs that working-class women had as mothers. The driving force behind the Six Point Group, the NUSEC's most important opposition, was Margaret Haig Mackworth, Lady Rhondda. Lady Rhondda was also the publisher of *Time and Tide*, the influential feminist weekly which began publication in 1920. The Six Point Group defined itself both as the voice of the younger generation of feminists and as the champion of a feminist position that placed equality for women at the centre of feminist belief and feminist activism.

The new feminism of the 1920s was not, in fact, new, nor were the criticisms it levelled at equal rights feminism. Before the First World War, groups like the Women's Industrial Council had been explicitly or implicitly critical of feminist preoccupation with issues like the suffrage, and had claimed for themselves a greater understanding of the ways in which class cleavage and exploitation affected the majority of British women.[1] New feminism was the postwar incarnation of this position.

In the postwar period, equal rights feminists vigorously defended their own commitment to social justice for all women, and mounted both specific and general criticisms of new feminism. The general criticisms included an analysis of the new feminist position as a retreat from feminism, in so far as it ignored or downgraded the centrality of equality for women, and an attack on the new feminist claims that they alone represented the interests of working-class women.

From the time that Vera Brittain and her closest friend, the writer Winifred Holtby, were introduced to the Six Point Group in March 1922, Brittain identified herself unequivocally with equal rights feminism.[2] She was an early and enthusiastic reader of *Time and Tide*,[3] and she soon became active in the Six Point Group, serving on its executive from 1926.[4] The fact that she also gave active support to the birth control movement, that she believed a better understanding of the needs of mothers was central to feminism, and that she became a member of the Labour Party (new feminism considered that it had a special link to Labour) underscores the fact that new feminism had, in reality, no monopoly on feminist support for social justice or for women's needs as mothers.[5]

Brittain's uncompromising and vigorous adherence to equal rights feminism had its origins in the way in which feminism had entered her consciousness during her girlhood. From her own justly famous account in *Testament of Youth* of her escape from the confines of her conventional upper-middle-class upbringing through the achievement of admission to Somerville College, Oxford, it is clear that even as a young girl, Brittain was sustained by a fierce desire for autonomy. She was, indeed, one of those women who was born feminist, in that she responded with a spontaneous sense of outrage when confronted with the confines of the feminine role. As soon as she discovered it, feminism allowed her to articulate that outrage.

Writing from the vantage point of the 1920s, she likened her introduction to feminism to a conversion experience, and associated it with the reading of one significant book, Olive Schreiner's *Woman and Labor*.[6] 'For many of us . . . "Woman & Labour" sounded with a note that had the authentic ring of a new gospel',[7] she wrote, and she was not exaggerating the extent to which Schreiner's work influenced her, both when she was a young girl, and during the 1920s and 1930s. Schreiner's championing of work as woman's right, and as woman's liberator, her claim, on behalf of women, to 'take all labour for our province', her condemnation of the narrow, confined 'parasitic' nature of the middle-class woman's role in modern industrial society, spoke directly to the young Vera as she struggled to escape the confines of 'provincial young ladyhood', and continued to speak to the mature Brittain's belief that while feminism was of course about the achievement of social and political equality for women, at its heart lay a commitment to woman's full autonomy, and a rejection of Victorian notions of femininity. It was because of these beliefs that Brittain aligned herself with equal rights feminism.

In the inter-war decades, Brittain's feminist journalism appeared in a variety of publications, including the *Yorkshire Post*, the *Manchester Guardian* and *Time and Tide*.[8] In this work, she most often took up issues that related directly to her own experience. As a professional woman, she was an incisive opponent of the customary and legal barriers that still confronted women in the postwar years, and she wrote extensively about the difficulties educated middle-class women experienced as they attempted to combine motherhood with a career.

While she wrote about lingering prejudice and discrimination, the dominant tone of Brittain's feminism in the 1920s was one of optimism. Indeed, a large part of the hopefulness that characterized her outlook in the immediate postwar years sprang from her belief that while there were still feminist battles to be fought, the barriers that had fallen offered women revolutionary new opportunities. She believed that women need no longer be confined to the narrow world of Victorian and Edwardian femininity and they now not only had the right but also the responsibility to participate fully in politics and in social, economic and professional life.

One major theme of Brittain's inter-war journalism was the assertion that it was work, above all else, that would allow women to enjoy these new opportunities. 'Work . . . has been the twentieth century's great gift to woman, it is dignified work which puts her, as far as the chance of happiness is concerned, upon the same level as men', she wrote in a 1927 article for *Time and Tide*.[9] Work gave women a chance to test themselves, and to gain respect in the public arena. Work also brought with it independence, and if the first principle of Vera Brittain's feminism was respect for work, the second was independence. In Brittain's view, it was the dependent position of the Victorian woman, as wife or as daughter, that had so often caused her to become an idle and frustrated creature. But the successes of feminism meant that women need no longer be prisoners of the parasitic domesticity that had developed as a result of industrialization, a domesticity that had led 'a whole generation of middle class women . . . [to produce] . . . vast debris of useless products . . . pathetic . . . crochet mats . . . waxflower models'.[10]

Brittain was appalled by the fact that even in the 1920s there were many women who clung to the false security provided by such outmoded definitions of femininity, and she developed an analysis of the dangers of an excessive preoccupation with domesticity. She was especially concerned to attack the internal and external pressures that led too many middle-class women in the 1920s to reject new patterns, or technological developments that would simplify housework. Women who avoided the new freedoms and the new possibilities were 'guarding themselves against life's problems by means of life's trivialities', she believed.[11]

When discussing the burden that domesticity placed on women, Brittain was not insensitive to the fact that it weighed much more heavily on working-class than on middle-class women. In one of her most effective pieces, 'I Denounce Domesticity! A Protest Against Waste', published in 1932, she wrote:

> [T]he wage-earning classes of this country still live in badly planned, inconvenient little houses which harbour dirt, involve incessant labour, and are totally unequipped with the most elementary devices for saving time and toil . . . [T]he home is the one place upon which sufficient capital has never been spent, with the result that . . . women with poor tools and no modern equipment fight a perpetual losing battle against the ever-accumulating detail of domesticity.[12]

In this critique of domesticity, and in her proposed solutions – that society should recognize the importance of improving the home, for the sake of women of all social classes, and that women themselves must no longer take a sentimental view of housework, and must be more open not only to technological change, but to collective solutions which might free them from unnecessary labour – Brittain reveals herself as an inter-war representative of a feminist tradition that had its roots in early twentieth-century thinking, but that also anticipated mid and late twentieth-century feminist analysis.

Brittain herself was well aware that in formulating her analysis she drew on Olive Schreiner. From our own vantage point, we can see that she looks forward, most obviously to the critique of domesticity offered by Betty Friedan in *The Feminine Mystique* (1963), but also to more recent feminist analyses of housework which point to the continuing influence of an association of domesticity with femininity.[13]

From the perspective of such recent work, Brittain's comments may appear flawed: for example, the belief that household technology would automatically serve to liberate women has been effectively demolished by such recent analysis. Nonetheless, in her critique of the sentimentalization of housework, of society's indifference to the waste of women's labour, and of the reluctance of men and women alike to seek collective or co-operative solutions to housekeeping, she was far-seeing.

After her own marriage in 1925, and the birth of her first child in 1927, Brittain became especially concerned with the problems women faced in 'combining marriage and a career'.[14] Indeed, she came to perceive the challenge of combining professional work with marriage and motherhood and of creating feminist marriages as the most important feminist task of the postwar era. In her journalistic writings she opposed such specific barriers as the regulation that prevented the employment of married teachers in the state school system,[15] but she is at her most passionate and effective when she took on the even more damaging but still pervasive attitude that a married woman ought not to be gainfully employed. For Brittain, a wife's right not only to work, but to have her work regarded as equal in importance to that of her husband, was the key issue on which any genuinely egalitarian marriage must rest. Without full recognition of the married woman's need to work, women would be faced with what she called an 'intolerable' choice:

> [I]n effect it is this: Shall a woman who loves her work . . . continue it throughout her life at the sacrifice of marriage, motherhood and all her emotional needs? Or shall she marry and have children at the cost of her career, and look forward to . . . intellectual starvation and monotony? . . . Each normal person, whether man or woman, is endowed . . . with a mind and a body, and is intended . . . to fulfil the needs of both . . . the woman for whom mental atrophy has been the price of marriage is no more normal and complete than she who had foregone husband and children for . . . career.[16]

Brittain realized that the most acute problem facing the married woman with a career was that of combining the career with motherhood. She formulated a definition of feminist motherhood, and defended it against two different kinds of inter-war critics, the traditional anti-feminists, who clung to Victorian notions of maternalism, and the critics who drew their support from newly powerful ideas in psychology, which they claimed provided 'scientific' proof that feminism was responsible for producing a new kind of woman, who was hostile to heterosexuality and to motherhood.[17]

In opposition to such biological determinism, whether 'scientific' or sentimental, Brittain offered a new alternative, a vision of the modern feminist mother. She believed that the primary role that educated professional women ought to perform for their children was that of moral and intellectual guide. Unlike the ideal mother of the nineteenth century, who had been a 'self-sacrificing . . . infant nurse,' the twentieth-century mother, Brittain believed, would serve her children best by providing responsible professional care for them in infancy, and by continuing her own work. As a fully developed, productive member of society, she would then be a better mother, better able to oversee her children's development as they grew to maturity.[18]

Brittain also advocated that modern feminist motherhood should be *informed* motherhood. The old view that motherhood was instinctive had been proved wrong, she asserted, and 'mothercraft is a science which has to be taught'. As she pointed out, reformers had recognized the necessity of teaching working-class women how to mother, and had set up infant welfare centres to assist them. Brittain insisted that middle-class mothers needed this help too, and to this end, she welcomed an organization she herself called 'the first welfare centre for middle-class mothers', the Chelsea Babies' Club.[19]

The Chelsea Babies' Club was a well-baby clinic, staffed with a physician and a nurse, to which subscribers paid a fee of five guineas a year. Such a scheme might seem to possess little social importance, and at first glance to reinforce rather than challenge class differences. However, its egalitarian position that parents of all social classes needed the advice of experts represented a significant challenge to the customary practices of well-to-do families. Certainly, Brittain believed this to be the case, and she not only publicized the clinic, she used it for her own children, and she served on its board of management.[20]

In the 1980s, when a mistrust of the medical profession and of the claims to expertise advanced by the social sciences is a dominant element in feminist discourse, and indeed in radical discourse generally, Brittain's faith in the value of professional expertise may seem naïve, superficial and fundamentally conservative. But in the context of the 1920s it was part of the postwar revolt against Victorianism, and in a specifically feminist context it was a revolt against traditional beliefs in women's lack of rationality. Rejecting such beliefs was part of Brittain's feminist creed. Moreover, she did not regard a reliance on professional expertise as an anti-feminist acceptance of a male-dominated intellectual establishment: she advocated that women not only use experts, but that they become experts, and she herself sought out women professionals wherever possible.[21]

Brittain not only advocated modern, feminist motherhood; she also advocated feminist fatherhood, believing that one solution to the modern woman's dilemma of combining employment with motherhood lay in greater participation on the part of men as husbands and fathers: 'The good husband of the future will be the man who understands how to play the part of equal comrade . . . Such a husband will realise that, if life's prizes are to be accessible to men and women alike, the practical and domestic obligations of marriage must be reduced to a minimum for each by being shared by both.'[22]

A clear vision of equality in marriage, of wife and husband as comrades, sharing equally in the responsibilities of child-rearing, and no longer encumbered by the weight of Victorian assumptions, emerges from Brittain's writing on the subject. That vision can of course be criticized as limited in its understanding of social and economic realities, for while she did on occasion write perceptively about the problems of working-class women, Brittain's attention was focused primarily on women of her own class, and her solutions were sometimes of use only to the affluent. For example, the delegation of some parenting tasks to paid professionals still meant, during these years, a resort to the traditional upper middle-class pattern of employing domestic servants.[23]

Brittain's lack of sensitivity concerning class differences, her insufficient awareness that her own milieu and that of those she addressed through her writings made up only a small part of British society, was of course not unique to her. It is generally agreed that the First World War had done little to bridge the gulf between the upper classes and the working class, and that Britain in the 1920s and 1930s was almost as divided by class cleavage as it had been at the turn of the century. And while the new feminist activists who devoted their energies to promoting policies like the 'endowment of motherhood' were more conversant with the problems of working-class mothers, their perspective accepted the limited horizons that were the lot of such mothers. Such an acceptance is fundamentally patronizing. Brittain, at least, was never patronizing, and she did believe that her vision of a far-reaching equality in marriage and in parenting had the potential to benefit all women.

As well as writing about the difficulties of combining employment with marriage, Brittain also wrote frequently about the disabilities and the opportunities that confronted women in the labour market, whether they were married or single. She was a vigorous defender of equal pay for equal work, and equal opportunity for education and employment, and attacked the legislated inequality that women still faced, for example as teachers and in the civil service. But she also insisted that young women must make wise occupational choices, and in 1928 she published a handbook, *Women's Work in Modern England*, to help them do so. Its primary objective was to encourage women to reject stereotypical definitions of women's work, and avoid 'overcrowded professions' by seeking out what today are called 'non-traditional' areas of employment.[24]

One enthusiastic reader of *Women's Work in Modern England* was Elizabeth Abbott, the chairman of the Open Door Council (ODC).[25] The ODC had been formed in 1926, with the specific purpose of opposing all restrictive legislation directed at women workers. Its platform, 'To secure that a woman shall be free to work and protected as a worker on the same terms as a man, and that legislation and regulations dealing with conditions and hours, payment, entry and training shall be based on the nature of the work and not upon the sex of the worker',[26] was one that Brittain wholeheartedly endorsed. She was an early supporter of the Council,[27] and remained a supporter right up into the 1960s.[28] She served on the ODC executive[29] and some of her most effective feminist pieces were written in support of the Council's position, a position clearly opposed to that of the new feminists, who viewed legislation placing limits on women's work as 'protective' rather than restrictive.[30] Brittain effectively opposed this position, pointing out that it was based on 'a deep rooted misunderstanding of feminist aims'. Feminists, she explained, were not indifferent to the need for legislation controlling hazardous work. What they opposed was basing such legislation on sexual difference.[31] Brittain pointed out that the demand for the 'protection' of women was often based upon prejudice, not on knowledge, and she called for rational, 'scientific' investigation of problems relating to women's work:

If we are bent on discovering whether a real need for restrictive legislation for women exists, such questions as the following . . . most read-ily occur. How many women, compared with men, have suffered from accidents due to the cleaning of machinery? How much physical weak-ness among women is due to natural disability, and how much to under-pay and under-nourishment? How many women, compared with men, have been injured by carrying heavy weights?[32]

In the inter-war decades, the issues of marriage, motherhood and women's work had both general and specific connections to debates among feminist groups. As we have seen, on all these questions Vera Brittain believed that women's autonomy and independence were of central importance. Where there were spec-ific disputes – the best example being the debate over restrictive legislation – Brittain unequivocally rejected the maternalism of new feminism and advocated the right to independence of women of all social classes.

While restrictive legislation divided feminists in the 1920s, one issue that united them was the denial of the vote to women under thirty. It served as a rallying point for feminists in the 1920s,[33] with an active campaign being mounted from 1926 until the passage of the 'Flapper Act' in 1928.[34] This brief campaign provided the 1920s feminist movement with the opportunity to revive some of the drama of the pre-war suffrage struggle, including the excite-ment of large-scale public demonstrations. Vera Brittain took an active part in this campaign.[35] She believed an equal franchise to be of importance, but for her it was a symbolic rather than a substantive issue. As she put it in July 1927, on the occasion of one of the large franchise rallies held during these years: 'Women still hold political demonstrations because the incompleteness of the English franchise is again a symbol – a symbol of the incom-plete recognition of women as human beings.'[36]

And in a piece written in March 1928, she contrasted the impending passage of the Franchise Bill into law with the 'anti-feminist reaction' reflected in the refusal of some London hospitals to accommodate women medical students:

Does [this final triumph] signify the final triumph of the feminist idea . . . or . . . is the acquiescence in equal franchise due more to a growing scepticism as to the importance of votes than to a growing conviction as to the justice of women's rights? Have we really rounded seraglio point? Or have we merely concluded that votes do not matter very much?[37]

For Vera Brittain, it is clear, 'rounding seraglio point' would occur only when women had achieved a thoroughgoing equality with men. The fact that women's gains in medicine were being eroded just as equal suffrage was finally becoming law – an erosion which she saw as dangerous not only for women doctors but also for their women patients – underscored the need for continued feminist activism.

In the 1920s Vera Brittain was active not only as a feminist, but as an internationalist, working to promote the League of Nations, and to encourage it to develop into a genuine force for peace.[38] As an informed observer of League activities, she regarded its lukewarm commitment to the equality of women with dismay, and she therefore eagerly took an active part in an international campaign of the late 1920s and early 1930s to challenge the League's anti-feminist bias. The chief specific goal of the campaign was to secure passage by the League Assembly of an Equal Rights Treaty, whose main clause was to read: 'The Contracting States agree that upon the ratification of this Treaty, men and women shall have Equal Rights throughout the territory subject to their respective jurisdictions.'[39]

In this campaign, the Six Point Group was the leader among British feminist groups.[40] Vera Brittain contributed to the campaign effort by producing two important statements about it, both of which became Six Point Group pamphlets,[41] by acting as a liaison between the American Woman's Party and the Six Point group,[42] and in organizing support for the Treaty among the English delegation to the League Assembly in 1929. On 10 August 1929 she organized and led a delegation of women to speak to Lord Cecil, the head of the British delegation to the Assembly, to encourage his support for the Equal Rights Treaty.[43] Her work for Equal Rights International, which allowed her to combine her support for the League with her support for feminism and thus link the two political causes that were of most importance to her, marks the high point of her involvement with feminist activism.

From 1929 until its publication in 1933 Vera Brittain was at work on *Testament of Youth*, her autobiographical account of the years 1900–25. Before its publication, her reputation rested largely on her journalism and non-fiction. The two novels she had published in the 1920s (*The Dark Tide* and *Not Without Honour*) had achieved little recognition. But the success of *Testament of Youth* established Brittain as an important author, and allowed her to devote herself to the longer, more serious work she had always wanted to do, and it was through such works that her feminist voice was heard in the 1930s.

As the most successful work she ever wrote, *Testament of Youth* represents her most important single contribution to feminism. Brittain's account of her compelling desire to escape the bonds of 'provincial young ladyhood' and find a milieu in which her love of hard work, and her ambition, would win her respect rather than disapproval, was an impassioned defence of the middle-class woman's right to autonomy, to test her powers and to defy the limits of the Edwardian feminine ideal. The book's feminism inspired many readers in the 1930s, and in the late twentieth century it is acknowledged as a feminist classic.

After completing *Testament of Youth*, Brittain devoted her creative energies to a novel, *Honourable Estate*.[44] In its foreword Brittain explained that the novel was intended as a political statement, and that feminism – or the 'women's revolution' – was the book's central theme: '*Honourable Estate* purports to show how the women's revolution – one of the greatest in all history – combined with the struggle for other democratic ideals and the cataclysm of the War to alter the private destinies of individuals.'[45]

Brittain constructed *Honourable Estate* in a way that allowed her to express her thoughts about women and change, and about the institution of marriage. It contains two feminist characters: first, the unfortunate Janet Rutherston, unhappily married in 1893, at nineteen, who becomes a mother unwillingly but finds some emotional and spiritual comfort in the suffrage movement. Janet and her husband quarrel bitterly over her feminism, and she eventually leaves her marriage, only to die shortly afterward. The portrait of Janet Rutherston is one of a woman whose temperament fitted her for achievement, but who is forced to conform to the limited model of Victorian wifehood. She escapes, but her escape is paid for in bitterness, and she dies of exhaustion. She has gained her right to autonomy, but at too great a price.

Brittain based the character of Janet on her husband's mother.[46] The other feminist character in *Honourable Estate*, Ruth Alleyndene, is based on Vera Brittain herself. Ruth is a generation younger than Janet. Like Brittain, she attends Oxford, and serves as a nurse in the First World War. In the novel's concluding section she marries Denis Rutherston, Janet's son, has twins, and also runs successfully for Parliament as a Labour candidate.

Concerning feminism, *Honourable Estate*'s clear message is that Ruth is able to achieve a life that encompasses Janet's unfulfilled desires because of the lessening of prejudice against feminist women.[47] The character of Ruth Alleyndene represents the fictional embodiment of that optimism about feminism that informed Vera Brittain's feminist journalism in the 1920s. It is, however, written with a painful awareness that times were changing in the 1930s, and that the rise of Fascism and the return of militarism marked a reaction in politics, and that this reaction included a revived hostility to feminism. But as she said, 'the fact that we are now living in a period of reaction makes it the more important to contemplate that which was gained during the four decades which ended in 1930'.[48]

Brittain consciously modelled the fictional character Ruth on her best self. And she also believed that in real life she was indeed an exemplar of modern feminism, because of her ambition, her determination to succeed and her capacity for hard work, but also because of the nature of her personal relationships. There was first of all her feminist friendship with Winifred Holtby and, second, there was her feminist marriage.

The friendship with Winifred Holtby began in 1920 when both were at Oxford after the war, and it continued until Holtby's premature death from kidney disease in 1935. When she memorialized the friendship in *Testament of Friendship*, her biography of Holtby, Brittain emphasized its feminist significance:

> From the days of Homer the friendships of men have enjoyed glory and acclamation, but the friendships of women . . . have usually been not merely unsung, but mocked, belittled and falsely interpreted. I hope that Winifred's story may do something to destroy these tarnished interpretations, and show its reader that loyalty and affection between women is a noble relationship.[49]

This friendship was unquestionably central to Vera Brittain's life. After Oxford, and until Brittain's marriage, the two women lived together, and sustained each other during their early years as aspiring novelists and journalists. And when Vera Brittain did marry, the marriage disrupted but did not destroy either their friendship or their living arrangements.

In 1925 Vera Brittain married G. E. G. Catlin, a political scientist. From its beginning, the couple's relationship was openly and self-consciously feminist. During their courtship they engaged in negotiations about how a future marriage could be genuinely feminist. After marriage Vera Brittain kept her own name – an unusual symbolic action in the 1920s – and even more important, she never subordinated her career to that of her husband. During the early years of their marriage Catlin was teaching at Cornell University in the United States. During these years Brittain maintained a home for herself and their two children (John was born in 1927 and Shirley in 1930) in London. Winifred Holtby made up part of this household, with Catlin joining them for part of the year. Brittain called this arrangement, which allowed them both to pursue their respective careers, 'semi-detached marriage', and she frequently wrote about it and other aspects of her marriage, clearly believing that her marriage provided a model for other women, and was in itself a contribution to feminist solutions to the problems of combining marriage, motherhood and career.[50]

Brittain supported feminist marriage, but she questioned neither the institution of marriage itself nor the dominance of heterosexuality. In recent historical writing, the connection between feminism and changing sexual mores in the 1920s has been a subject of controversy. While some assert that the development of greater sexual frankness increased access to birth control and the growth of support for companionship in marriage that followed the First World War benefited women,[51] others have emphasized the negative side of these changes, and assert that whereas in the Victorian and Edwardian periods, feminism could sanction close bonds between women without fear of censure, and could offer women a genuinely viable alternative to heterosexuality, the picture changed radically in the course of the 1910s and the 1920s. As psychological discourse gained hegemony, and homosexuality was defined by the discourse of sexology as a dangerous illness, love between women became stigmatized and feminism lost its power to resist the dominance of heterosexuality. Some go further, condemning the period's sexual radicals, and claiming that the women among them sold out feminism to heterosexuality.

In one such analysis – that of Sheila Jeffreys in *The Spinster and Her Enemies* – Vera Brittain is characterized as just such a reprehensible 'modernist'. Jeffreys condemns Brittain for her own heterosexuality, and for her failure to defend lesbianism.[52] Jeffreys's analysis is an insufficiently developed construct imposed on a complex set of issues, and the way in which Vera Brittain's personal life and writings have been used by her and others underscores the underdeveloped nature of historical speculation about sexuality in the inter-war period.[53]

Although Brittain herself hints that many contemporaries believed that she and Holtby were lesbians, not only was she not a lesbian but the subject made her acutely uncomfortable.[54] Her own discomfort did not prevent her from becoming a courageous defender of Radclyffe Hall, when Hall's lesbian novel *The Well of Loneliness* was condemned as 'obscene',[55] but it was nonetheless present, and it is characteristic. Although she advocated openness in sexual matters, and supported 'scientific' sexology, her public modernism was imposed on a personal sensibility that remained in most respects Victorian. And even publicly she did not in fact support sexual radicalism: in *Halcyon: or the Future of Monogamy*, her contribution to the 'Today and Tomorrow' series, she defended monogamous marriage.[56]

But did her position on marriage contribute to the denigration of independent women, and the conscripting of women into heterosexuality, as Jeffreys claims? It is true that Brittain did accept the view that the women's movement had in its 'early days' reacted against marriage, and that this had been unfortunate. It is true that she saw herself and other married professional women as illustrating that it was possible to combine 'the best of both worlds', namely marriage and career, but in doing so she believed that she was widening the scope of feminism, not narrowing it.[57] Given the anti-feminist opposition to married professional women that was endemic in the 1920s, her point of view offered a radical challenge to established norms.

And while it is true that Brittain did believe that feminist marriage was preferable to singleness, she also wrote several spirited defences of single women, and clearly recognized that attacks on 'the spinster' – which she identified as a 'favourite theme of the opponents of feminism' – were anti-feminist. In response to those who wrote of 'the lamentable incompleteness of the unmarried woman', she asserted that the 'married woman who deliberately neglects the intellectual side of her humanity is incomplete in a far more serious sense than the spinster worker who is using the energy of her trained mind for the welfare of society'.[58]

In a touching letter that F. Pethick-Lawrence wrote to Vera Brittain when Winifred Holtby was dying, he told her of the importance that both Brittain and Holtby had for himself and his wife Emmeline:

> If you will forgive me for being very personal, may I tell you in what special way I regard herself & yourself & those others of your generation who are holding aloft with such courage and determination the noblest emblem of modern womanhood? . . . As we have no children of our body, so I always feel that those who fulfill [*sic*] the vision are children of our spirit.[59]

That assessment of Brittain's contribution to feminism by one of the leading figures of the pre-war suffrage movement can serve as a conclusion to this analysis. Brittain's feminism had its limitations, but as a feminist in the inter-war decades, she did indeed 'fulfill the vision'. For her, feminism meant an assertion of personhood for women in its fullest sense, and her commitment to internationalism and social justice flowed directly out of her feminist convictions. At her best, she represents the best in the liberal humanist feminist tradition.

Notes

1. Ellen Mappen, *Helping Women at Work: The Women's Industrial Council, 1889–1914* (Hutchinson, London, 1985).
2. Vera Brittain, *Testament of Youth* (Macmillan, New York, 1933), p. 583.
3. See e.g. Vera Brittain to Winifred Holtby, 4 November 1921, Winifred Holtby Collection, Hull Central Library, Hull, Humberside, England (referred to hereafter as Holtby Collection).
4. The Six Point Group Collection at the Fawcett Library, London, is sparse for the 1920s, but correspondence confirms that Brittain was a member of the executive: for example in a letter of 8 May 1927, from Vera Brittain to Miss Vernon, Brittain mentions her membership. Unpublished letter, Vera Brittain Archive, William Ready Division of Archives and Research Collections, McMaster University Library, Hamilton, Ontario (referred to hereafter as VBA).
5. For her birth control activism, see *Testament of Youth*, p. 582, and see her diary entry for 3 February 1932, where she mentions attending 'Marie Stopes' Executive Committee as a member'. Brittain's 'Reflective Record' is in VBA. The diaries of the 1930s have been published: Alan Bishop (ed), *Chronicle of Friendship: Vera Brittain's Diary of the Thirties, 1932–1939* (Gollancz, London, 1986). On her membership in the Labour Party, see e.g. *Testament of Youth*, p. 647. Alan Bishop and Paul Berry interpret Brittain's multiplicity

of interests as meaning that she was sympathetic to new feminism as well as equal rights feminism: 'Her feminism represented a creative reconciliation of "old" and "new" feminist priorities, both of which she forwarded', they say in their 'Introduction to Vera Brittain's journalism', in Berry and Bishop (eds), *Testament of a Generation: The Journalism of Vera Brittain and Winifred Holtby*, (Virago, London, 1985) pp. 37–8. This statement implicitly accepts the new feminist position that equal rights feminism was narrow.

6.   Olive Schreiner, *Woman and Labor* (Frederick A. Stokes, New York, 1911).

7.   Vera Brittain, 'Olive Schreiner', *Nation and Athenaeum*, 23 October 1926, G23, in VBA.

8.   In *Testament of a Generation* Berry and Bishop provide a useful selection of Brittain's journalism, with helpful introductions and notes.

9.   Vera Brittain, 'Woman's place: the passing of the married woman's handicaps', *Time and Tide*, 25 November 1927. G79 in VBA.

10.   Vera Brittain, 'The girl baby has her day', *Yorkshire Post*, 2 December 1927, G82 in VBA.

11.   Vera Brittain, 'Wasted women and the tyranny of houses', *Manchester Guardian*, 10 June 1927, G55 in VBA.

12.   'I denounce domesticity! A protest against waste', *The Quiver*, August, 1932, G385 in VBA. Reprinted in *Testament of a Generation*.

13.   See for example, Ruth Schwartz Cowan, *More Work for Mother: The Ironies of Household Technology from the Open Hearth to the Microwave* (Basic Books, New York, 1983).

14.   Vera Brittain, 'The leisured woman of America', *Yorkshire Post*, 12 November 1926, G25 in VBA.

15.   See for example her 'Of prejudice or knowledge? Fields for women's research', *Manchester Guardian*, 28 June 1927, G58 in VBA.

16.   Vera Brittain, 'Semi-detached marriage', *Evening News*, 4 May 1928, G107 in VBA. Reprinted in *Testament of a Generation*.

17.   Charlotte Haldane's *Motherhood and its Enemies* (Chatto & Windus, 1927) provides a good example of the latter. Brittain wrote a witty and perceptive review of this book: 'Mothers and feminists', *Time and Tide*, 18 November 1927, G78 in VBA.

18.   Vera Brittain, 'What is a good parent? Changing motherhood', *Manchester Guardian*, 6 May 1927, G46 in VBA.

19.   Vera Brittain, 'Welfare for middle-class mothers', *Time and Tide*, 30 March 1928, G97 in VBA.

20.   See her reference to the Clinic in Vera Brittain, *Testament of Experience: An Autobiographical Story of the Years 1925–1950*, (Virago, London, 1979: first published in 1957), p. 51. For references to her use of the clinic, see e.g. Vera Brittain to Winifred Holtby, 25 September 1928, Holtby Collection. For reference to serving on the board of management, see Reflective Record, 24 April 1932, VBA.

21.   For her public advocacy see her 'Women and architecture', *Yorkshire Post*, 30 January 1928, G91, VBA where she advocates more women architects, and her 'Maternal mortality and medical women', *Nation and Athenaeum*, 31 March 1928, G98 in VBA, where she asserts that there would be fewer maternal deaths if there were more women physicians attending births. In her private life, Brittain sought out women professionals. E.g. see her letter to her husband, 23 February 1929, where she mentions using a woman insurance agent. Vera Brittain to G. E. G. Catlin in VBA.

22.   Vera Brittain, 'Future husbands and fathers', *Manchester Guardian*, 1 February 1929, G179 in VBA.

23. Some analyses of Brittain's feminism have concluded that her insufficient awareness of class differences seriously damaged her feminist contribution. E.g. Yvonne A. Bennett, in her 'Vera Brittain: feminism, pacifism and the problem of class, 1900–1953', *Atlantis*, vol. 12, no. 2 (Spring 1987), pp. 18–23 states that 'Brittain's writings . . . were arguably often clouded by deeply engrained class perceptions'. Bennett, while critical of Brittain, is fair and balanced. Marvin Rintala is considerably more harsh, asserting that Brittain's claim to be a socialist was essentially fraudulent: 'Chronicler of a generation: Vera Brittain's testament', *Journal of Political and Military Sociology*, vol. 12, (Spring 1984), p. 25. For Rintala, the fact that Brittain and her husband employed domestic servants and sent their children to fee-paying schools is evidence of hypocrisy. If so, it was a hypocrisy shared by many upper-middle-class Labour Party supporters during these decades.
24. *Women's Work in Modern England* (Noel Douglas, London, 1928), pp. 1–2.
25. See Elizabeth Abbott to Vera Brittain, 29 April 1928 in VBA. She calls the book 'admirable', and says it will be very helpful in ODC work.
26. The statement of policy appears on ODC letterhead. See Elizabeth Abbott's correspondence with Vera Brittain in 1933, VBA.
27. Vera Brittain, 'Woman's record in 1927', *Yorkshire Post*, 30 December 1927, G88 in VBA.
28. See the Open Door Council and the Open Door International files in VBA.
29. For her membership of the executive, see Vera Brittain to Winifred Holtby, 25 September 1928, Holtby Collection.
30. On 'new' feminist support for such legislation see *Time and Tide*, 5 March 1926, pp. 220–1.
31. Vera Brittain, 'Women in industry: restrictive legislation again', *Manchester Guardian*, 13 December 1927, G85, VBA. Reprinted in *Testament of a Generation*.
32. Vera Brittain, *op. cit.* note 15.
33. From 1926 a wide-ranging spectrum of groups and individual feminist supported this last suffrage activism. See *Time and Tide*, 2 July 1926, p. 605.
34. On opposition to the extended enfranchisement, see Noreen Branson, *Britain in the Nineteen Twenties* (Weidenfeld and Nicholson, London, 1975), pp. 203–8.
35. Brittain was involved in planning the 3 July rally, at which she was asked to speak and serve as a marshal on behalf of the Six Point Group. See her letter to Winifred Holtby, 28 March 1926, Holtby Collection.
36. Vera Brittain, 'Political demonstrations: why women still hold them', *Time and Tide*, 26 July 1927, p. 686. The article appeared first in the *Manchester Guardian* on 14 July 1927.
37. 'Women, the vote and the hospitals', *Nation and Athenaeum*, 31 March 1928, G99.
38. See Bennett, *op. cit.* note 23, and my unpublished paper, 'Vera Brittain and the Great War' (Canadian Historical Association meeting, Montreal, 1985).
39. See Vera Brittain, 'A memorandum showing the connection between the status of women and the relations between countries published by the Six Point Group' (n.d. but 1929), p. 8, G264 in VBA.
40. The Equal Rights Treaty was drafted at a conference in Paris in 1926 by a group of English and American women, including Lady Rhondda and American women from the National Women's Party. See 'The Six Point Group makes history', *The Woman Teacher*, 22 November 1929, p. 51. Clipping in the Winifred Holtby Collection. See also, the Equal Rights International

collection, Fawcett Society Library, London, clippings and correspondence in Box 331.

41. One is cited above. The second, which first appeared in two parts in *Time and Tide*, as 'Feminism at Geneva', parts I and II, on 25 January and 1 February 1929 (they are G177 and G178 in VBA) was reprinted as a Six Point Group pamphlet entitled 'Geneva – the key to equality'.

42. That she was involved as a liaison with the Americans is clear from Brittain's correspondence, when she was visiting her husband in Ithaca, New York in 1927. See Vera Brittain, writing from Ithaca to Miss Vernon (of the National Woman's Party), 8 May 1927. Letter in VBA. See also Lady Rhondda to Vera Brittain, 20 August and 4 September 1928. Letters in VBA.

43. This effort is fully described in her letter to Lady Rhondda dated 11 August 1929, in VBA. However, Brittain's active involvement with the Equal Rights International apparently ended in 1929. See the letter to Helen Archdale from Winifred Mayo, dated 9 November 1930. Letter in Foundation File, Box 331, Equal Rights International collection, Fawcett Library.

44. Vera Brittain, *Honourable Estate: A Novel of Transition* (Macmillan, N.Y., 1936).

45. *Idem*, pp. xi–xii. For a different view of the significance of *Honourable Estate*, see Lynne Layton, 'Vera Brittain's Testament(s)', in Margaret Randolph Higonnet *et al.* (eds), *Behind the Lines, Gender and the Two World Wars* (Yale University Press, 1987), pp. 70–83.

46. See *Testament of Experience*, p. 124.

47. Brittain says this explicitly. See *ibid*.

48. *Honourable Estate*, xiii.

49. Vera Brittain, *Testament of Friendship: The Story of Winifred Holtby* (Macmillan, London, 1940; Fontana Paperbacks in association with Virago, 1981), p. 2.

50. While there were more tensions between them than Brittain was ever willing to reveal in public, the experiment must be accounted a success: the marriage lasted until Brittain's death in 1970, and produced two successful children. For a personal portrait of the couple, see the account by their son, John Catlin, *Family Quartet* (Hamish Hamilton, London, 1987), and see also Hilary Bailey, *Vera Brittain* (Penguin, London, 1987).

51. See for example Jeffrey Weeks, *Sex, Politics and Society* (Longman, London, 1981).

52. Sheila Jeffreys, *The Spinster and her Enemies: Feminism and Sexuality 1880–1930* (Pandora, London, 1985), pp. 123–4 and 189.

53. In contrast to Jeffreys, Lillian Faderman assumes that Brittain must have been a lesbian: *Surpassing the Love of Men: Romantic Friendship and Love between Women from the Renaissance to the Present* (William Morrow, N.Y., 1981), p. 310.

54. In the voluminous correspondence between Holtby and Brittain, there is no evidence that Brittain was a lesbian, or that the Holtby–Brittain friendship involved sexual passion. Indeed, there is evidence to the contrary, expressed for example in a letter to Winifred of 5 September, 1929, Holtby Collection. In it Brittain comments about the views of a mutual acquaintance who believes that women have a greater chance of happiness in a homosexual relationship than in marriage. Brittain calls such views 'dangerous in the extreme'.

55. Brittain supportively reviewed *The Well of Loneliness* in *Time and Tide* on 10 August 1928; she was present in the court when the book was on trial in October; and she later wrote an account of the case: *Radclyffe Hall: A Case*

of Obscenity? (Femina Books, London, 1968). See the letter from Radclyffe Hall to Brittain thanking her for being present at the trial. Letter of 15 November, 1928 in VBA.

56. Vera Brittain, *Halcyon or the Future of Monogamy* (Kegan Paul, Trench, Trubner, London, 1929).

57. See her 'Mothers and Feminists', *op. cit.* note 17. In private she went further: 'If it seems arrogant to say that the success of our marriage matters to the world, to society, to politics, to feminism, I can only reply that it is the kind of arrogance that one ought to encourage in one's self. Today, as in the past, one happily married wife and mother is worth more to feminism, and to the whole course of social morals, than a dozen gifted and eloquent spinsters.' Brittain to Catlin, 8 March 1929, in VBA.

58. Vera Brittain, 'The incomplete woman: wives and spinsters', *Manchester Guardian*, 19 October 1927. G74 in VBA.

59. F. Pethick-Lawrence to Vera Brittain, 28 September 1935, VBA.

7 Eleanor Rathbone and the Economy of the Family

Hilary Land

The passing of the Family Allowance Act, Miss Rathbone's permanent memorial on the Statute Book, was probably the most notable personal triumph in legislation since the Act which celebrates the Plimsoll line. In her life-long campaign on behalf of the 'disinherited family', Miss Rathbone displayed all her most characteristic qualities: her preference for a cause neglected by the powerful organised interests, economic or political; her detachment from all political parties which all had to be educated into agreement; her insistence on finding out and facing the facts which wedded the advocacy of reform inseparably with the practice of research; and the tireless, disinterested, passionate and compassionate fervour which added strong emotional force to her equable and good-humoured appeal to reason.

Thus wrote *The Times* in a leader launching an appeal for a Memorial Fund entitled 'Thanks to Miss Rathbone', on 1 October 1946, nine months after her death. Sadly, although Eleanor Rathbone had lived to see the Family Allowance Act reach the statute book in 1945, she did not live long enough to see the first family allowances paid the following August.

Family allowances, now called child benefit, are still part of the social security system in the United Kingdom, although their future is by no means certain. The threat to cash allowances for all children comes not only from a hostility to universal provision of any kind and a perception of public expenditure on welfare as a burden on the economy, but also from a refusal to accept Eleanor Rathbone's arguments, which stemmed from one of her core feminist principles. She was firmly of the view that legal equality was 'but a fleshless bone' if a woman 'has no income of her own and is prevented by the burden of family cares or the jealousy of male competitors from earning one'.[1] To her, therefore, the case for family allowances did not rest solely on the need to prevent poverty in large families; to encourage women to have more children; or to maintain male work incentives at the same time as avoiding allegedly inflationary wage increases. These were important concerns and won many over to the support of the introduction of a national scheme of family allowances, but to Eleanor Rathbone much more was at stake: women should not be forced into economic dependence upon their husbands and fathers of their children. Women as mothers together with their children were entitled to *direct* provision from the state.

This is why, to her, the question of to whom the family allowance should be paid -- the mother or the father – was not just an administrative issue but one of principle. In 1945 Eleanor Rathbone, as an MP, declared that she would vote against the Family Allowance Bill, currently being debated in the House of Commons, if the allowance was to belong to and be paid to the father, as was proposed. Eva Hubback, the secretary of the Family Endowment Society, recalled later that Eleanor Rathbone organized 'a lightning conference of women's organisations who insisted that the allowance should be paid to the mother unless she was proved unfit'.[2] After a free vote in the House of Commons the government conceded that the family allowance would be paid to the mother and in spite of attempts to change this thirty years later, when family allowances and child tax allowances[3] were combined to form, in effect, a tax credit for children called child benefits, cash allowances for children are still paid directly to the mother. Eleanor Rathbone's legacy therefore still has tangible consequences for every mother in the United Kingdom.

Eleanor Rathbone, however, also made and left for us an important contribution to feminist theory. In many ways this is as relevant to the issues confronting feminists today as it was ninety years ago when, while an undergraduate at Somerville College, Oxford, she sketched out for a college society, arguments

especially those relating to the social disadvantages of the present system and its bearing on the relation between men's and women's labour and concluded that the remedy was for society to 'substitute a system of more direct payments of the costs of its own renewal' for 'the arrangement by which the cost of rearing fresh generations is thrown as a rule on the male parent.'[4]

At that time she was already 'a fierce feminist', some of her

Somerville contemporaries later recalled, and this college society was, as Mary Stocks, her biographer, later wrote:

> not a cross-section of the undergraduate population. They were a selected few: a small circle of first-rate minds distilled from a student body which in those far-off days of pioneer female education was itself a distillation of young women emanating from abnormally enlightened homes and impelled by abnormally serious purpose.[5]

In time she brought much more than 'fierce feminism' to her analysis of the inadequacies of the wages system and support for children and their mothers. Before discussing in more detail her analysis of the problem of providing sufficient resources for the next generation within a wages system, which has other and conflicting economic functions, and the associated issue of the relationship between men and women within the family and between the family and the state, I want briefly to describe some of the other influences and experiences which she brought to bear on her work. It is then easier to see how her analysis contributed to the debates being conducted within feminist and socialist circles at the time and vice versa as well as understanding why she took a rather more benign view of state support and intervention than some of her contemporary working-class sisters.

Eleanor Rathbone came from a wealthy, radical family who for six generations had been prominent in the political and economic life of the city of Liverpool. On her mother's side also there was a history of philanthropy and an enlightened attitude towards women, stemming in part from their membership of the Society of Friends. The women as well as the men on both sides of her family had been active in public life. Not surprisingly she became involved in civic affairs in Liverpool as soon as she graduated. She had no need to seek paid employment (indeed throughout her life she also had sufficient resources to pay for domestic and secretarial support and to sustain various organizations to which she was committed, notably the Family Endowment Society). As Mary Stocks put it: 'of what use to spend unnecessary effort on money raising activities when fate had endowed one with an income greatly in excess of an abstemious spinster's reasonable needs?'[6]

During 1897 she became a visitor for the Liverpool Central Relief Society, a manager of a council school and honorary secretary of the Liverpool Women's Industrial Council. She also became parliamentary secretary to the Liverpool Women's Suffrage Society, thus becoming associated with the non-militant wing of the suffrage movement. In 1909 she became the first woman councillor on Liverpool City Council, standing as an Independent. She undertook social research and studied Merseyside docks and the causes and consequences of casual labour and underemployment. She also undertook a study of family budgets for the Women's Industrial Council.[7] Her methods were as painstaking and thorough as her older contemporaries, Beatrice Webb and Charles Booth. Her work as a council member gave her an intimate knowledge of housing problems. Mary Stocks sums up the decade leading to the outbreak of the First World War thus:

> Eleanor did not become exclusively or even predominantly a suffrage worker. She kept all her pots boiling, and indeed an ever-increasing number came to simmer under her busy hands. To the world outside as well as inside Liverpool, she appeared rather as an expert on social problems and local government than as a prominent speaker or agitator for the suffrage cause.[8]

This invaluable experience was consolidated still further during the First World War, when she became heavily involved in the welfare of the families through the Soldiers' and Sailors' Families Association (SSFA). Moreover, not only did she acquire a broader picture of working-class family life, but the scheme of separation allowances paid directly to the wives and mothers of serving men demonstrated the advantages of adjusting family income to family size *and* paying allowances directly to the woman in the family. To quote Mary Stocks again:

> This picture revealed something which seemed almost to give an audible click, as it dropped into place in the structure of her thought about the economics of motherhood. Here was the final stage of her argument. Here was the experiment whose result was to provide the empirical case for family allowances: the working experiment. War and family disruption was [sic] a sad business, but here for all to see was a new element of security in the lives of working mothers: a family income that bore some relation to the burden of family expense. The separation allowances were meagre enough. Even at 1918 prices, a weekly allowance of 12s 6d for the mother and 5s for the first child and 3s 6d for each subsequent child did not ensure the barest margin of subsistence. But it possessed the unfamiliar virtue of expansiveness,

and it represented spending power in the mother's own hands: hers by right, the essential tools for the work the nation expected her to do.[9]

How far was Eleanor Rathbone's evaluation of the scheme shared and what issues arose during the First World War in relation to separation allowances and how did they relate to wider debates about social welfare occurring at the same time? Separation allowances – involving almost half a billion pounds paid during the five-year period of the war to millions of wives and mothers – were the largest programme of direct payment the government had ever made to women. The administration of these allowances involved many controversial issues and are important to discuss briefly because they were subsequently raised in the campaign for family allowances, and not all feminists agreed with Eleanor Rathbone's views.

First, there was the problem of administering the allowances: who should do it and what conditions, if any, should be imposed on the women receiving the allowance? Second, were the payments made, as the suffragist journal *The Common Cause* asked, 'to be regarded as part of the soldier's wage or as a payment to the wife and mother for the work that falls on her'?[10]

These were important and related questions for in the early weeks of the scheme, the War Office gave local police authorities lists of women receiving allowances and issued a circular saying that the wife of a soldier or sailor should be arrested if found drunk and disorderly, kept at the police station until sober and then should be warned: 'Of the serious consequences including the loss of separation allowances that must ensue if she persisted in such irregularity of conduct and urge upon her to prove herself worthy of the husband who is fighting for his country.'[11]

The police were also given authority to enter their homes. This met with widespread outrage. The Women's Co-operative Guild organized conferences in Manchester and London, for example, passing resolutions opposing such a measure, and in mid-December 1914, the day after receiving a delegation from leading feminists and socialists, including Mary Macarthur, Margaret Bondfield, Susan Lawrence and Marion Phillips, the War Office officially apologized and withdrew the circular.[12] However, the question whether or not the separation allowance was really part of the soldier's remuneration, handed over to his wife in his absence by the War Office for practical reasons, or whether it represented recognition by the state that the work of home-maker had an economic value to the state remained unresolved.

This was an important question because it influenced the extent to which Eleanor Rathbone's argument, that the wartime scheme of separation allowances was analogous to a state scheme of family allowances, was accepted. Some argued that an employer paid wages to a man irrespective of the worthiness of his wife. Others, on the other hand, argued that as a man had no obligation to maintain his wife under common law if she committed a single act of adultery (and that remained the case in England and Wales until 1978), then the state, on her husband's behalf, did indeed have an interest in a wife's moral behaviour.

Of more direct concern to Eleanor Rathbone and those who through the SSFA helped to administer the scheme was whether voluntary organizations or local government should be organizing this work. In the early days of the war the SSFA was directly involved in paying out the allowances. At first the War Office had thought to use the Poor Law machinery, but the stigma associated with that was such that this was immediately and universally rejected by serving men and their families. Eventually payments were made through the Post Office, leaving the SSFA with the job of adjudicating difficult cases with respect to serving men's wives. Customs and Excise officials were asked to assess the needs of dependants other than wives (that is, mainly mothers and common law wives).

For Eleanor Rathbone, this meant she 'learnt the inner history of several hundred cases of matrimonial breakdown',[13] which Mary Stocks later speculated may have contributed 'to the instinctive aloofness which characterised her attitude to sex problems'.[14] It may well have contributed to her thoughts on what she called 'the Turk Complex' or men's desire to dominate women. Perhaps more importantly it convinced her that women 'by nature and experience' were best suited to do this 'exceedingly difficult and sensitive work'.[15]

However, she did not want the work to be done using untrained workers, however well meaning. She wrote: 'The new field of social effort is essentially one where the trained and expert woman social worker ought to play her part.'[16] Moreover, although active within local government herself, she disagreed with the Labour

Party whom she saw as having 'a craze for piling every conceivable new function upon already overworked town councils'[17] and wanting by this means to circumvent the charitable organizations. She was very resistant to the state usurping the latter's role in welfare administration and, as Susan Pederson suggests, this may also have been because she feared, with good reason, that women would be marginalized as a result.[18]

Others shared her concern about the importance of including women in the administration of welfare, but wanted *working-class* women to be involved. For example, in the debate during the First World War about the development of welfare services for mothers and babies prior to the passing of the Maternity and Child Welfare Act 1918, the Women's Co-operative Guild argued very strongly that the point of view of 'the independent working woman was more important than ladies "sitting on charity committees" and therefore "the working woman" should be given a voice in shaping policy.'[19] They in particular had fought hard to enable working-class women to become members of the national insurance committees created by the 1911 national insurance legislation, by insisting, for example, that travelling expenses of members should be paid. The issue therefore went beyond the matter of training as some other contributors to *The Common Cause* recognized. For example, one article headed 'At the Mercy of Volunteer Investigators' criticized SSFA ladies because some were 'of mediocre ability, narrow-minded, or prejudiced against the working classes' and most voluntary workers anyway were 'nearly all drawn from the middle and upper classes and many have not the wide experience necessary'.[20] Another contirbutor advocated a Service Wives Union who until public departments could be established would administer the scheme.[21]

Eleanor Rathbone's lack of experience of ever having been on the receiving end of welfare, whether provided by the state or by a charitable organization, also made her much more sanguine than some other feminists about state supervision of allowances in principle. Although she was suspicious of state paternalism (preferring instead what might be called philanthropic maternalism), she was certain that the principle of making the receipt of allowance conditional was a right one. As she wrote in *The Common Cause* in 1915:

> Even in the case of a widow with children, even if the State is acting
> *in loco parentis* it has a right to be satisfied that they are being properly
> looked after. It seems to me to be a pseudo-feminism which assumes
> that all mothers are good mothers and denies and ignores the principle
> that to take money from the State for discharging a certain duty
> involves a responsibility to the State and justifies such supervision as
> is necessary to see that the duty is being properly carried out.[22]

She was very clear that the continued payment of allowances
should be contingent upon 'the proper performance' of the functions of motherhood.[23] How 'proper performance' was to be
defined and by whom was, and remained, a contentious issue, but
Eleanor Rathbone never subscribed to the view that 'proper'
mothers gave up paid employment and stayed at home to look
after the children full time. As she wrote in 1924:

> Such a condition would be strongly resented by independent women
> and would defeat its own end. Some women, including some of those
> most capable of producing desirable children, are not fitted by tempera-
> ment for an exclusively domestic life. If they prefer to use part of the
> allowances to engage domestic help for the care of the children and
> seek paid work better suited to them, they should be free to do so as
> well-to-do women are now, so long as they can show that their children
> are properly provided for.[24]

Although she considered paying a separate allowance to the
mother, she decided against because, as she explained later to the
Beveridge Committee, who reviewed the social security system in
1941, 'we felt the case was really stronger if you leave out the
wife'.[25] As she had written in 1924: 'the functions performed by
the working mother do not all arise out of her maternity. She is
also her husband's housekeeper; a service equally needed by the
unmarried or childless man, and for which he should be able to
pay out of his wages.'[26] It was therefore better to set minimum
wages for men and women at a level sufficient for the maintenance
of two people. She did not, however, agree with feminists like
Anna Martin who, along with some members of the Fabian
Women's Group, wanted a woman to have a legal right to half
her husband's income. (Anna Martin thought this proposal would
strengthen men's responsibilities instead of weakening them like
family allowances to which she was opposed.)

She had in any case, since her student days, taken a keen
interest in women's employment and was firmly committed to the

achievement of 'equal pay for equal work' and became convinced
this objective was closely related to the question of family endowment. In 1924 she summarized her analysis of the causes of
women's restriction to a narrow range of occupations deemed
less skilled and therefore less well paid than predominantly male
occupations. She concluded that this was due:

> much less than is generally supposed to the free play of economic
> forces, which select from the available supply of labour the more
> efficient sex for the more skilled and the less efficient for the less
> skilled, and much more to the steady pressure of men's hostility to
> women's competition. [She identified four factors contributing to this
> hostility:] . . . the age-long tradition of masculine domination . . . the
> inevitable resentment felt by vested interests at a new class of
> competition . . . the conviction that men have a right to all the best
> paid jobs, because they have to support wives and children out of their
> pay; partly to the fear that women, because they have no wives and
> children to support, can afford to take less, will be forced to take less
> and so will undercut men.[27]

The first two factors she briskly dismissed as 'unreasonable,
selfish, anti-social' but she believed that in order to challenge
them, the other two factors had to be removed. Before the war,
men organized in trade unions and professional bodies had
attempted to reduce the competition from women and so strengthen their case for 'a family wage' or 'living wage' (that is, a
wage sufficient to support a wife and three children, the standard
family) by excluding married women from the labour market
altogether. Both the Trades Union Congress's and the Labour
Party's annual conferences had debated resolutions to prohibit
married women from keeping or taking up paid employment outside the home. These resolutions did not succeed but marriage
bars requiring women to resign on marriage had been introduced
in the professions, notably teaching and the civil service, and in
some areas manual occupations too. In the years prior to the
outbreak of war there was considerable debate in the popular
press on the subject of women's employment, and reading it leaves
no doubt that the hostility some men felt towards women workers
was very real.

During the First World War criticism of the married woman
worker was muted because she was needed in the war effort and
the issue of equal pay, particularly in those occupations previously

reserved for men, became more pressing, not least because men wanted to reduce women's potential for undercutting their wages. Eleanor Rathbone's analysis led her to the conclusion that women would be able to enforce equal pay and equal opportunities only in a market economy, either when there was a government with the political will and power to intervene in setting wage levels or in times of exceptional expansion of trade or shortage of labour, as had occurred in certain trades or occupations during the First World War.

In more normal conditions even with the statutory regulation of wages, her analysis led her to the conclusion that if equal pay was achieved the effect would be to intensify the existing tendency of the two sexes to become segregated in different occupations. She therefore disagreed with those who 'couple together equal pay and equal opportunity as though they were as inseparable as concave and convex'.[28]

Just as important, however, was her conclusion that the achievement of equal pay would do little to ensure that wages bore some relation to the needs of all families whatever their size. Even if trade unions did successfully bargain for wages for a five-member family, she calculated that 'provision would be made for 3 million phantom wives and for over 16 million phantom children in the families containing less than three children, while, on the other hand, in families containing more than three children those in excess of that number, 1¼ million in all, would still remain unprovided for'.[29] This was clearly an extremely wasteful way of providing for the next generation, but in the absence of any other mechanism for allocating resources to meet the needs of the next generation, men's objections to equal pay had to be taken very seriously: the healthy survival of society depended upon it. She therefore proposed that:

> the only possible solution is through a system of direct provision or family allowances that will, once and for all, cut away the question of the maintenance of children and the reproduction of the race from the question of wages and allow wages to be determined by the value of the worker's contribution to production, without reference to his family responsibilities.[30]

Eleanor Rathbone's analysis of women's weak position both in the labour market and in the family, confirmed by her experience of family welfare during the war, linked two issues which concerned feminists in the first two decades of this century and has led to a single solution: family allowances. When in 1917 she got together a small committee to take the idea further, their first pamphlet, published in 1918, was entitled *Equal Pay and the Family: A Proposal for the National Endowment of Motherhood*. The Family Endowment Committee was soon renamed the Family Endowment Society and the campaign for family allowances was launched. The six other pioneer members, Maude Royden, Kathleen Courtney, Mary Stocks, H. N. Brailsford, Emile and Elinor Burns, unlike Eleanor Rathbone, were either members of the Labour Party or in sympathy with it. They were all feminists.

This was an opportune moment for such a campaign to begin. The Act giving women aged thirty or older the vote reached the statute book in November 1918, three weeks before a general election. Having achieved a large part of their main aim, the suffrage movement was having to redefine its objectives and strategies. Ray Strachey, the parliamentary secretary of the largest suffrage society, the National Union of Women's Suffrage Societies (NUWSS) at the time, recalled later:

> Some felt that it must abide strictly by its 'feminist' objectives, and work only for the removal of the remaining disabilities of women and the extension of the franchise on equal terms. Others, and these were slightly in the majority, felt that there was much more waiting to be done. All the 'causes' which had made them care to possess political power rose up in their minds, and they wanted to work within the organisation they knew and loved so well for all sorts of aspects of the betterment of humanity – for the welfare of children, the improvement of health, education and sanitation, the improvement of international understanding and the general education of women in the duties of citizenship. The first group urged that there were many other organisations through which to advocate these things, their own duty as a feminist body lay along the plain equality line on which they all agreed. The others answered that this was a dry, academic view; what was the use of having the vote if they were not to use it for all the causes they believed in.[31]

There was a compromise for a while, not least because there were still many legal injustices and inequalities to be removed and in the early 1920s they had some success in achieving changes in the laws concerning, for example, divorce and maintenance, guardianship of children and inheritance. However, to use Ray

Strachey's words again: real equality of liberties, status and opportunities 'is an easy phrase to use, but its translation into terms of life in a world where men are still supposed to support their wives and children, is a harder thing'.[32] Eleanor Rathbone had the answer in her analysis of the claim for equal pay. This could be achieved only by acknowledging that men and women had *different* needs and that this difference arose from the fact that women were mothers or potential mothers.

Eleanor Rathbone, who had become president of the NUWSS in 1919 when Millicent Fawcett resigned from that position and the Society changed its name to the National Union of Societies for Equal Citizenship (NUSEC), was in a strong position to broaden the aims of the Society to include the introduction of a national scheme of family endowment. In her presidential address to the NUSEC in 1925 she brought to the fore the debate between the equal rights feminists and the 'new feminists' who included welfare and social reform in their programme to take account of women's special needs. The time had come, she said, when 'at last we can stop looking at all our problems through men's eyes and discussing them in men's phraseology. We can demand what we want for women, not because it is what men have got but because it is what women need to fulfil the potentialities of their own natures and to adjust themselves to the circumstances of their own lives.' She went on to say that, like manual workers in the last century, women had to realize

> that the privileges and the formulas that had been shaped to meet the needs of the classes that had hitherto held dominion were not necessarily sufficient in themselves to bring real freedom, real equality of opportunity . . . [they] . . . must work out for themselves a whole new science and art of living that would enable them not merely to copy the manners and customs of their betters, but to shape their own destinies.[33]

It was against the background of this speech that the NUSEC was asked formally to support the principle of family allowances. It had already been discussed at NUSEC local meetings all over the country, and there had been articles in the Society's journal *The Woman's Leader* and the majority of the executive, two of whom had been members of the original Family Endowment Committee, were in favour. Eva Hubback, who had replaced Ray

Strachey as parliamentary secretary in 1920, had become secretary also to the Family Endowment Society in 1924 (and remained involved until it ceased to exist after Eleanor Rathbone's death) and Elizabeth Macadam, Eleanor Rathbone's lifelong partner, had been honorary secretary since 1919. Not surprisingly the resolution was carried by 111 votes to 42. Millicent Fawcett (by then a dame) was the leading opponent on the grounds that it would undermine parental responsibility.

Support for the principle of family endowment was one thing, agreement about when and how this principle should be put into practice quite another. Although there were no doubts that the allowance should be paid to the mother, among feminists there were considerable differences of opinion about the details of the scheme – the source of its funding; the extent of its coverage; its relationship to services and benefits in kind for children and their mothers and whether or not the main focus was mothers or children. Even within the Family Endowment Committee when it consisted only of seven members there was not agreement about the level of the allowance. Should it be the same for all children or paid at a higher rate to those in higher income groups in recognition of the fact that they spent more on their children? The majority were concerned more with vertical redistribution (from rich to poor), but two members attached more importance to horizontal redistribution (from those without children to those with children in every income or occupational group).

Eleanor Rathbone herself did not have a fixed position on all these questions. She always had a preference for a state-financed scheme as this was simpler but was prepared to consider a contributory or occupation-based scheme as a first step if that was the only way to have the scheme accepted by 'a people so instinctively conservative as the British'.[34] As she explained in 1940 in the introduction to her book *The Case for Family Allowances*:

> The case for Family Allowances does not rest on any one concrete scheme. It rests on a principle which, as we shall see, can be and is embodied in a variety of schemes . . .
>
> The concrete schemes . . . may appear differently to readers according to their differing political views or class outlook. Some who are attracted by one scheme may repudiate others. But fruitful discussion of the whole subject is only possible if the question of the principle is not confused with that of any particular method of embodying

it . . . Our proposal is not a substitute for greater productivity, or more goodwill or workers' control, or socialism, or any other 'ism'. It is neither dependent on nor antagonistic to any of these things. It aims only at meeting a particular need which would continue even if all these other ends are achieved – will continue indeed so long as the institution of the Family continues.[35]

Among feminists active within other political parties, and in particular within the Labour Party and the trade union movement, not only were there different views on these questions but also different opinions about the impact the introduction of cash allowances might have on other desirable social and economic reforms. They had loyalties to their class as well as to their gender. In the Labour movement, like their brothers, some were fearful that the principle of direct provision for children in the form of cash allowances by creating divisions between men with families and those without, as well as divisions between women and men, might indeed be antagonistic to the *achievement* of socialism.

This view is summed up in a joint report of the Labour Party and Trades Union Congress in 1922:

Children's pension from birth to working life would require for its successful and economic administration, considerable changes in the wages system as well as a very great increase in taxation and must therefore be held over for later consideration when Labour in power has been able to re-organise and stabilise Society on a better basis.[36]

When in the 1930s some senior Conservatives, notably Leo Amery, began to advocate a scheme of family allowances in the context of concern about a falling birth rate; a rearming Germany, which was adopting pro-natalist policies; and the alleged disincentive effects of too small a gap between low wages and unemployment insurance levels, their suspicions seemed confirmed. As Ellen Wilkinson, a former suffragist organizer who in the 1920s had been among the first women in the Labour Party to support the idea of family allowances, wrote in 1938, by which time she was an MP: 'What the Amery-type want is to feed the existing and potential cannon fodder with the greatest economy and lack of waste. Pay the money for the upkeep of each child, don't give it to the individual workman who may have few or no children. In short apply the means test to wages.'[37]

To some feminists their analysis led them to adopt a strategy which would extend and develop social services for children and their mothers and not to strive, in the first instance, for the introduction of cash allowances for all children. This was the view that the National Labour Women's conference took when in 1923 it rejected a resolution supporting the principle of family allowances, favouring instead 'endowment in kind' as the next step. Describing the conference, Mary Stocks later wrote that the resolution had failed 'at the instance of the Party bureaucracy'.[38] Certainly there was a strong strand of opinion in favour of cash allowance and two years later the conference voted in favour of a state-financed scheme of cash family allowances.

The reasons for giving the development of social services priority varied. Some, in agreement with some of their fellow male trade unionists, focused on economic issues.[39] Others believed that while social conditions were so unequal, such a small allowance as five shillings a week would hardly give mothers the purchasing power to acquire better housing conditions, increased access to education or higher standards of maternity and infant welfare services. In the view of Gertrude Tuckwell, a prominent trade unionist who was very involved in issues concerning women's welfare, this was 'the overwhelming reason'[40] for preferring services. There was also evidence that 'the belief in the effectiveness of social services is much greater in places where there is a Labour majority'.[41] It was not therefore the case, as Eleanor Rathbone asserted, that behind the reluctance of all those unable to commit themselves to family allowances was 'a certain distrust of the working-class mother and an itch to supersede her by "experts"'.[42]

On the contrary, the Women's Co-operative Guild, for example, as already discussed, was very aware of the issues of the control and accountability of state-provided services and benefits. While there was support in general for family allowances (the Guild's national conference had passed resolutions in favour in 1924 and in 1926), there was also a strong strand of opinion in favour of extending the payment of maternity benefit. After that there would be nursery schools where meals would be provided, as well as in schools. This would be preferable to a smaller cash allowance paid over a longer period. The Guild had taken a particular interest in the double burden facing so many working-class women who were driven to take up paid work while their children were still very young. In pressing for a mixture of cash benefits and services, however, it stressed that 'while the money might be spent well in a communal way, do not let it go forth that the view is held that the mother could not spend it better'.[43] In all the Guild's work during this period, whether campaigning to have maternity benefit paid directly to the mother (for the first two years after its introduction in 1911 it was paid to the *father*) or to reform the divorce laws, it strongly believed that 'the woman's work in the home as a wife and mother is not recognised' and this was so of 'even the best of men'.[44]

Central to Eleanor Rathbone's campaign for family allowances was also the improvement of the status of women as wives and as mothers. But in some respects, like most new feminists, her views of the family were very traditional. (Some of the equal rights feminists, like Winifred Holtby, challenged the division of labour within the family.) She firmly believed that children needed *two* parents and were best cared for *within* their own homes even if it was not always the mother who did the caring. In the 1920s, when the provision of such services as school meals was being presented as an alternative to cash benefits, she did not accept that this would be a cheaper way of meeting children's needs. In 1924 she wrote: 'Those who rely on the general principle of the economy of large scale production forget that in this case it means a duplication not a substitution. The home and the mother are there anyhow, not to be eliminated except by communalising the whole existence of adults as well as children.' She was clearly not in favour of this not just because of economic arguments. She goes on to ask:

> . . . would this barrack existence be good for all children of all ages? Its promoters assume that children are like Ford cars, best and most cheaply produced by standardising all the elements of their well-being, instead of infinitely various and individualised human beings. Communal life might suit the healthy child of average ability. But would it suit the backward and repressed child, the delicate and the nervous, the able and imaginative? Would it encourage development of the qualities of initiative, resource, personality that have given this nation its present position in the world?[45]

Nearly twenty years later she was of the same view. In 1941 she wrote:

It is difficult to see how the economic burden of parenthood could be substantially lightened by communal provision unless we adopted a system something like that of the Jewish collective colonies in Palestine . . . it is difficult to imagine our individualistic and privacy-loving people taking to such a life, unless of course we were reduced by defeat in war to the position of a nation of serfs.[46]

Those who supported communal provision, however, were not thinking only of the *economic* burden of parenthood: they were thinking of how to share the *work* of motherhood differently. They presented a rather more positive picture of the possibilities of combining communal care with equal pay and cash benefits for children. Mrs Arnot Robinson, a member of the Woman's Labour League, for example, had written in *The Common Cause* in 1914, commenting on Eleanor Rathbone's proposals for motherhood endowment:

> Children not motherhood should be endowed. Every child should have a grant out of public funds sufficient to cover maintenance etc. Every penny of the grant would be spent on the child . . . if the mother determines to become the nurse and trainer of her children, the money would be paid to her. She might if she chose become a nurse to the children of other women who, although mothers, do not feel themselves specially fitted to develop the best that was in their children, and who therefore continue to work outside the home after marriage and motherhood.
>
> Were the value of women's labour increased in the labour market, houses would be designed to save the brutal unnecessary labour, which drains the vitality and strength of many women. Washing would be a skilled trade, and a laundry would be built for every dozen houses or so. Labour saving appliances under the management of a skilled staff of women advisers would be available. There would be airy, well-furnished nurseries, where the women who are good nurses would look after the children of wage-earning mothers and kitchens where it would be possible to get good meals at a moderate cost.[47]

This went far beyond Eleanor Rathbone's solution to removing the drudgery from women's domestic work. She proposed improving housing standards and amenities and in order to make better housing accessible to families, she advocated and – in true Rathbone tradition – successfully campaigned in the 1930s for the introduction of rent rebates which adjusted rents to take account of family size and income.

Eleanor Rathbone's analysis of the defects of the wage system as a mechanism for providing for mothers and children includes a number of powerful insights into how and why women's time and therefore women's work both in the home and outside it is not even noticed, let alone valued. As discussed above, she saw the introduction of a national scheme of family allowances as one way both to begin to place a value on women's work as mothers in the home as well as to increase its value in the labour market. Her focus was always centred on the economic arguments, perhaps because early on she believed that 'the economic soundness of state endowment of maternity has always appealed to me even more strongly if possible than its humanitarian and eugenic advantages!'[48] Her analysis and experience had also led her to the conclusion that 'the economic dependency of the married woman is the last stronghold of those who, consciously or unconsciously, prefer women in subjection, and that perhaps this is why the stronghold is proving so hard to force.'[49] She wrote that over fifty years ago and the stronghold remains in place – a little weaker but not yet broken. Her work helps us, as well as generations of earlier feminists, to understand why that is so. Her life is also a demonstration of what women can do when their energy and commitment is untrammelled by domestic cares and responsibilities and they have not only money of their own, but also that most precious of all resources – time.

Notes

1. E. Rathbone, Foreword in E. Reiss, *Rights and Duties of Englishwomen* (Sherrratt and Hughes, Manchester, 1934), p. viii.
2. E. Hubback, 'The family allowances movement 1927–1948', in E. Rathbone, *Family Allowances* (Allen & Unwin, London, 2nd edn, 1949), p. 285. Family allowances worth five shillings were paid for every child except the first.
3. In 1909, Lloyd George introduced a graduated system of income tax. Tax was levied on income above a certain threshold. The threshold for each person liable for tax was his tax allowance. If he had any children, his allowance was increased by a fixed amount for each child. Fathers benefited from these tax allowances because the Inland Revenue did not (and until 1990 will not) recognize married women as taxpayers in their own right. In 1978 taxpayers lost their child tax allowances, which, together with cash family allowances, which had been taxable, were replaced by a tax-free cash allowance – child benefit – paid on behalf of every child. For a detailed account of this change, see H. Land, 'The child benefit fiasco', in K. Jones (ed), *The Year Book of Social Policy, 1976* (Routledge and Kegan Paul, London, 1977). Also S. Fleming, introduction to republished edition of E. Rathbone, *The Disinherited Family* (Falling Wall Press, Bristol, 1986).
4. Rathbone, *op. cit.* note 2, p. 132.
5. M. Stocks, *Eleanor Rathbone*, (Gollancz, London, 1949), p. 46.

6.   *Idem*, p. 101.
7.   Liverpool Women's Industrial Council, *How the Casual Labourer Lives* (1909).
8.   Stocks, *op. cit.* note 5, p. 67.
9.   *Idem*, p. 76.
10. Notes and News, 'To whom is the payment due?' *The Common Cause*, 24 Dec. 1914, p. 617.
11. C. Macmillan, 'The liberty of the (woman) subject', *The Common Cause*, 11 Dec. 1914, p. 591.
12. *Daily Citizen*, 8 Dec. 1914, Gertrude Tuckwell Papers.
13. Stocks, *op. cit.* note 5, p. 76.
14. Rathbone, *op. cit.* note 2, p. 214.
15. E. Rathbone, 'Pensions and allowances', *The Common Cause*, 22 Jan. 1915, p. 664.
16. *Ibid.*
17. *Ibid.*
18. S. Pedersen, *Separation Allowances in Britain during the Great War* (1986), mimeo.
19. Co-operative Women's Guild, *Memorandum on the National Care of Maternity* (1917).
20. 'At the mercy of voluntary investigators', *The Common Cause*, 27 Oct. 1916, p. 364.
21. 'A service wives union', *The Common Cause*, 1 Jan. 1916, p. 625.
22. Rathbone, *op. cit.* note 15, p. 664.
23. E. Rathbone, 'Separation allowances: an experiment in the state endowment of maternity', *The Common Cause*, 17 Mar. 1916, p. 649.
24. Rathbone, *op. cit.* note 2, p. 239.
25. Public Records Office, *Beveridge Committee Minutes of Evidence*, CAB 8/87, Q.3029, 2 June 1942.
26. Rathbone, *op. cit.* note 2, p. 219.
27. *Idem*, p. 103.
28. *Idem*, p. 108.
29. *Idem*, p. 15.
30. *Idem*, p. 93.
31. R. Strachey, *The Cause* (Virago, London, 1978), p. 369.
32. *Idem*, p. 370.
33. Quoted in Stocks, *op. cit.* note 5, pp. 116–17.
34. Rathbone, *op. cit.* note 2, p. 221.
35. E. Rathbone, *The Case for Family Allowances* (Penguin, Harmondsworth, 1940), pp. x–xi.
36. Joint Research and Information Department of Labour Party and TUC, *Motherhood and Child Endowment* (1922), p. 4.
37. E. Wilkinson, *Tribune*, 8 July 1938.
38. Stocks, *op. cit.* note 5, p. 101.
39. For a fuller discusssion of the economic issues related to family allowances, see J. Macnicol, *The Movement for Family Allowances* (Heinemann, London, 1980), and H. Land, *The Family Wage*, Eleanor Rathbone Memorial Lecture, 1979.
40. G. Tuckwell, letter to Living Wage Committee, 15 July 1928, TUC Records File, 117.
41. Dr Marion Phillips taking evidence from Women's Co-operative Guild, 15 Mar. 1928, TUC Records File, 117.
42. Rathbone, *op. cit.* note 2, p. 242.

43. Mrs Barton, Women's Co-operative Guild, evidence to Living Wage Committee, 15 Mar. 1928, TUC Records File, 117.
44. *Ibid.*
45. Rathbone, *op. cit.* note 2, p. 241.
46. Rathbone, *op. cit.* note 35, p. 49.
47. A. Robinson, 'Women as mothers and homemakers', *The Common Cause*, 20 Mar. 1914.
48. Rathbone, *op. cit.* note 23, p. 648.
49. Rathbone in Reiss, *op. cit.* note 1, p. ix.

8   The Women of the British Labour Party and Feminism, 1906–1945

Pat Thane

The female membership of the British Labour Party has been given little credit for making a positive contribution to feminist thinking or to extending the limits of women's public role. They have been interpreted, rather, as essentially subordinate to the males who dominated the party and to male ways of thinking. This has been said to have been especially so after women were given a formal place in the party constitution in 1918.[1]

Female support for the Labour Party was first organized in the form of the Women's Labour League. This was established in 1906 as an autonomous 'organization of women to work for independent Labour representation in connection with the Labour Party and to obtain direct Labour representation of women in parliament and in all local bodies'.[2] The League became an 'affiliated organization' in 1908.[3] The 1918 Constitution incorporated the League fully into the party, transforming its branches into 'women's sections' of local party branches, giving women full party membership, a party official, the Chief Woman Officer, and four members on the National Executive Committee of the party, to be elected by the annual party conference.

The reality of male dominance in the party is unquestionable, but its use as a framework for interpreting the role of women in the party does less than justice to their organizational importance and independence of mind, to the coherence of their analysis of the role of women in society and of their strategies for change. The justification for including the Labour women in any study of twentieth-century feminism, at least for the years before 1945, is that views which were plainly held by a majority of the membership consistently through the period from 1906 to 1945 were feminist, on any but a very narrow definition of the term. Yet they were women who chose to work for feminist as well as for other goals in a mixed-sex organization. They were fully aware of the difficulties which would and did result. Their reasons for making this choice, their attitudes to and relationships with single-sex feminist organizations, their strategies in relation to male members of the party, and their outcome, merit examination.

The numbers of women involved were large and cut across class boundaries. In 1914 the membership of the Women's Labour League was probably no more than 5000.[4] After the vote was given to most women above the age of thirty in 1918, women joined local Labour Party branches in proportionately larger numbers than men.[5] By 1923 membership of the women's sections was about 120 000;[6] between 1927 and 1939 it fluctuated between 250 000 and 300 000.[7] In the inter-war years women composed at least half the individual membership of the party and in some branches more, for example three-quarters of the Cardiff party membership in 1930 was female.[8]

The membership of the relatively small pre-1914 Women's Labour League may have been proportionately more middle class than the much larger membership of the inter-war women's sections and it was strongly influenced by the middle-class female socialists who initiated it, such as Margaret Macdonald, wife of the party leader, and Katherine Bruce Glasier. But even in these early years the main strength of the League was in northern industrial areas and it established branches in decidedly working-class districts. In Benwell in the north-east coalfield in 1909, 'the League meeting was an event in the lives of the miners' wives, some of whom walked miles to attend the meetings'.[9] The branch at Liscard on Merseyside held 'lectures and drawing room meetings' at first but felt by 1907 that these were not attracting 'the right people'. Instead they started a clothing club, which brought in more and poorer members.[10] Nor, as this example suggests, can the social composition of the membership be interpreted as primarily drawn from the secure élite of the working class. Many members, whatever their current social position, had at some point in their lives directly experienced severe poverty.

There are signs that the League and the women's sections, like other female Labour organizations, sought more vigorously and effectively than their male equivalents to draw in and work with the poorest. They gave notably active support to strikers and their families, helping them to hold out in some of the prolonged strikes of the pre- and inter-war period, such as the dockers' strike of 1913 and the long miners' lock-out which followed the General Strike of 1926.[11] The support networks of the miners' wives in the British coal strike of 1984 lay in a long tradition within the British Labour movement. The cancellation of the 1926 Conference of Labour Women because too many members' families had lost too much in the General Strike and the lock-out to be able to afford to travel, and the fall-off in paid-up membership (though not necessarily in active participation) in regions of heavy unemployment in the inter-war years suggest how many members lived in or close to real poverty.

The Labour women were, however, as proud of their middle-class as of their poorer membership. They regarded it as a definite asset that their membership included women in paid *and* unpaid occupations, housewives, manual workers *and* professional women; women employed professionally or voluntarily in social services and caring occupations (doctors, nurses, health visitors, housing managers) *and* their clients.[12]

The chairman (the term always used by the Labour women, as it was in single-sex feminist organizations at this time) of the Conference of 1911 commented:

> The wage-less home worker and the almost homeless wage-earner meet here for mutual benefit, and the woman of leisure can find abundant scope for her energies in our ranks. Class distinctions need make no barrier if the principle and enthusiasm dominates [sic] the minds of women and membership is open to all who will unite in the great work of regaining for those who labour a more just reward for their toil.

The biographical material on membership to be found in conference speeches and in the publications of the organization suggests that both the social mix and the belief that it was an asset to the organization continued at least until 1945, though perhaps a majority of members throughout the period identified themselves as primarily workers in the home. The Labour women sought to use the variety of expertise and experience in their ranks in the efforts, which they saw as a major part of their function, to assess, analyse and propose remedies for important social problems. They circulated questionnaires to gain information on the experience and views of members and their neighbours on, among other things, divorce in 1911,[13] maternity hospitals in 1924,[14] malnutrition in 1936,[15] housing design and equipment in 1942.[16] These formed the basis of policy proposals pressed upon the party and on governments.

How did the Labour women perceive and analyse the position of women in society? They certainly emphasized the need to enhance society's valuation of woman's maternal and domestic role. This could be interpreted as a restatement of an ideology of 'separate spheres' whose inevitable outcome must be the reinforcement of male power. This emphasis was not unusual among feminists of the period, and like others the Labour women saw it as a means to assault rather than to reinforce male power. Like other feminists they sought equal rights, opportunities and status for women with men in all spheres where it was lacking and *also* equal status for the domestic with other social roles. This should not be misinterpreted, as it has been, as a prescription that woman's place *should* be in the home. This would be to misread the implications of their pragmatic assumption that most women were and were likely to continue to become wives and mothers. Statements can be found such as: 'we must admit that the chief significance of life for a woman finds itself in love marriage and motherhood'.[17] But they were supported by a distinct minority of the membership. They are far less representative, even in peace-time, than those expressed by Dorothy Thurtle in *Women – An Oppressed Class*.

> . . . women are still not regarded as human beings with equal rights and duties. And the reason for this seems to me to be found in the doctrine that the prime function of woman is to bring forth children and perpetuate the race. It would be idle to deny that this is an important function that can only be performed by a female. Modern conditions have proved conclusively however that this is not necessarily a full-time occupation and in most cases should not be.[18]

The range of views among the Labour women in the early days on this key area of debate in the feminism of the first half of the twentieth century was evident in a debate at the 1909 Conference on 'Endowment of Motherhood and Married Women's Work'. Katherine Bruce Glasier opened with the view which she was not to abandon through her long years of activism in the Labour Party: 'the home where it existed, the influence of the family . . . were the greatest humanizing factors we possessed . . . a woman who has a home to make should not be compelled to work outside it from economic necessity . . . she would even be inclined to prohibit married women's work'. She was alone in a debate which expressed a full range of views among leading members of the organization, though Margaret Macdonald came close to sharing Glasier's position. Margaret Macmillan denied that working mothers harmed their children, while Dr Ethel Bentham 'thought that . . . it was not the labour of married women in factories that was so harmful as the effects of overwork on young people not yet come to maturity'.

In March 1934, when it was being widely argued that married women should leave the labour market to release jobs for men in the depths of the Depression, an essay competition for readers of *Labour Woman*, on the topic 'Should Married Women Work?' attracted over a hundred entries, three out of four in favour of the right of married women to work. This reflected the balance of opinion in the organization throughout the period.[19] Rather than offering prescriptions for women's conduct of their lives the Labour women were engaged in a long process of debate about the roles of women in society and about the development of strategies for maximizing their choices about these roles.

Broadly uniting the majority who did not believe that woman's place was necessarily in the home, throughout the period, was a clear awareness of the nature of contemporary gender roles, of their interaction with state policies and social and economic structures, of how they might be changed, and of the potential role of women as agents of change, using their growing citizenship rights. They had few illusions that such change would come easily or that significant male support would readily be forthcoming, indeed they recognized that male opposition, including that within the party, posed their greatest problem.

They assumed that most women were and would continue to wish to be wives and mothers and that many, at least in the immediate future, would make this their primary occupation at least for a substantial proportion of their lives. Also that both social and economic conditions and women's aspirations were changing in such a way as potentially to increase opportunities for freedom of choice in the conduct of their lives. This was, after all, a period in which the birth rate fell decisively and the marriage rate rose, in which the range of paid employment available to women expanded, especially in the 1930s, a time of changing technology affecting work in and out of the home and changing housing styles in the direction of smaller size and easier manageability. They aimed to enable women to take advantage of these changes in order to assert greater control over their lives, above all to create conditions in which women made a genuine choice whether to work in the home or in the paid labour market, rather than having the decision imposed upon them due to poverty or pressures of custom, convention or male authority; and in which unpaid work in the home was valued equally with paid work outside it.

That this, however idealistic it may have been, was no mere rhetoric, the expression of a male-dominated 'false consciousness', is suggested by the vigour, clarity and consistency of their proposals. At its base was the conviction that the home should and could provide the base for the liberation of women rather than for their inescapable bondage. It currently was, but need not always be, a site of domestic slavery. Though in the present the primary responsibility for children might lie with the mothers who bore them, this need not constitute a mother's sole or leading role. Strategies could be developed to give women more flexible control over their lives. The Labour women advocated, among other things, day nurseries not only for the children of mothers active in the paid labour market but for those working in the home, to allow them space free from child care and domestic responsibility to devote to their own leisure, education, political or voluntary action – for self-development. They insisted that work in the home was in no way different – except in often being harder and the hours longer – from work in the paid labour market and was certainly as vital to the national economy. In 1911 Margaret Macdonald complained that according to the new National Insurance Act:

> All women who are not wage-earners working for employers are 'non-workers' . . . this sets up a quite erroneous standard of useful 'work', for the woman who looks after her house and family usually works quite as hard and contributes quite as much to the family wealth as her wage-earning husband.[20]

In April 1920 Marion Phillips stated: 'The Labour Party is the party of the workers and so it realizes the needs of women, for who are workers to such an extent as they?'[21] In 1944 Mary Sutherland, Marion Phillips's successor as Chief Woman Officer, launched a 'Charter for Housewives and Mothers' based on their right to good conditions of work and their right to adequate leisure. It was to include 'Good labour saving homes', good health services, 'Social security for the wife and mother as for other members of the community', family allowances, home-help service, nursery school holiday and leisure facilities at moderate cost and 'expansion of communal services – e.g. restaurants and laundries'. She declared that:

> The right of a married woman to earn outside the home must be insisted on; and equally her right not to be forced to work outside the home through economic necessity if she wants to make home and children her work. (In the past outside employment for married women has meant the burden of two full-time jobs instead of one.)[22]

Throughout the period the Labour women were impressively careful in their use of language to avoid the equation of work with paid work in the formal labour market. They saw one of their roles as that of a collective body through which home workers, the largest occupational group in the country, could strengthen their position and acquire a public voice, as trade unionists strengthened that of paid workers. Their determination to reduce hours of work and improve conditions for women in the home led to campaigns which were especially active in the 'reconstruction' periods of both wars for improved housing design and increased and improved house-building at low rents.[23]

They could see no virtue in women being forced to bear the double yoke of domestic and paid labour if they did not wish to, and assumed, realistically enough, that this was the meaning of paid work for most mothers in the present, whatever might be hoped for in the future. Women, they argued, *could* effectively achieve personal dignity and public influence from their home base and should be given time and encouragement to do so. Their presence and experience would strengthen and humanize public life and the priorities of politics. The woman who took her domestic role as her primary work need not become submerged in the home and cut off from public affairs; one of their aims was to urge and to help her not to become so, but rather to contribute her vital perspective to public debate.

They complained, not always justly, that women in suffrage organizations had sometimes become so absorbed in the struggle for the vote that they were not assisting women to use it when they got it. Their aim, even from 1906, was to help women to use their growing civil rights by seeking election, co-option or appointment to the growing number of public bodies open to some of them even before 1918.[24] They were also encouraged to observe and demand improvements in the local administration of services.[25] The scale of such encouragement grew in the inter-war years. *Labour Woman* provided briefing articles on new legislation and main policy areas and the women's sections offered classes on public speaking and political and administrative education through pamphlets, lectures and summer schools attended by hundreds of women annually. Margaret Macdonald told the 1907 conference how: 'at their meetings many women had shown powers of organizing and speaking which they had not shown when attending meetings where men took part and they were able to express their opinions as women on matters of which they had a special knowledge'. The women's sections provided a supportive sub-culture which enabled women to enter the public sphere, to take action to improve their own lives and that of society more generally. Women should not be slaves to their families but the formal labour market was not their only escape route. Those who chose to do so could be active from places of paid work, others, helped by one another, could use the domestic base as a source of strength, a springboard into the outside world rather than a haven from it.

In this view attaining the vote was an essential step towards a feminized democracy, characterized, ideally, by gender roles and relationships so modified as to bring to society and politics the benefit of all that was good in the characteristics which both males and females had acquired over time.[26] This implied changed attitudes to the marriage relationship and to the male role. Their vision was of a world in which women ideally lived in mutually supportive partnerships with men and mothered children, but in which their lives were not exclusively defined by the domestic role. *Labour Woman* was early to support the idea of the companionate, sexually fulfilling marriage.[27] They had nothing to say about women who lived with women though a number of their leading members did so; their obituaries referred to these friendships and there is no sign that they were disapproved of.[28] Nor did they imagine that all or even most marriages, or equivalent relationships, were currently supportive. They recognized the numbers of women trapped in unfulfilling marriages and pressed vigorously and with some success for improved divorce, separation, maintenance and custody laws to diminish the very considerable barriers to a woman's escape from a bad marriage and to her achieving economic independence free from it.[29] They campaigned that society should treat the unmarried mother and her child on the same basis as the married,[30] and that women should have maximum control over reproduction and conditions for safe childbirth, to maximize her control over her own life and health.[31] The marriage relationship and even dependence upon male earnings need not necessarily subordinate and silence women, if they were conscious of their *right* to share those earnings by virtue of their domestic labour and to assert their independence as human beings within the marriage relationship.

Women, however, needed emotional and institutional support if they were to take this new command of their lives and, ideally, also some independent financial resources; hence the support of the Labour women for family allowances. The way forward, they believed, was not to seek to dismantle the established framework of family relationships, but to build on them and modify them, to increase the autonomy of women within and outside the home; to work for change from where most women were rather than from an abstract, ideal position. In this context it was also suggested that the role and responsibility of fathers for children should be strengthened, rather than weakened. Some feared that the latter might be the effect of the introduction of family allowances; their payment directly to mothers might reinforce the notion that children were primarily the responsibility of the mother. A strong strand of argument within the Labour Party was that direction of state resources, instead, into provision of improved housing, nursery and higher level schools, health and welfare services would directly benefit children and increase the opportunities of the 'housemother' for independence by reducing her domestic burdens, whilst avoiding this danger.[32]

For the Labour women, just as important as enabling women to use the home as a base for liberation was the need to improve their access to paid employment and their conditions of work and pay. They campaigned vigorously against the marriage bar, which spread through industry and the professions in the inter-war years.[33] Though supporting male strikes to ensure that male incomes were sufficient to support a family where necessary, they opposed the concept of the 'family wage', and far more serious effort went into promotion of female trade unionism, statutory improvements in women's pay and working conditions and social service support for mothers in paid and unpaid work. It was as rare to find a defender of the 'family wage' among rank and file speakers at the annual conferences as among the leadership. Majority (though of course not unanimous, on this as on any other issue) support was for the 'rate for the job' regardless of the sex of the worker.

Most important, they demanded not merely equal pay, which, they argued consistently from at least 1918 to their evidence to the Royal Commission on Equal Pay of 1946, could be restricted to the very few areas of precisely equal work between men and women, but that women's wage rates in all occupations, especially those defined as exclusively female, which were notably low paid should be raised to comparable levels with those of men. From as early in 1913 the annual conference opposed the argument that males merited a 'family wage' to meet the needs of their dependants: many women had dependants to provide for, many men had not; in any case wages should not be determined by such criteria but by evaluation of the job itself. Mrs Mottram of Leigh (a textiles town in Lancashire) told the conference that

> women were entitled to the same wages as men no matter how they spent it. So long as the employer is satisfied with the work done, it is not his business to say that because the employee is a woman she should get less money. Nor is it his business to consider whether the worker is married or single.

The 1930 Report, *Equal Pay for Equal Work*, the fullest expression of the attitudes of women in a range of Labour organizations on this subject, expressed plausible scepticism as to whether men's higher pay did indeed derive from the tacit or explicit acceptance in industrial bargaining of male family responsibilities or from higher levels of organization among male workers. They were well aware that male trade unionists were often false friends on this issue, demanding equal pay because they were fully aware that it would reduce women's opportunities in the sectors of equal work with men. And they were equally conscious that what appeared to be extensions of work opportunities for women could be employer strategies for reducing wage rates for men and women. This was seen especially to be a danger in both world wars when employers were suspected, with some justice, of using the shortage of male labour and pressures for 'dilution' as opportunities permanently to subdivide, reclassify and pay at lower rates tasks previously assigned to higher paid men. In the First World War in particular Labour women had few illusions that what appeared to be extensions of opportunities for women in manual work were as they seemed. The women were aware that they were fighting on two fronts, against both employers and male workers, including men in their own movement. The 1930 Report stressed the need to overcome the antipathy in the Labour movement to married women's work. It also interestingly, and probably accurately, observed that the real problem was not, as often asserted, that men feared their wages being undercut due to female competition. In most occupations most of the time in peacetime this was not a danger given the reality of sexual division of labour. Rather they were indifferent; women had to organize to change this. They recognized too that higher male pay could not be attributed to the higher skill content of male work: highly skilled work normally performed by a woman attracted lower pay than work of equivalent skill performed by a man. The way forward was organization by women in trade unions and also politically, as a united body within the Labour Party, to fight for legislated equality.[34]

Many of these aims and analyses they shared with single-sex groups. Why did they seek to promote them within an organization of both sexes, and why this one? Most active Labour women related the changes they desired in the situation of women and in gender roles to a broader vision of social change; they varied in the relative prominence they gave to it and some, of course, could not be defined as feminist at all. Many of them had concluded that the desirable changes for women could be attained only by political means and hence by activity within a political party; the Labour Party was the best vehicle available for achieving their goals. Also, they were women who believed that in a real mixed-sex world it was necessary to work with men, as they lived with them, and patiently to seek to convert and persuade rather than to confront them; to enter and change 'male' institutions armed with female values. They believed that a viable feminism must acknowledge the complementarity of male and female lives. Like most of their party they were pragmatic, reformist and gradualist. They did not necessarily have high hopes of how far or fast the men could be pushed.

An important part of their role they defined as bringing to the attention of men in the party issues they had neglected or underestimated, mainly in the social policy sphere. Margaret Macdonald told the first conference in 1906 that 'there were many questions on which women's knowledge was more extensive such as the feeding of children, women's work and wages, old age pensions and many other things which closely affected the home life'.

The first 'maiden speech' in the House of Commons by a female Labour MP, Susan Lawrence in 1924, concerned school feeding, which, she proclaimed 'is one of the many things for which we felt women to be especially needed in the House'.[35]

In the short run women were encouraged to emphasize social issues and those directly affecting women, not because the Labour women had an 'essentialist' view of women's interests and capabilities but because men had grossly neglected them and they were urgent; but they were aware of the danger of 'ghettoization' and believed that in the longer run this focus on 'women's' questions would be largely unnecessary.[36] Barbara Ayrton Gould told the 1943 conference: 'The more women they could get into parliament the sooner they could eliminate women's questions as women's questions and they would all become universal questions.' Though many believed that there were essential differences between men and women, their precise dimensions were unclear, and that there was likely always to be a distinctive woman's point of view.

Some members devoted most of their time to issues not directly within the female sphere, though few ignored them entirely. Most of the female labour MPs elected before 1945 devoted a significant portion of their political effort to questions concerning women's rights or women's welfare. Of the three female Labour cabinet ministers of the period, Ellen Wilkinson had been a suffragist and was an active supporter of women's causes in the 1930s, notably 'equal pay, whilst denying in public that it was a sex question, but emphatically a class question'.[37] Susan Lawrence campaigned against the 'marriage bar' among other things. Margaret Bondfield more perfectly than most embodied the collective commitment of the Labour women to helping women to fulfil their potential both as public and private beings, both as individuals and in partnerships with men, and fought for causes some of which did and some did not centrally concern women, while like her colleagues she abhorred 'extreme' confrontationist feminism – a hostility which perhaps originated in distaste for the pre-war activities of the WSPU, which they believed had harmed the women's cause.[38]

The women's sections encompassed believers both in equality and in the essential difference between the sexes and many who blended both beliefs. They contributed both to the further promotion of equal rights feminism *and* were early proponents of the new feminism which sought to change society to reflect women's experience rather than just to open up opportunities previously claimed by men.[39] But most were less concerned with abstract speculation about woman's nature or her ideal political role than with seeking solutions to urgent current problems. These they were convinced could not be achieved without the help of men in the real political world. By the time of the Second World War when there were prospects that the worst poverty might be receding they showed greater interest in more abstract consideration of gender roles.[40] In the inter-war years they were critical of the women in single-sex organizations who they felt focused too exclusively upon the needs of women, ignoring the importance of their interdependence with men, indeed conventionally they confined the term 'feminist' to such women, in a pejorative sense still familiar today. Whether this held them back from a more thorough-going re-evaluation of gender roles than characterized the single-sex organizations is doubtful.

There was of course a certain overlap in membership with such organizations as the National Union of Societies for Equal Citizenship (NUSEC) but also considerable tension between members such as Dora Russell, who gave much of their allegiance to a more confrontational style of feminism and to left-wing socialism, and the mainstream of the women's Labour movement.[41] The clash was most evident in the battle of the 1920s to persuade the party to adopt a policy of allowing local authority maternity and child welfare clinics to give free birth control advice. In this often described but much misinterpreted episode[42] the women of the party supported this policy with large majorities, but were unable to persuade the first Labour government of 1924. The national conference voted in favour in 1926 before retreating in the following year under firm orders from Ramsey Macdonald on the grounds that this was an issue of conscience on which a party statement was inappropriate.[43]

This is generally interpreted as a battle between male and female values within the party as a whole, and among the women between those who were and were not subservient to the men. This is too simple. There is evidence of strong male support for free birth control advice in local party branches.[44] An important reason for the leadership's refusal was almost certainly very active pressure from the Catholic Church, which had considerable power in a number of key urban constituencies; together with the fact that the minister responsible for such measures in the 1924 government, John Wheatley, was an active Catholic. In Labour's next period of government with Arthur Greenwood at the Ministry of Health, the Ministry very quietly in 1930 enabled clinics to give free advice 'in cases where further pregnancy would be detrimental to health'.[45] This has been criticized for inadequacy,[46] but even the Communist militant campaigner for birth control Stella Browne thought that 'medical grounds' could be broadly interpreted and that it opened the door to the effective provision of free advice. The disappearance of the agitation thereafter suggests that she may have been right.[47] By 1930 the government was under pressure on this issue from a wide range of sources, including the Church of England, the British Medical Association and numerous local authorities,[48] though it was the women of both the 'feminist' organizations and the women's sections who played the most prominent part.

The difference between the women in the party was also less one of principle than of tactics. Marion Phillips and Ethel Bentham had reservations which Dora Russell had not as to the health risks associated with certain birth control devices – and in view of the subsequent history of birth control techniques who is to say that they were necessarily wrong? There is no evidence that they failed to support or to promote the majority view in the women's sections. The difference was essentially between the determination of Russell and her associates to confront male party leaders and the more persuasive style of Phillips and the majority. As Phillips put it: 'We have much propaganda to do. It is no use complaining. We do not want a dictatorship of women: we want to explain to men (and women) the meaning of the proposal and convince them of its justice.'[49] It has been too readily assumed that Phillips's avoidance of confrontation equated with acquiescence with the male view; arguably the persuasive approach contributed at least as much to the limited victory of 1930 as did more outspoken tactics.

The other issue which divided Russell and her associates in and out of the party from the mainstream of the Labour women was that of protective labour legislation. From before the First World War egalitarian feminists had argued that protective legislation restricted women's work opportunities and should be abolished. This pressure continued in the inter-war years, promoted by the NUSEC, which presented such legislation as a conspiracy by trade union men to keep women out of better-paid jobs.[50]

It was a view which won notably little support among working-class women and was strongly opposed by leading female trade unionists. Ada Nield Chew and other textile workers pointed out that in cotton weaving where such legislation was longest standing women were closer in pay and levels of employment to men than in any manual trade. Selina Cooper, no longer a manual worker and active in the NUSEC, opposed legislation but the attitudes of the Lancashire millworkers among whom she lived were, at best, much divided. Barbara Drake claimed the number of women in protected industries had risen in the previous three-quarters of a century, while those in unprotected trades had fallen.[51] Mary Macarthur argued in 1918 that removal of protective legislation during the war had exposed women to greater exploitation and health hazards.[52] Julia Varley argued vigorously that while women were relatively unorganized only legislation could protect them from exploitation by employers; the need was to extend protection to men not to cut back on one of the few gains made by the working class. In the long run all hoped that differential legislation would disappear, but for the moment it was needed. Women had more to gain from promoting it than from an abstract hope of future social equality if they did not.[53] Hence Labour and trade union women pressed for extended statutory maternity leave and such measures as the Lead Paint Act 1926, the latter due to the proven effects of lead in causing miscarriage; while also arguing that it be extended to men whose health was also affected. They pointed out that in the past protective legislation for women and young people had been the first step to protection for all workers.[54] As Olive Banks has pointed out, Eleanor Rathbone attempted in 1927 to bring the NUSEC's position on protective legislation closer to that of the trade union women, but the outcome was a split and secession from the NUSEC of the most determined opponents of protective legislation.

In an outburst of impatience Marion Phillips expressed the majority view of the Labour women:

> Why is it that being democrats they so entirely ignore the views of women organized in trade unions and their representatives? Have they really such a contempt for women that they believe that so soon as they are in any way associated with men they take the men's view and not the women's?[55]

Similarly, supporters of family allowance among the Labour Party women questioned whether Eleanor Rathbone, its foremost proponent, understood the real world of working-class women. Her readiness to countenance payment of the allowances by employers in a package incorporating pay cuts for childless workers at a time, in the 1920s, when trade unionists were struggling against wage cuts, was criticized for failing to relate questions concerning women and welfare to some of their wider and longer-term consequences. It was hard for Labour women to believe that strengthening the hands of the employers against the unions in any respect could be in the long-term interest of working-class women or men, or of society as a whole. Nor was this a straightforward instance of Labour women giving primacy to class over sex interests; the two were inextricably intertwined: if existing structures of (male) economic power were reinforced both women as a sex and workers as a class would suffer.[56]

A reading of the words and actions of the Labour Party women which seeks to place them in the context of their times and does not judge them for failing to speak the precise language of their granddaughters reveals that they anticipated that language surprisingly often and had a coherent body of ideas and strategies that can reasonably be defined as feminist. They continued to promote feminist causes even in the 1930s when feminism has been described as collapsing into home-centred welfarism.[57] Their demands in particular for equal opportunities for women to enter and remain in the labour market and for equivalent training and pay at all levels with men certainly went beyond welfarism as normally defined.

But however admirable their ideas, what did the Labour women achieve? There is insufficient space to substantiate the case here, but it can be argued that they put welfare more firmly on the Labour Party agenda before 1945 than would otherwise have been the case. They played a substantial role in building the party organization and its growing vote in the inter-war years. They brought more women into public life, chiefly at local level, though a handful of women were voted into Parliament. They were notably more successful in London than elsewhere. In the local elections of 1934, which were generally good for Labour, of 729 Labour borough councillors elected in London 150 were female: 15 of them on Bermondsey Council, 15 in Hackney, 16 in Southwark, 12 in Poplar, all poor boroughs.[58] Larger numbers were co-opted on to statutory authorities as Labour's power grew in municipal government. Sixty-one Labour women were among the first female magistrates appointed in 1920.[59] It is highly probable that the influence of these women on public bodies was greater than their numbers due to the newness of their ideas, their dedication and enthusiasm; in particular they played an important part in the improved levels of health care in Labour-controlled authorities.[60] In these as in other ways they did something to expand women's opportunities and male expectations of their capabilities.

Compared with their ambitions, however, it was a minimal achievement. There was a fundamental difference between the political vision of most of the Labour women and that of most of the men; when they collided the male vision generally won. The party gained immeasurably from the numbers, energy and policy innovations of the women but the undoubted ability of the women in the party was not put to use proportionate to their numbers. The national conference not only held their birth control policy at bay but refused to endorse the 1930 equal pay report, sticking to the narrow 'old-fashioned' commitment to 'equal pay for equal work', and differed from the women on the family allowances issue. The women were well aware that their proposals were given less weight than those backed by males and protested against male control.[61]

The story of the Labour women illustrates the age-old regularity with which women have demonstrated independence of mind and to a limited degree exerted power at the personal and local level and show every potential for exerting it more comprehensively and at higher, national levels, but are blocked by the crude exercise of male power. This approach provides a more satisfactory framework for analysis than one which interprets the Labour women, or any similar group, as puppets of male leaders or as traitors to a feminist movement which in the period considered here offered no more successful route to unseating male power.

Notes

1. Sheila Rowbotham, *A New World for Women: Stella Browne – Socialist Feminist* (Pluto Press, London, 1977). Harold Smith, 'Sex vs. class: British feminists and the Labour movement, 1919–1929', *The Historian*, vol. 47 (Nov. 1984), pp 19–37. Christine Collette, 'An independent voice. Lisbeth Simm and women's Labour representation in the North-West, 1906–1914', *North West Labour History*, vol. 12 (1987).
2. Report of the First Conference of the Women's Labour League, 1906, p. 4.
3. Collette, *op. cit.* note 1, p. 80.
4. *Idem*, p. 86.
5. R. McKibbin, *The Evolution of the Labour Party, 1910–1924* (Oxford University Press, 1974), p. 141.
6. Labour Party, *Report of Annual Conference, 1923*, p. 60.
7. See Annual Reports of the National Conference of Labour Women for each of these years.
8. Report of Annual Conference of Labour Women (hereafter ACLW) 1930. See also McKibbin, *op. cit.* note 5, p. 141.
9. ACLW Report 1909.
10. ACLW Report 1907.
11. ACLW Reports 1912, 1913, 1927. *Labour Woman*, April, June, Oct. 1926.
12. See also Collette, *op. cit.* note 1, p. 83.
13. ACLW Report 1911.
14. *Labour Woman*, May 1924.
15. *Labour Woman*, July 1924.
16. *Labour Woman*, Sept. 1942.
17. *Labour Woman*, July 1915. Editorial.
18. *Labour Woman*, May 1945.
19. *Labour Woman*, March, April, May 1934, March 1942.
20. ACLW Report 1911.
21. *Labour Woman*, April 1920.
22. *Labour Woman*, February 1944.
23. *Labour Woman*, Feb., March 1918, Feb. 1942. ACLW Report 1943, among others.

24. See Patricia Hollis, *Ladies Elect. Women in English Local Government 1865–1914* (Oxford University Press, 1987).
25. See Pat Thane, 'The working class and state welfare in Britain, 1880–1914', *Historical Journal*, vol. 27, no. 4 (1984) p. 890.
26. See Sandra Stanley Holton's discussion in chap. 1 in her *Feminism and Democracy. Women's Suffrage and Reform Politics in Britain, 1900–1918* (Cambridge University Press, 1986).
27. *Labour Woman* carried a very favourable review of Marie Stopes's *Married Love* in May 1918.
28. E.g. the obituary of Margaret Llewellyn Davies in *Labour Woman* in July 1944 by Margaret Bondfield referred to Davies's long and close relationship with Lillian Harris.
29. For example, the first Labour government in 1924 was persuaded to introduce a Separation and Maintenance Bill, enabling a woman to claim maintenance while still living under the same roof as her husband, so that she no longer had to make herself homeless before maintenance was available, if the husband would not himself leave: *Labour Woman*, July 1924, July 1925.
30. E.g. in the payment of 'mothers' pensions' for which they campaigned in the 1920s. They never succeeded in persuading the males of the party to include unmarried mothers in these proposed pensions.
31. See below.
32. See debates at annual conferences in 1922 and 1929. ACLW Reports, *Labour Woman*, June 1928.
33. E.g. *Labour Woman*, Nov. 1930; ACLW Report 1935.
34. Report of the Standing Joint Committee of Industrial Women's Organizations (an advisory committee on women's issues which included representatives of the Women's Co-operative Guild and female trade unionists as well as Labour Party women), *Equal Pay for Equal Work*, in ACLW Report 1930.
35. *Labour Woman*, February 1924.
36. Marion Phillips (ed), *Women and the Labour Party* (Headley Bros., London, 1918), pp. 10–11.
37. ACLW Report 1930.
38. This assessment is based on a thorough reading of the frequent contributions of all three women to *Labour Woman* and to annual conference debates, and the reports of their activities in *Labour Woman*. Brian Harrison gives a somewhat different picture in chap. 5 of his *Prudent Revolutionaries* (Oxford University Press, 1987), which deals with these three women. He represents Lawrence and Bondfield as having relatively little interest in women's issues.
39. Olive Banks, in *Faces of Feminism* (Blackwell, Oxford, 1981), describes Eleanor Rathbone as fully 'opening up' new feminism in Britain in 1925 (p. 167); it appears to me to be evident and openly discussed among the Labour party women earlier.
40. Among other things in October and November 1943 *Labour Woman* reprinted a lecture by Margaret Mead, 'Science, women and the problem of power'.
41. Dora Russell, *The Tamarisk Tree. My Quest for Liberty and Love* (Elek, London, 1975) gives her account of her relationship with the Labour women at this period. It should not be read uncritically.
42. Audrey Leathard, *The Fight for Family Planning* (Macmillan, London, 1980), pp. 28–50; Jane Lewis, *The Politics of Motherhood* (Croom Helm, London, 1980), pp. 197–8; Rowbotham, *op. cit.* note 1, pp. 31–8; Smith, *op. cit.* note 1, pp. 25–7.
43. *Labour Woman*, June 1924, July 1923, March 1926.

44. Leathard, *op. cit.* note 42, pp. 30, 34, 40, provides evidence of Labour-controlled local authorities both establishing birth control advice centres and demanding ministry permission to do so before 1930. S. Fielding, 'The Irish Catholics of Manchester and Salford: aspects of their religious and political history, 1890–1939' (unpublished PhD thesis, University of Warwick, 1988) describes birth control literature on sale at Labour Party meetings in the early 1920s and the strong Catholic Church pressure against it. I am also grateful to Cornelie Usborne for allowing me to see her unpublished Open University BA dissertation, which is a notably subtle and well-researched study of this episode and which contains further evidence of support for birth control from mixed-sex local Labour parties and local authorities, and from other organizations which were neither feminist nor radical, such as the Church of England.
45. Leathard, *idem*, pp. 44–50.
46. Lewis, *op. cit.* note 42, p. 212.
47. Rowbotham, *op. cit.* note 1, p. 58.
48. Leathard, *op. cit.* note 42, pp. 44–8.
49. *Labour Woman*, March 1926.
50. See discussion in Smith, *op. cit.* note 1, pp. 33–5.
51. See debate at 1910 ACLW; *Labour Woman*, Feb. 1925, among others.
52. ACLW Report 1918.
53. *Labour Woman*, June 1924.
54. *Labour Woman*, January 1930. See also the debate on equal pay at the 1930 ACLW, Report, pp. 48–9.
55. In an article entitled 'The pet bogey of extreme feminism. Protective legislation for women workers', in *Labour Woman*, March 1929.
56. See debate on motherhood and child endowment, at ACLW, Report 1922; *Labour Woman*, June 1928, Feb. 1931, June 1933.
57. By Olive Banks, *op. cit.* note 39, p. 172.
58. *Labour Woman*, Dec. 1934.
59. *Labour Woman*, August 1920.
60. *Labour Woman*, October 1929.
61. In particular at the way that branch parties, in which women were strong, could be outvoted at the annual party conference, the body which decided party policy, by the massive block votes of the affiliated trade unions. See debates on the relationship between the women's sections and the party at ACLW 1927, 1928, 1929, 1930, 1931, 1935.

9 Domesticity and the Decline of Feminism, 1930–1950

Martin Pugh

'Modern women', confessed Ray Strachey in 1936, 'know amazingly little of what life was like before the war, and show a strong hostility to the word feminism, and all which they imagine it to connote.'[1] This seems a surprisingly pessimistic comment by one who was steeped in the work of a women's movement between the wars. Yet Strachey's sentiments were echoed by many other feminists in the two decades after 1930. By the 1950s it was hard to escape the conclusion that the movement had suffered an inexorable decline; and some historians have gone so far as to suggest that feminism had virtually ceased to exist as a result of the combined effects of the depression and the Second World War.[2] Without fully accepting such gloomy prognostications this chapter will consider in what sense British feminism had declined, and examine the reasons for its changing fortunes.

In 1930 the women's organizations in Britain were still largely under the command of activists who had served their apprenticeships in public life during the Edwardian, or even Victorian, period. Their work reached a climax in the immediate aftermath of the First World War. At that time the formal, political changes that had come about seemed to be highly advantageous to the cause of feminism. In the optimistic mood of the early 1920s it was easy to overlook the famed capacity of British political and social institutions for adapting and absorbing the challenges presented by radical movements without surrendering what was essential to their own power; feminism was by no means the first reforming cause to be somehow frustrated by the British system at the time of its greatest triumphs.

As Ray Strachey's remarks suggest, the feminists' fundamental problem lay in mobilizing the younger generation of women. Millicent Fawcett, the former president of the National Union of

Societies for Equal Citizenship (NUSEC), bemoaned the new women's pages in the popular newspapers during the 1920s for their 'inane observations on the length of skirts or the shape of sleeves'.[3] Her successor, Eleanor Rathbone, did have one characteristic in common with the 'modern girl': she smoked heavily and in public. But that apart, Rathbone brought a similarly severe, intellectual approach to the cause, evincing no interest in clothes and the other frivolities of life. Not surprisingly the feminists of her generation were often shocked by the habit among young women of using cosmetics freely in public places, and were, moreover, dismayed by the realization that this behaviour was due to a desire to gratify the opposite sex.[4] In this way a gulf of incomprehension and disappointment began to develop. The so-called 'flappers' of the 1920s appeared to the serious-minded to be determined to take advantage of the freer *social* life for women after the war, but to be largely uninterested in exploiting the political opportunities which their predecessors had fought so hard to win. Nor were the heirs to the militant tradition in the women's movement any more in tune than the more staid constitutionalists with the ordinary women of the inter-war period. Lady Rhondda, who was a leading figure in the new Six Point Group, sought to advance the cause by means of her new feminist journal, *Time and Tide*, which was launched in 1920. But her approach was sternly up-market: 'a first-class review is read by comparatively few people,' boasted Rhondda, 'but they are the people who count, the people of influence'.[5] This was a strikingly élitist strategy to adopt at a time when over eight million women had obtained the vote; an attempt to establish a popular feminist paper was not even to be made, and the anti-feminist forces were allowed an open field. When confronted with magazines actually read by ordinary women in the 1930s Lady Rhondda was, in the words of the editor of *Woman*, 'completely mystified'.[6]

Yet it was from the ranks of the younger women that feminists had to draw recruits if they were to survive, let along grow in influence, for between the wars the natural pattern of death and retirement steadily thinned the ranks of the movement's leaders. Particularly among the militant organizations leading figures such as Mrs Pankhurst and her daughters, Christabel and Sylvia, were soon lost to women's causes after the war, while others such as Emmeline Pethick-Lawrence maintained only nominal involvement. In contrast the constitutionalists sustained their campaign more effectively, at least in the 1920s. However, they too suffered somewhat from a diversion of talent and energy into the political parties, disarmament and the League of Nations Union, and even the women's institutes and townswomen's guilds. During the Victorian era this kind of activity by women had promoted their acceptance in the public sphere. But by the 1920s and 1930s it is less clear that it was any longer helping to advance their cause; for women's participation was often at the cost of subordinating their feminism.

Of course, the decline of feminism during the 1930s was in part simply a reflection of its success in the previous decade. Between the Sex Disqualification (Removal) Act in 1919 and the Equal Franchise Act in 1928 a whole series of women's measures was enacted. After that, however, momentum was difficult to maintain. Rathbone herself felt that issues like the right of a peeress to sit in the House of Lords or the right of a woman to enter the diplomatic and consular service could not provide the focus for a major campaign. Though the Women's Freedom League and the Six Point Group persisted with the 'equal rights' tradition, they remained small and peripheral; even *Time and Tide* had abandoned its feminist contents by 1930. On the other hand, the NUSEC followed Rathbone's lead by shifting the emphasis from equal rights to the 'new feminism'. In many ways this was a shrewd and perceptive approach which capitalized on politicians' belief in the necessity for social reform in the new, democratic era, and on their initial fears that women might establish a separate party if all their demands were rebuffed.

However, the flaw in Rathbone's strategy lay in the fact that it sought to advance feminism by using 'welfare feminism' as a Trojan horse. After a few general elections the politicians regained their confidence, and saw that while measures such as widows' pensions were popular, there was no great pressure to go beyond this to such feminist causes as equal pay, the bar on the employment of married women, birth control, the equal moral standard, or even family allowances. Consequently, by 1929 legislative progress for women had virtually ground to a halt in spite of the fact that women now comprised 52 per cent of the total electorate. Moreover, by the 1930s the optimistic spirit of reconstruction engendered in 1917–18 had largely evaporated. Prolonged depression and mass unemployment had steadily whittled away male tolerance of female aspirations, and had consolidated traditional assumptions about the importance of a 'family wage' for the male head of each household. Like the 1890s, then, the 1930s fostered a climate rather hostile for feminists, which was due, fundamentally, to the pervading sense of shrinking economic opportunities.[7]

Nonetheless, the NUSEC attempted to counter the danger of marginalization by extending its reach into the ranks of the majority of women who had never been involved in the struggle for the vote before 1914. Already many of its local societies had amalgamated with branches of the Women's Citizens Association, which had itself been formed with the object of educating women generally for their future political role. However, the affiliated societies of the NUWSS/NUSEC shrank from a peak of 478 in 1914 to 220 in 1920 and 90 by 1929.[8] Hence the fresh initiatives of December 1928 which were designed to divide the work of the organization into two.[9] First, there was to be a National Council for Equal Citizenship (NCEC) which would specialize in political work for feminist causes much as before; and, second, it was proposed to establish a National Union of Guilds for Citizenship which would educate women as citizens, foster social contact between them, and promote the skills and interests of women as housewives – or 'home-makers' in the contemporary phrase. This latter body, known from 1932 as the National Union of Townswomen's Guilds, was intended to extend the NUSEC's influence by blending its feminist tradition with the socialization function of the women's institutes (WIs). The WIs, which had originated towards the end of the war, were proving to be a great success, and the NUSEC saw an opportunity to exploit a gap for similar organizations in communities whose population exceeded 4000, which was the upper limit for a WI.[10] Perhaps because the WIs were led by a known feminist, Lady Denman, and had attracted the participation of figures like Margaret Wintringham, Britain's second woman MP, they seemed more susceptible to feminist influence than was really the case.

It certainly cannot be said that the townswomen's guilds achieved the objectives of their founders in the 1930s. On the one hand the old feminist organization continued to diminish, dropping to sixty-seven societies by 1932. A leading society in Glasgow was wound up in 1933, blaming the depression, the competition from other women's organizations and an underlying loss of purpose for its demise.[11] Also in that year the NUSEC's journal, *The Woman's Leader*, folded and was absorbed by the *Townswoman* – a highly symbolic development. The steep fall in income was at least checked during the 1930s, but the NCEC was left with less than £1000 revenue each year. It is scarcely surprising that it did not last much beyond the Second World War. However, the NUSEC tradition did survive in the London Society for Women's Service, which specialized in employment questions; it later gave rise to the Fawcett Society and the Women's Employment Federation, which continue to exist.

Meanwhile the townswomen's guilds flourished, though their growth was less rapid than that of the WIs. But they failed to channel a new body of recruits towards feminism, and it is very questionable whether they really reflected the thinking of their founders at all. Certainly the guilds were endowed with several leading figures from the NUSEC, notably Margery Corbett Ashby as chairman, Mary Stocks, Eva Hubback and Gertrude Horton.[12] Despite this the guilds grew away from their origins. Even in the first few years their local activity was overwhelmingly concentrated upon handicrafts, home-making and gardening; questions relating to the status of women scarcely figured at all in the programme.[13] At least one of the founders, Eva Hubback, recognized this as inevitable: 'the time is past when "equality" can be the rallying cry for a powerful organisation'.[14] Shorn of the impediment of feminism the new groups succeeded in establishing themselves widely among the female population. Membership of the guilds reached 54 000 in 1939 and approximately a quarter of a million after 1945; the WIs numbered 238 000 by 1937 and nearly half a million by the 1950s. Yet this progress seemed only to deepen the gulf between them and feminism. By the 1940s it had become the policy of the guilds to reject any form of association with feminist organizations such as the National Council of Women. During the 1950s an interesting debate took place within the guilds on the subject of juvenile delinquency. The prevailing view was that the problem had grown as a result of more mothers going out to work. Corbett Ashby found herself a rather lonely opponent of this way of thinking.[15]

Thus despite the size of the movement the townswomen's guilds must be seen in the long run less as an extension of the NUSEC tradition than as a departure from it. Not that the women recruited into the guilds and the WIs were devoid of political interests. But the *proper* questions with which they concerned themselves tended to be village water supplies, cheap electricity and rural education;[16] they would not go beyond such things as the provision of midwives and infant welfare clinics in the direction of feminism. Instead they remained rooted in the home, family and motherhood. The all-embracing domesticity which was the hallmark of their activities was not easy for feminists to come to terms with. If they tried too hard to lift women's aspirations beyond the purely domestic they could seem disparaging of the housewife; but to concentrate simply on the welfare of the housewife brought the danger of being swallowed up in the ideology of domesticity. This dilemma was all the more acute because the inter-war period saw a marked revival of anti-feminist forces in British politics and society which sought to capitalize upon domesticity as an alternative ideal to that which feminists wished to promote. Government attitudes after 1918 reflected this concern quite blatantly; for example, the perceived need to replace the manpower lost in the First World War pointed unambiguously to a return to marriage and motherhood.[17] As we shall see, the strategies adopted by the political parties for harnessing women's support conformed strongly to this thinking. What, however, is less often appreciated by historians is the more pervasive interests of a commercial kind which were also reaching out to the mass of women in their homes during this period.

Their influence can be seen most graphically in the vast and growing array of popular magazine literature sold to women.[18] Such material was not new in the inter-war period. For several decades popular commercial papers such as *Home Chat* and *My Weekly* had been published, relying on a simple formula of romantic fiction slightly leavened with articles on fashion, cookery and household tips. Their chief theme consisted in preparing for and anticipating the delights of marriage. With this winning formula the magazines made no attempt during the 1920s and 1930s to extend their readers' interests beyond the state of marriage, except perhaps to take more notice of actresses, titled ladies and members of the royal family. The 1920s had seen a considerable increase in the number of magazines catering to married and soon-to-be-married women: *Modern Woman, Woman and Home, Modern Home, Wife and Home* to take some typical examples. Whether aimed at middle-class or working-class women the whole range of popular papers showed striking similarities in terms of content and character. The only changes, apart from the growth in number, took the form of a development of two aspects of the existing publications.

The first of these reached its fullest form in *Good Housekeeping*, which was published in Britain from 1922. 'We are on the threshold of a general feminine awakening', announced the enthusiastic editors.[19] Yet the awakening to which they referred involved no new role for women so much as an improved competence in performing their existing one. Through *Good Housekeeping* middle- and lower-middle-class women could in effect follow a correspondence course in home-making, learning how to manage their resources, raise the quality of their cooking and needlework, and take full advantage of the new products, especially mechanical household aids, which were tested in the Good Housekeeping Institute. In short, it aspired to elevate household management to the status of a profession. This was, perhaps, flattering, but also very practical at a time when many of its readers had lost the domestic servants on whom their mothers had depended for the successful running of the household. Yet although it claimed to be taking the drudgery out of women's lives, *Good Housekeeping* tended rather to add to the burdens of the housewife by raising her standards and filling up the time she might have devoted to interests outside the home. This did not altogether preclude wider horizons. The early years of the magazine brought contributions by feminists and articles by and about women who had become successful in spheres beyond home and motherhood. But this was never a major element in *Good Housekeeping*, and it diminished during the 1930s. By the 1950s few articles of wider interest were published and the magazine had moved closer to the lowbrow journals. Nonetheless its reach was formidable: by 1950 half the women in households whose income fell within the £400–1000 range read *Good Housekeeping* regularly or occasionally.[20]

The second development which occurred in the 1930s was the emergence of a new wave of magazines, notably *Woman's Own* (1932), *Woman's Illustrated* (1936) and *Woman* (1937). Though in the tradition of *Home Chat*, these publications were better produced, boasted superior colour illustrations and eventually achieved sales in the millions rather than merely hundreds of thousands. However, they should not be thought of merely as bland and glossy compilations of fiction, recipes and dress patterns; for in this period at least, they sometimes carried the ideology of domesticity more blatantly and energetically than the older publications. Perhaps the best example of a magazine which actively campaigned for domesticity was *Woman's Own*, which from the outset devoted itself to the belief that marriage was the best job for a woman. Indeed it argued that paid employment was acceptable for girls only in the period before marriage and preferably as a *route* to marriage, to which end it helpfully drew attention to the jobs most likely to lead a woman to meet a satisfactory husband.[21] In addition, the staple elements in the magazine – such as articles on cosmetics and fashion – were made to serve a similar function in that they were remorselessly directed towards the chief purpose of a woman's life, namely acquiring and keeping a husband. Thus, for example, in the early years of *Woman's Own* the beauty page regularly appeared under the title 'Looks Do Count After Marriage'.[22] It also endeavoured to make the readers feel guilty for ignoring the advice given. A typical sermon by a female writer in 1935 cautioned wives against allowing their innocent husbands to be ensnared by the attractions of typists or shop assistants: 'stop to think how often these lapses are due to the fact that their wives refuse to dress up for them'.[23]

The only obvious point of contact between such publications and the world of feminism concerned issues pertaining to marriage, such as the changes in the law on divorce. Here the popular magazines repeatedly urged upon their readers that it would be folly for women to take advantage of easier divorce to rid themselves of unfaithful husbands, the ultimate justification for this view being simply that 'a bad husband is better than no husband'.[24] Not all the magazines adopted so blatantly an anti-feminist line as this; and even *Woman's Own* lost some of its crusading quality by the 1940s. But all reflected the same character and underlying assumptions about the ideal of domesticity and dependence for the female sex. It is of course possible to argue that women bought these magazines for the fiction or the recipes without in any way subscribing to the message they contained. However, there is, as we shall see, some evidence that readers actively approved of the attitude espoused by the magazines and reacted against any departure from it. In any case the sheer quantity of sales strongly suggests that the proprietors had tapped a *growing* demand for the cult of domesticity. Even journals which had formerly tried to promote women's employment, for example, seem to have allowed this to dwindle in response to their readers' interests in the inter-war period.[25] The most successful of the new publications was *Woman*, which from its foundation in 1937 won sales of 750 000 copies by 1939, and reached 3.5 million by the late 1950s.

Nonetheless, this literature was prescriptive, and it cannot be assumed that women necessarily followed the advice given. For example, in spite of the propaganda rather more people did seek divorces in this period, although this should be seen in its context: a higher proportion were getting married in the first place. The pattern of employment is particularly interesting. By the 1930s many of the *new* jobs being created in the economy were offered to women. In addition male unemployment inevitably drove some women out to work from sheer necessity regardless of the blow to male pride. But, since an unemployed man could secure eight shillings a week in benefit for a dependent wife in 1931, she would have to be sure of earning over this amount before taking work outside the home. By the early 1930s rather more young women were taking paid employment than in the early 1920s. But in the age groups above thirty-four the pattern was reversed, with fewer women going out to work.[26] This behaviour is compatible with the view propagated by the women's magazines. More strikingly, the evidence of oral history now suggests that the *attitudes* of the women towards work strongly reflected those expressed in the popular papers.[27] Though often obliged to work when young, the working-class women of this period seem to have been keen to abandon their jobs, and had little or no ambition to achieve permanent or full-time employment. For the majority of them progress and emancipation consisted precisely in being able to return to the home when children came, or when their husband's income improved, and in remaining there for the rest of their lives.

Moreover, the 1930s were a decade in which the realization of the domestic ideal became more attainable for many women. For the majority, whose husbands were in employment, the fall in prices made for a rise in the standard of living. The expansion in house-building and the production of consumer goods such as vacuum cleaners, which were sold almost entirely in the home market, helped to make tangible the alluring vision presented by the magazines: an improved domestic and family life was within reach. Such trends help to make explicable the especial difficulties facing feminist organizations in appealing to working-class women in this period. However, this is somewhat less true in regard to middle-class women. After the war it was more widely accepted that a middle-class girl should establish a career of her own, partly because of the presumed difficulties of finding a husband, and because of the greater difficulties many fathers experienced in providing for their daughters financially. With the trend towards marriage at a younger age, even middle-class wives frequently worked for a few years at least while their husbands were still struggling on low salaries in the professions. But in due course, they, too, expected to be able to concentrate solely on the home.[28] Consequently, the natural recruiting ground for feminist organizations remained, as it had been in the Victorian era, the middle classes. To grow much beyond that meant meeting the anti-feminism on the left; but, as before 1914, there was a tendency to see feminists in terms of their class and thus to regard them as somehow enemies, or at least obstacles, to the progress of the Labour movement, even though they held progressive views on such matters as social welfare.

Thus, with only minor qualifications, it does seem that the popular women's press achieved its success in the 1930s by simply pulling with the tide which ran strongly for domesticity and marriage. Rare attempts even by the popular *Woman* to venture beyond the staple fare into articles on social problems were rewarded only by a prompt drop in sales.[29] Moreover, the magazine felt obliged to be especially careful to distance itself from such subjects as birth control, if only for fear of antagonizing Catholic readers. The part of *Woman* which, to the editor Mary Grieve, represented 'our main source of danger' was the Evelyn Home problem page, where such topics would give offence if allowed to appear.[30] At a time when many couples evidently were limiting family size this cautious attitude is surely revealing. At the best, the magazines ran safely behind the pace of change, avoiding radical ideas until sure that they were no longer contro-

versial; at the worst, as in the early *Woman's Own*, they campaigned actively against change in women's lives. Thus their overall contribution was to blunt the cutting edge of feminism both
by setting up a positive, alternative goal in the form of a skilful and
rewarding domesticity, and also by drawing a gloomy caricature of
the career woman, grimly fending for herself and sadly isolated
from male society.[31]

This informal role of the women's magazines complemented
the more formal bias towards domesticity exerted by the political
parties between the wars. Interestingly enough, both the left and
the right looked enviously at the long reach of *Woman* and showed
a desire to woo the paper and its readers.[32] *Woman*, however,
avoided the embrace of either, even to the extent of refusing to
accept advertising from both the *Daily Mail* and the *Daily Herald*:
no doubt for the proprietors the commercial motive of maximizing
the market remained uppermost. Yet the important point is that
both left and right thought it desirable to capitalize on the magazines' approach to women, for it was perfectly consistent with
their own concept of the female sex in the political sphere.

It might well be thought that one reason for the formal decline
of feminist organizations was simply a movement among women
activists into the political parties after 1918, and thus into a more
not a less influential position. Clearly a few women did pursue
political careers, though a number of the early women MPs,
especially the Conservatives, had no history of involvement in the
pre-war suffrage campaign. Nor were the numbers of politically
ambitious women apparently *growing* by the 1930s. Between sixty
and seventy women stood in the general elections of 1929, 1931
and 1935, and fourteen, fifteen and nine were elected respectively
at those elections. Naturally the parties made strenuous efforts to
mobilize their female support after 1918. In the late 1920s both the
Labour Party Women's Organization and the Women's Unionist
Organization reached a peak, the former with around a quarter
of a million members and the latter with one million.[33] Then,
during the early 1930s both lost membership a little, and the
situation then stabilized as the novelty and excitement of the first
decade wore off.

What did this signify for the cause of feminism? The Six Point
Group persistently argued that since no political party was yet
prepared to treat women fairly and equally, women should abstain

from joining any of them.[34] The NUSEC felt obliged to be more flexible in its attitude, since it contained Liberal, Labour and Conservative women, and in any case valued its contacts with the parliamentary world. But it, too, was noticeably drawn to the idea of women as a cross-bench force in politics; and to this end many of the local societies encouraged women to seek election to municipal authorities independently of political parties.[35] At the parliamentary level the only success occurred in the university constituencies, where Eleanor Rathbone was elected as an independent in 1929.

The difficulty for the feminist strategy lay in the fact that they had not been able to start with a blank sheet in 1918. Since the 1880s women had been steadily integrated into the political system through local government and party activity in the Primrose League, the Tariff Reform League, the Women's Liberal Federation, the Independent Labour Party (ILP) and the Women's Labour League. The effect of their work had been to complement the official party's effort at and between elections rather than to pose any challenge to male control or to male political priorities.[36] To some extent it seemed unnecessary to rock the boat because politics was steadily moving in the women's direction. Having established their own expertise in the essentially domestic concerns of local government, women found, after the turn of the century, that these same areas were increasingly absorbed into the realms of national government. Standards of living and social welfare in general, and fears about the birth rate and the quality of the British population in particular, began to occupy politicians in all parties; and if children were frankly recognized as assets to the state, could their mothers be far behind?[37] The steady advance of women into politics under cover of motherhood and domesticity culminated in the politicians' willingness in 1918 to confer the vote, not upon the young war workers, but upon the women over thirty years of age – who were presumed to be largely wives and mothers. Thus, up to a point, the cult of domesticity had already assisted women in penetrating the political system; but it was not easy, or even natural, to escape from the domestic ideology subsequently, even when women had the electoral power to do so.

The conventional thinking continued to be a main element in the enactment of the women's legislation of the 1920s. Though the NUSEC naturally saw the reforms as another success for feminism, this scarcely squares with the motivation of the politicians at this time. It is significant that *both* Conservative and Labour Parties backed the reforms, indeed they almost entered into a competition to prove their sincerity. In the event the measures were passed by Conservatives, who enjoyed the advantage of being in office for most of the decade. Yet one would be dubious, on this account, of using a concept such as 'Tory Feminism' as an explanation. A similar caution is in order before resorting to 'Labour Feminism'. Any credible explanation must take account of the politicians' fears about losing the new voters in the early 1920s when they were still an unknown quantity; but it must also recognize the perspective which each party brought to reforms such as the Widows' Pensions Act of 1925. Conservatives, male and female alike, could justify such a measure on the grounds that it strengthened the *family* and thereby helped ensure the stability of society and the state.[38] In this way women's legislation could be regarded as complementing, not undermining, Conservative ideology. For its part, Labour saw widows' pensions as an important aspect of its overall policy for raising the standard of living of the working class by means of state social reform. Thus, without in any way modifying or departing from their different perspectives and ideologies the parties converged upon an essentially bipartisan policy for women. *Neither* felt obliged to subscribe to a feminist rationale, or to depart from their view of women as wives, mothers and household managers.

This is corroborated by the common hostility of Conservative and Labour to further demands by feminists over such matters as equal pay, the employment of married women, birth control and family allowances. Of course, this is not to deny that all parties contained some feminists within their ranks. On the Tory side Lady Astor naturally occupied the role of feminist gadfly, and was succeeded during the 1930s and 1940s by other MPs, notably Mavis Tate, Irene Ward and Thelma Cazalet-Keir. But the conferences of Conservative women rejected proposals for family allowances and birth control, the debate being couched in terms of what was, or was not, in the best interests of the state at the time.[39]

On the Labour side the inter-war period saw an intermittent struggle between the orthodox party loyalists like Marion Phillips,

Margaret Bondfield and Susan Lawrence, who put party and class before sex, and the proponents of feminism such as Dora Russell and Dorothy Jewson who usually emerged from an ILP background.[40] The official view, as expressed by the party's Chief Woman Officer, Marion Phillips, was that Labour women should not dissipate their energies by involving themselves in any non-party women's organizations, including even the women's institutes.[41] The Labour movement proved particularly hostile to feminists over the question of 'protective legislation', and was divided internally by such issues as the employment of married women, equal pay and birth control.[42]

The question which most clearly demonstrates the non-feminist character of Labour's approach to women was family allowances. In Eleanor Rathbone's original conception family allowances were regarded as a step towards paying a wage to women for their work for their families; she argued that the system of industrial bargaining would never produce a high enough income for large families. Naturally her brisk dismissal of the cherished trade union concept of the 'family wage' proved difficult for the Labour movement to swallow. Even a woman like Bessie Braddock adopted the union line that family allowances were undesirable because they would encourage employers to reduce the men's wages.[43] However, a majority of Labour women voted at their own conference in favour of the reform; but for many years they failed to persuade the party itself to do so. When the wartime coalition government eventually decided to introduce family allowances it excluded families with only one child from the scheme. However, it was important to *feminist* supporters of the measure both that the allowances should be paid to mothers, not to fathers, and that a woman with a small family was as much entitled to her wage as any other. Yet Labour women rejected the proposal to extend allowances to one-child families, arguing that they were less likely to be in need of assistance.[44] There could be no clearer indication of the distinction between the welfare socialism that by the 1950s had come to dominate their thinking and the feminist approach.

This outlook did not, of course, constitute a weakness in Labour's approach to women, rather the reverse. Both parties seemed determined to mine the rich vein of domesticity in the women's electorate, and each benefited according to political circumstances. During the 1930s Labour developed its policy for women in terms of improvements in social welfare, standards of house-building and design, children's health, food supply and price controls. By 1939 these were the topics that absorbed the women's organization, while the feminist issues formerly put forward by the ILP had dropped away. It was when war broke out that Labour's strategy began to pay dividends. Mass evacuation and civilian bombing rapidly concentrated attention on mothers and children, so that the long-term pressure for the provision of cheap milk now began to seem patriotic common sense: 'there is no finer investment for any community than putting milk into babies', declared Churchill.[45] Food rationing was a good example of an innovation which combined women's interests with socialist planning of the nation's resources. By 1942 even the TUC had joined William Beveridge in endorsing family allowances. Yet as in the 1920s women's reform depended on an ill-assorted alliance of feminist and anti-feminist support. What, for example, coloured Beveridge's thinking on family allowances was his concern over the birth rate, which had been declining for several decades and reached its low point in 1941, hence the appointment of a Royal Commission on Population in 1944. It appeared that women required encouragement from the state to remain at home and rear children. Family allowances seemed to Beveridge a simple and efficacious means of promoting that objective. The subsequent welfare measures enacted after 1945 were conceived in this spirit, that is, they were designed to support woman in her capacity as wife and mother.

However, both wartime and post-1945 conditions placed British governments on the horns of a dilemma in this respect; for against the domestic ideal they were forced to weigh the acute need to bring more women into the labour force. They gave way, reluctantly and belatedly, to this pressure but, as in the First World War, the wider employment of women during 1939–45 does not appear to have emancipated them in any lasting or fundamental way.[46] Even when mobilization was at its height in 1943 the majority of women remained as housewives. For those who took up paid employment the experience was not by any means new, which helps to explain why many were reluctant to volunteer for war work. They resented the imposition of industrial conscription by Ernest Bevin, and according to the survey conducted by Mass Observation, some three-quarters of the women workers wanted to give up their jobs as soon as the war was over.[47] This is explicable in terms of the positive preference for life at home, and also the negative reaction against work. As in the First World War women encountered hostility from both employers and trade unions; and, as in the past, government connived in the various expedients adopted in industry to deny them equal pay.[48] Thus, as far as their attitudes and aspirations are concerned it would seem that women continued to regard domesticity as the ideal. This is corroborated by their behaviour. The proportion of the population which was married had been rising during the 1930s and reached a record level in 1939–40; it dipped slightly after this peak, but rose sharply again by 1945 and was sustained during the postwar decade, thereby giving rise to the so-called 'baby boom'. In this way the Second World War, like the First, appears to have helped to consolidate rather than to undermine the conventional role of women. There is, consequently, a strong sense of continuity between the pre- and postwar situation; the popular purveyors of the domestic cult flourished as never before, the political parties intensified their existing strategies for women, and organized feminism continued its apparently inexorable decline.

One qualification ought, however, to be made here. Under the stimulus of the war the embers of the feminist organizations flickered into life again. The women MPs began to act as a cross-bench pressure group in a way that they had rarely done in peacetime. By June 1940 a bipartisan Woman Power Committee had been established in order to chivvy the government over its manifest reluctance to mobilize women for the war effort. The MPs also took up a flagrant case of discrimination by the government: its decision to pay compensation to men for their war injuries at a higher rate than women; by 1943 they had succeeded in forcing the authorities to back down.[49] Outside Parliament the Six Point Group under Dorothy Evans began to argue that if women were to be conscripted like men then the principle of equal treatment should be extended to all areas of life; they proposed a comprehensive measure known as the Equal Citizenship (Blanket) Bill to achieve this. But the campaign launched in support of the bill in 1943 was not backed by the trade unions because of the implications for protective legislation; many feminists thought it too ambitious and impractical a proposal, and no political party would take it up. This drew attention back again to the heart of the problem, and generated fresh attempts by Theresa Billington-Greig and the 'Women At Westminster' group to persuade each party to adopt more women candidates in time for the next election. The idea was to encourage the women within each constituency party to nominate a woman themselves, so as to avoid the impression of outside interference by feminists. Even this, however, was apt to backfire. When the Labour Women's Conference debated a motion urging the adoption of more women in 1942, delegates 'deplored the fact that they had any resolution on the agenda which had any suggestion of feminism or asked for special treatment for women'.[50] Whereas similar proposals in the 1920s had met with a sympathetic response, now the resolution was defeated by women themselves.

Above all, the wartime discussion of womanpower and conscription put fresh life into the issue of equal pay. Under the chairmanship of the Conservative MP, Mavis Tate, a new campaign committee was set up. Unfortunately, though it was widely supported by women's organizations, the Labour movement, represented by the Standing Joint Committee of Working Women's Organizations, refused to participate, exposing once again the crippling gap between the working class and middle-class feminism.[51] As a result the initiative, at least initially, was seized by W. J. Brown and several Tory members, notably Tate and Sir Douglas Hacking, and their campaign concentrated upon the civil service pay structure. This had the advantage of providing an unambiguous example of identical work by men and women; it was also subject to the direct control of the government, unlike industrial employment. However, the campaign's only real success came, fortuitously, in 1944 when Cazalet-Keir put down an amendment to give equal pay to teachers under R. A. Butler's Education Bill. To the surprise and consternation of the House her amendment was approved by 117 votes to 116. Churchill immediately moved to kill the idea by means of a vote of confidence in his government. No less extraordinary was the support given to him by Labour ministers; Bevin and Chuter Ede, for example, announced they would resign if Butler's bill were not restored to its original condition.[52] The amendment was duly quashed, the government offered to appoint a Royal Commission on equal pay, which did not report until October 1946, and meanwhile the parliamentary campaign was suspended.

However, the general election of 1945 proved advantageous for women in spite of the parties' attitudes. Although the number of women candidates increased only marginally, from sixty-seven in 1935 to eighty-seven, those elected rose from nine to twenty-four. This was because the landslide for Labour swept in a number of women in constituencies which the party would not have expected to win. Thus, after 1945 the Tory advocates of equal pay were reinforced by several Labour MPs: Elaine Burton, Eirene White and Leah Manning. The campaign sprouted local branches, argued its case at by-elections, and subjected political speakers of all parties to cross-questioning.[53] In 1947 White secured a four-to-one vote in favour of equal pay at the Labour Party Conference. All this, however, made little impression upon the Attlee government.

The new cabinet was badly torn between a desire to boost the birth rate and an urgent need to increase industrial production and exports. As a result it pursued contradictory policies towards women. On the one hand it embarked upon a great propaganda campaign designed to encourage women to seek employment.[54] On the other hand it closed down the wartime nurseries and withdrew funding for local authority nurseries; nor was there any pretence that the women workers were replacing men – they constituted cheap labour on a strictly temporary basis. Successive Chancellors of the Exchequer resorted to the economic crisis to justify their refusal to implement equal pay even in the civil service, arguing that wage stability and a reduction in inflation were essential. This firm line clearly inhibited Labour supporters of equal pay, and the party's Chief Woman Officer, Mary Sutherland, did her best to quash the issue by claiming that no popular demand for it existed. Consequently, at the 1950 general election the Equal Pay Campaign Committee obtained much more support from Conservative than from Labour candidates.[55] However, the closeness of the 1950 result probably caused an upsurge in backing from Labour candidates in 1951, though after that election only 122 MPs were pledged to unqualified support for equal pay; the majority claimed to support it in principle but refused to act until permitted by the party whips.[56] It was not until 1954 that the Conservative Chancellor, Butler, agreed to implement equal pay for civil servants. This may have been partly an attempt to outflank the Labour Party in the run-up to the 1955 general election.

But it also reflected the belief that the concession over civil servants would not have to be extended, except perhaps to teachers.

In a sense this was correct, for the women's success over equal pay in 1954 stands out as a rather isolated example. The Equal Pay Campaign Committee simply dissolved itself, perhaps recognizing that it had won by concentrating on a very limited case, and that there was as yet no momentum for the general application of equal pay in industry. It had been a triumph won against the tide, for the 1950s saw the reassertion of domesticity as never before. Amid the trend towards marriage and the baby boom the women's magazines threw themselves back into the task of discouraging women from seeking careers.[57] According to Mary Grieve the underlying reason for the new peak in sales achieved during the 1950s was the dramatic growth of material opportunities for women in this decade.[58] Although these opportunities led rather more married women to take up employment, this only reflected the traditional behaviour pattern. Whereas the Edwardian woman had gone out to work in order to keep her family from starving, her 1950s counterpart sought to enable the family to enjoy its share of consumer goods, suburban homes, motor cars and foreign holidays. Work remained a temporary expedient not a vocation, and as in the 1930s the politicians chose to work with this trend not to resist it. During the late 1940s the Conservatives rebuilt their women's strategy by means of a relentless campaign against food shortages, controls and rationing, promising wider choice, easier hire purchase and the greater provision of privately built housing. As before this was justified in terms of 'strengthening family life'.[59] Battered by the propaganda of the Housewives' League, Labour found it difficult to counter this; having devoted itself to the cause of the housewife-in-politics the party was loath to change its approach to women even when the consumer boom seemed to present its opponents with all the best cards.[60]

But for the scattered remnants of feminism, women such as Margery Corbett Ashby, Dora Russell and Rebecca West, the apathy and indifference of the women of the 1950s represented an even more dismaying prospect. From their perspective the problem was not just the prosperity of the many, but also the complacency of the politically aware minority from whom support might have been expected. In the words of Marghanita Laski: 'I was born too late for the battle. Older and nobler women struggled that I should be free, and did their work so well that I've never even bothered about being bound. Rights for women, so far as my generation is concerned, is a dead issue.'[61]

When these words were written, in 1952, the women's movement had passed through two cycles. The first had seen the rise of the 1860s and the decline of the 1890s; the second spanned the upsurge associated with the Edwardian period and the prolonged retreat from the 1930s to the 1950s. Yet by the end of that decade another generation was already on the brink of a third cycle which was not only to revive something of the old equal rights tradition but to produce new expressions of feminist thinking.

Notes

1. Ray Strachey (ed), *Our Freedom and Its Results* (Hogarth Press, London, 1936), p. 10.
2. Olive Banks, *Faces of Feminism* (Blackwell, Oxford, 1981), p. 203.
3. Quoted in Brian Harrison, *Prudent Revolutionaries* (Clarendon, Oxford, 1988), p. 21.
4. See Mary Agnes Hamilton, in Strachey, *op. cit.* note 1, p. 271.
5. *Good Housekeeping*, March 1957, p. 162.
6. Mary Grieve, *Millions Made My Story* (Gollancz, London, 1964), p. 143.
7. See the discussion in Brian Harrison, 'Women's suffrage at Westminster, 1866–1928', in M. Bentley and J. Stevenson (eds), *High and Low Politics in Modern Britain* (Clarendon, Oxford, 1983).
8. See Harrison on their dwindling annual income, *idem*, p. 88.
9. Annual Council Report, 'Proposed lines of expansion for the NUSEC', 1928.
10. Mary Scott, *Organisation Woman: the Story of the National Union of Towns-women's Guilds* (Heinemann, London, 1978), p. 10.
11. Minutes, Glasgow Society for Women's Suffrage, 16 and 30 January 1933.
12. See the discussion on the careers of Corbett Ashby and Hubback in Harrison, *op. cit.* note 3.
13. Stott, *op. cit.* note 10, p. 24.
14. *Idem*, p. 18.
15. *Idem*, pp. 169–70.
16. See Gervas Huxley, *Lady Denman* (Chatto and Windus, London, 1961), p. 88.
17. Martin Pugh, *Electoral Reform in War and Peace 1906–18* (Routledge and Kegan Paul, London, 1978), p. 144; Anna Davin, 'Imperialism and mother-hood', *History Workshop Journal*, vol. 5 (1978), p. 43.
18. See Cynthia L. White, *Women's Magazines 1693–1968* (Joseph, London, 1970).
19. *Good Housekeeping*, March 1922, p. 1.
20. Mass Observation Survey, in *Good Housekeeping*, January 1950, pp. 10–11.
21. *Woman's Own*, 4 March 1933, pp. 704–5.
22. *Woman's Own*, 15 and 22 October 1932 for typical examples.
23. *Woman's Own*, 5 January 1935, p. 449.
24. *Woman's Own*, 6 January 1934, p. 381.
25. White, *op. cit.* note 18, p. 100.

26. Ray Strachey, *Careers and Openings for Women* (Faber and Faber, London, 1935), pp. 17–19.

27. Elizabeth Roberts, *A Woman's Place: An Oral History of Working-Class Women 1880–1940* (Blackwell, Oxford, 1984), p. 137.

28. Strachey, *op. cit.* note 26, p. 19.

29. White, *op. cit.* note 18, p. 112.

30. Grieve, *op. cit.* note 6, pp. 87–9.

31. *Woman's Own*, 6 January 1934, p. 381.

32. Grieve, *op.cit.* note 6, p. 53.

33. Figures drawn from reports of the annual conferences of the two organizations.

34. *Time and Tide*, 18 May 1923.

35. For a good example see Minutes, Cambridge Women's Citizens Association, 20 Sept. 1922, 23 May and 24 Oct. 1923.

36. Martin Pugh, *The Tories and the People 1880–1935* (Blackwell, Oxford, 1985), pp. 57–69.

37. Davin, *op. cit.* note 17.

38. Conservative Party Campaign Guides, 1922, p. 981; 1950, pp. 663–4; and the discussion in Martin Pugh, 'Popular Conservatism: continuity and change 1880–1987', *Journal of British Studies*, vol. 27, no. 3 (1988), pp. 264–8.

39. Reports, Women's Unionist Organization Conference 1926, pp. 33–7; 1931, pp. 45–50.

40. See Harold Smith, 'Sex vs. class: British feminists and the Labour movement 1919–29', *The Historian*, vol. 47 (Nov. 1984).

41. Conference Report, Labour Women's Organization 1920, pp. 77–8.

42. *Idem*, 1932, pp. 48–9, 59–60; 1926, p. 123; 1928, p. 27.

43. *Idem*, 1930, pp. 53–4.

44. *Idem*, 1954, p. 24.

45. Conservative Party, *Notes for Speakers and Workers* (1945), p. 150.

46. Harold Smith, 'The effect of the war on the status of women', in Harold Smith (ed), *War and Social Change* (Manchester University Press, 1986), pp. 211–14; Penny Summerfield, *Women Workers in the Second World War* (Croom Helm, London, 1984).

47. Mass Observation, File Report 2059, 8 March 1944.

48. See Harold Smith, 'The problem of "equal pay for equal work" in Great Britain during World War II', *Journal of Modern History*, vol. 53 (December 1981).

49. Papers of Megan Lloyd George, 20490E (National Library of Wales).

50. Conference Report, Labour Women's Organization 1942, pp. 44–5.

51. Equal Pay Campaign Committee, Minutes, 26 January 1944.

52. Anthony Howard, *RAB: The Life of R. A. Butler* (Cape, London, 1987), pp. 136–7.

53. EPCC, Minutes, 25 November 1947.

54. William Crofts, 'The Attlee government's pursuit of women', *History Today*, August 1986.

55. EPCC, Box 157, folder T.

56. EPCC, Box 259, folder B9/3.

57. White, *op. cit.* note 18, pp. 150–1.

58. Grieve, *op. cit.* note 6, pp. 196–7.

59. Conservative Party, *Campaign Guide* (1950), pp. 663–4.

60. Jean Mann, *Woman In Politics* (Odhams, London, 1962), pp. 172–3.

61. Vera Brittain, *Lady Into Woman* (Andrew Dakers, London, 1953), p. 77.

PART III

FEMINISM FROM THE SECOND WORLD WAR TO THE PRESENT

10 Myrdal, Klein, *Women's Two Roles* and Postwar Feminism 1945–1960

Jane Lewis

Late nineteenth- and early twentieth-century feminism was concerned above all to assert women's right to enter the public sphere. A majority of Victorian feminists were Liberals and for the most part accepted the idea that, if women chose to exert their right to enter the world of citizenship and paid work, they must compete on the same terms as men: their claim was to a fair field and no favour. In practice, of course, women were presented with a choice between either marriage and motherhood, or a career. Mainstream inter-war feminism made the private sphere and the needs of mothers (for family allowances and birth control) its first concern, but did not challenge either the idea that adult women had to choose between a family life and a career, or the way in which the work of the private sphere was organized. Myrdal and Klein's famous book, *Women's Two Roles*,[1] was the first to suggest, with extreme caution, that there might be a case for women 'having it all', albeit sequentially, becoming first workers, then wives and mothers, and finally re-entering the labour market to become workers again.

The idea that women should not necessarily have to choose between paid work on the one hand and unpaid work and motherhood on the other was potentially radical, especially in the context of the 1950s, when Parsons was developing his ideas about the functional superiority of the male breadwinner family model, in which husbands and wives 'specialized' in terms of roles, husbands becoming economic providers and wives carers and domestic labourers.[2] Despite the influence of Parsons's formulation within mainstream sociology, Myrdal's and Klein's views found more reflection in reality. The 1951 figures on adult women's employment in the United Kingdom showed the first hint of what Hakim has called the two-phase, or bimodal, pattern of female employment.[3] After a sharp drop in the economic activity rate in the twenty-four to thirty-four age group, there was a very slight increase for married women aged thirty-five to forty-four. By 1961 the bimodal patterns had emerged clearly and by 1971 older wives were more likely to be working than younger ones. It cannot be argued that Myrdal's and Klein's work played a part in causing the postwar revolution in married women's employment – *Women's Two Roles* was not published until 1956 – but their analysis helped to legitimize the change. In the early 1970s the book was still selling a steady 1500 copies a year. However, in later feminist analysis, Myrdal and Klein have received a bad press because of the limited nature of their claims on behalf of married women; their tendency to problematize women rather than men; and because their solutions required more in the way of adjustment by women than changes in either male behaviour or structures. Myrdal and Klein may have anticipated the second wave feminist analysis of the relationship between paid and unpaid work, but there remained a world of difference between their optimistic belief that women could and should combine 'home and work', and the later feminist belief that the burden of the 'double day' underpinned the subordinate position of women in society.

Myrdal and Klein (especially Myrdal) tended to subordinate the needs of women to those of nation in a manner not dissimilar from 1940s policymakers who talked about the need to meet the needs of motherhood, for the sake of the future of the race, rather than those of individual mothers. In particular, Myrdal's and Klein's approach may have been dictated by strategic consider-ations: *Women's Two Roles* was written when the memories of inter-war marriage bars in the professions were fresh in order to promote the idea that educated women need not give up work for ever on marriage. The way in which the argument of the book was constructed must also be assessed in the context of postwar concern to rebuild traditional family life. Nevertheless, the book reflected ideas that Myrdal and Klein had been developing before the 1950s about the historical relationship between work and the family and about what constituted equality for women. Myrdal and Klein were not alone among postwar feminists in wanting to eschew all notion of equality based on 'sameness', while also having reservations about making claims on the basis of 'difference'. But by opting for rational arguments about the contribution women might make to economic progress rather than for an argument that asserted women's claims on the basis of an analysis of their position in society, Myrdal and Klein also failed to make their plea for family *and* work into a call for the radical restructuring of both, settling rather for a limited extension of women's participation in paid employment on what remained essentially men's terms.

Myrdal and Klein

Early ideas: defining the postwar 'woman problem'
By 1950 Alva Myrdal was a well-established international expert on family and population policy. As she explained in her foreword to *Women's Two Roles*, it had been her involvement with the UN and UNESCO after the war that had stopped her finishing the book she had begun alone in 1946. In large measure Myrdal's reputation was built on her book *Nation and Family; The Swedish Experiment in Democratic Family and Population Policy*, published in 1941.[4] Against a backdrop of international concern about falling birth rates, predictions from demographers as to dwindling populations and warnings from social scientists as to their adverse implications for social progress; and finally, in 1935 in Sweden and in 1945 in Britain, the appointment of Royal Commissions to investigate the issue,[5] Myrdal succeeded in capturing the policy initiative. She both granted the importance of the problem and insisted that parenthood must be voluntary. She interpreted the population crisis as a crisis in the family as an institution: stripped of their education, protective and recreational functions in the modern world, families were no longer undertaking their reproductive tasks either. The design of a population policy, therefore, encompassed all social policy, with its aim being nothing less than the reintegration of the family into the larger society. Parents had to be enabled, rather than cajoled or forced, into having more children.

Myrdal's preoccupations were with the needs of state and nation and her approach was that of the social engineer. 'Democratic family policy' meant only that policymakers should respect public opinion, but public opinion was susceptible to manipulation and

Myrdal speculated freely as to the extent to which compulsory sterilization could be achieved by engineering democratic consensus when support for such a policy was narrowly based.

From this social planning perspective, the position of women in the family naturally assumed the dimensions of a social problem. Myrdal's chapter on women (entitled 'One Sex a Social Problem') put forward the idea that women were as yet improperly adjusted to the workings of modern industrial society and must be helped to 'catch up':

> The feminine sex is a social problem whether a woman is young or old, whether she is married or not, whether a wife works or not, she is likely to be a problem. This problem is largely economic in origin as marriage and family are as yet poorly adjusted to the new economic order. This is of vital importance to the individual and society as the family is the essential social relationship.[6]

Myrdal's conclusions – that more child care should be collectivized and that women should be encouraged to engage in paid employment with changes in the organization of the workplace and greater training opportunities – have remained goals for later feminists. But her method of arriving at them involved negating any claim based on individual rights and asserting instead that the needs of the state were inseparable from those of individual women: 'A population policy of democratic vision thus creates a new stronghold for married women's fight for their right to work. At the same time the frontier among feminist groups should be shifted in order to denote this new interlocking of individual and social interests.'[7] Myrdal's chosen mechanisms were designed to be genuinely enabling, but her faith in the benevolent state and rational planning, very much at one with the plans for the British welfare state based on the twin pillars of Beveridge and Keynes, could just as easily serve to perpetuate aspects of women's subordination within the family as undermine them, and just as easily permit the exercise of social control as promote individual freedom.

Myrdal promoted a particular vision of women's role in the family and in the wider society which she maintained served mid-twentieth-century society best. Like Eleanor Rathbone, she perceived the economic uncertainty that beset women and children as dependants on the family wage and advocated as a solution her version of a more genuinely companionate marriage, in which women were enabled to work outside the home and the natural superiority of men was no longer preached. Beyond the latter, she said little about any need for change in male behaviour, other than to praise what she felt was the greater domestication of men in the United States. Beveridge, on the other hand, while equally committed to companionate marriage and also concerned to improve the position of women in the postwar world, offered a competing vision of the role of a postwar welfare state, in which married women were rendered more securely dependent on their husbands for maintenance in the form of national insurance, pensions and national assistance.[8] A benevolent state could as easily sustain a traditional division of labour between husbands and wives as promote change, but Myrdal seemed not to realize the fragility of her vision, founded as it was on her faith in the power of rational argument to persuade.

While Viola Klein's perception of the crucial underlying problem (or 'dilemma' as both she and Myrdal termed it) facing women, was in many respects similar to that of Myrdal, her approach was rather different. Just as Myrdal identified a series of issues – vocational choice, domestic organization, and psychological well-being – impinging on women's choice of role as wife/mother and/or worker, so in her first book, *The Feminine Character* (1946), Klein described women's psychological state in terms of a dilemma arising from the contrast between a materially changed situation (in which adult women commonly went out to work) and the survival of traditional (domestic) ideologies and attitudes.[9] As a sociologist trained in Mannheim's school of interdisciplinary, qualitative research designed to achieve 'synthetic sociological knowledge', Klein was much more inclined to take a broadly based approach to the analysis of this central dilemma between home and work. Like Myrdal, she located it historically, using more care in delineating the stages of development in women's relationship to home and workplace than Myrdal with her sweeping idea of women's lagged adjustment to industrialization, but unhappily exercising no greater attention to historical evidence. In *The Feminine Character* technological change and falling family size were the great impersonal forces that determined changes in women's labour force participation. But Klein also dwelt at greater length on the conflicts experienced by individual women, who faced judgement in respect of both their public and private roles and who stood to be deemed failures in both. However, in *Women's Two Roles* the purpose became not to elucidate such conflicts, but rather by presenting a number of mechanisms, both individual and collective, for reconciling home and work, to deny that such conflict even existed.

Klein's primary purpose in writing *The Feminine Character* was to explore the concept of femininity and to show how the concept had changed in response to shifts in the material circumstances of women and how scientific knowledge was affected by the 'climate of the age'. In other words, unlike Myrdal, Klein's main focus was on the way in which gender has been socially constructed. Her conclusions were often perceptive. For example, on Freud and Weininger she wrote that despite their 'revolutionary attitudes against a world of taboos', they were 'children of the passing age in so far as they accept the relation between the sexes, as it prevailed in their special bourgeois social milieu, as eternally valid'. This conclusion has been echoed much more recently by Elizabeth Fee in her work on Victorian social scientists, whom she describes as using their own society as the model from which they formulated their ideas, which in turn justified the position of women as they found it.[10] Klein concluded that it was impossible to identify specific feminine characteristics; the concept of femininity had been subjected to constant change. But in her commentaries on the various authors she discussed, she revealed her own structure of beliefs about sexual differences and sexual equality. In all probability it was this gloss that caused the confused reception accorded the book. In the 1971 edition Klein avowed that her purpose was to study existing theories about feminine psychology rather than to write a psychological study of women herself, but there is nevertheless a substantial amount of Klein's own thinking in the book.

Notwithstanding her conclusion that there was insufficient evidence as to what comprised the feminine, Klein was cautious about throwing out the idea of sexual differences. Despite her convincing demonstration as to the social construction of femininity, she did not believe that it was a phantom likely to dissolve into nothing. Indeed, she clearly felt as strongly as had Herbert Spencer in the late nineteenth century that masculine and feminine characteristics (sometimes conflated in her comments with male and female) were necessary for social progress. In view of this she reserved her warmest approval for Margaret Mead's advocacy of 'democratic planning' for maximum variety and diversity in human behaviour. In this analysis it was wrong to plan either with the aim of perpetuating sexual difference, because this would deny the presence of masculine and feminine characteristics in differing proportions in all of us, or with the aim of achieving equal rights and a 'fair field and no favour', because this would deny the existence of differences and condemn women to adapting themselves to masculine patterns. Klein did not go on to explore the implications of her position on sex, gender and equality, but she had clearly reached a not dissimilar point to that of Myrdal, in that she believed in the importance of opening as wide a range of choices to women as possible. But she reached this position from a consideration of gender rather than of societal needs or development. Nevertheless, like Myrdal, her analysis lacked any consideration of the determinants of women's position beyond the operation of vast, impersonal social and economic forces.

Co-operators in research[11]
Viola Klein began work on the book that became *Women's Two Roles* in 1951 at the invitation of Alva Myrdal. Myrdal had been invited by the International Federation of University Women (IFUW) to conduct a cross-national survey of the needs of women who wanted to participate in both professional and family life, and had collected much of the empirical material, including questionnaires distributed through IFUW branches before joining the UN in 1949. Having read Klein's PhD thesis (which served as the basis of *The Feminine Character*), Myrdal asked her to help in the preparation of the manuscript. While very much the junior partner, Klein virtually prepared a new draft of the book single-handedly, while holding down what seems to have been a rather dreary job in the Foreign Office. She sent drafts to Myrdal for comment, correction and what Myrdal certainly considered to be all-important polishing.

The joint endeavour was a lengthy one for what proved to be a relatively slim volume; *Women's Two Roles* was not published until 1956. In large part this was due to the exigencies of Myrdal's international schedule. Klein wrote to Myrdal continuously, apologizing for seeming to press her, expressing worries about the amount of material appearing on a similar theme (and in particular fearing the competition from Judith Hubback's book on the careers of graduate women, which eventually appeared in 1953),[12] and explaining her need to see the book completed if she were to advance her own career. The joint project was certainly not the 'harmonious co-operation' referred to by Myrdal in her foreword. Klein's position as the junior research assistant was tenuous and Myrdal, very much the *grande dame*, evidenced little by way of sisterly understanding of it. Throughout 1953 and 1954 Klein asked for help in finding a new job, but received no positive reply from Myrdal. In 1952 Klein requested that the authorship on the proposed book become joint rather than in Myrdal's name alone and expressed her distress at Myrdal's intimation to her publisher that Klein had not contributed as much to the volume as had been originally anticipated. Klein protested that she could not see how her share could have been greater, while at the same time desperately seeking to assure Myrdal that she did not feel aggrieved: 'you are a very busy woman and it was clear to me from the start that most of the writing as well as the research would fall on me. Having accepted the collaboration on these terms I see no point in mutually measuring and comparing our individual share . . . I have enjoyed doing it and that is my main reward.'[13] Myrdal replied hastily that she had not meant to offend and that she had merely been trying to justify her own desire to go through the manuscript once more to her publisher. However, she continued to dither about joint authorship, explaining that the publisher had contracted with her alone and that she, after all, had funded the research.

Myrdal was a world-famous author, and consultant. Klein was relatively isolated and insecure. A more experienced writer, Myrdal undoubtedly worked faster than Klein, at one point revising three chapters in the three days between engagements. Their correspondence recorded no serious disagreement in terms of the ideas expressed in the book or of its direction. Indeed their skills seemed to have been largely complementary, Klein concentrating on setting out the nature of the issues and leaving the policy implications to Myrdal. Klein raised problems and suggested points of emphasis, while Myrdal accepted or rejected and redrafted, adding as Klein readily acknowledged 'accent and vitality'.[14] The project owed considerably more to Klein's labour than to Myrdal's and was undoubtedly central to Klein's identity in a way that it never was to Myrdal's. Yet it seems that Myrdal's influence steered the analysis more firmly in a direction that made it more strategically acceptable. Klein's book would have been more academic and more grounded in an analysis of sex roles. But just as Myrdal evinced little real sympathy with Klein's personal position, so her interest in the position of women remained at the level of an abstract social problem, rather than a desire to achieve greater analytical understanding. Of the two, Klein seems to have had both a greater grasp of women's position, born in part of personal experiences and a lonely struggle as a single career woman, and in part of a somewhat firmer grasp of the meaning of sex and gender. Their different concerns were reflected in their different evaluations of their book. When in 1954 Myrdal's publisher decided that the draft chapters lacked 'flare', Myrdal agreed and confessed that she had had difficulty working up any 'missionary zeal' for the book's message, other than in regard to one particular policy recommendation: that working hours should be shortened to give the working population more time for their families and to make possible a richer, creative family life.[15] Klein, on the other hand, felt that the most important aspect of the book was the one that stressed the different phases in a woman's life span and the idea that, by rational planning, women would be able to exert greater control over their lives.

The argument of *Women's Two Roles* in context

From the first, Myrdal and Klein were clear that what they wanted to do was to make a case for professional women's right to pursue a career and have a family. But it was difficult to decide how to construct their case and where to put the emphasis. In the end, Myrdal's emphasis on the needs of state and nation as the main justification for married women's work, rather than Klein's early analysis of sex, gender and equality, dominated the text. It would not have occurred to either to rely on an argument centred on women's rights.

The book argued that, historically, the employment of married women represented merely the final completion of women's long adjustment to industrialization. Myrdal's idea of women as 'late-comers in the evolutionary process' underpinned the historical chapter.[16] The increasing numbers of women entering the work-force were portrayed as recapturing positions that had been lost in the early phase of industrialization, when home and workplace had been separated, and the result romantically compared to the more 'balanced' family economies of the pre-industrialization period. Their view that industrialization caused a narrowing in women's role as the workplace left the home had more in common with Alice Clark's classic text on women's work in seventeenth-century England (which was not cited in their bibliography) than with the other classic treatment of women's work by Ivy Pinch-beck, which they did cite and which took an optimistic view of the increasing 'specialization' of roles between husbands as breadwinners and full-time wives and mothers.[17] In 1955 Myrdal suggested to Klein that they write of a two-phase revolution in women's relationship to the workplace during industrialization: first, the process by which they were squeezed out of economic activity and, second, the process by which they achieved re-entry, which was differently timed for working and middle-class women. Klein replied that they should write rather of two stages in the process of re-entry, first by unmarried women and later by married women.[18] This was essentially the line taken in the book. Myrdal and Klein did not in the end differentiate between social classes and their analysis fitted best the experience of the middle-class women who were the focus of their concern. Klein had in any case already made clear in *The Feminine Character* her (erro-neous) view that middle-class women had, in the guise of social investigators and social workers, spearheaded the movement of women back into the world of paid employment.

The idea of women reclaiming their rightful position in the public sphere was supported by the argument that women were increasingly available to undertake paid work because of the decline in family size and their greater longevity. Myrdal Klein calculated that childbearing and rearing now occupied only one-third of women's adult lives. Further, the postwar economy with its full (male) employment and steady growth needed more wor-kers and could not afford to tolerate female unproductivity. Nor, they warned, could women expect to claim the full rights of citi-zenship if they failed to make an economic contribution. As Klein's letters to Myrdal revealed early on in their joint work, she was clear that their argument hinged on the lack of any main source of labour other than married women. She was particularly struck by an early set of calculations which showed that if women worked through only half of their married life this would not only still leave them seventeen and a half years for child rearing, but would increase the total labour force of either Britain or the United States by 12.5–14 per cent, allowing the introduction of a five-day week with more leisure for everyone.[19]

Myrdal and Klein then sought to show that in a number of Western European countries and in the United States, married women were already too prominent in the workplace to be wished away. Women wanted to work for economic and psychological reasons, but the demand factors were argued to be stronger still. The economy required the skills women possessed, but because of their family commitments married women were less reliable workers in terms of their greater absenteeism, turnover rates and lack of flexibility. The answer, they maintained firmly, lay in treating the organization of work rather than the women workers as variable. This sounded promising, but in terms of policy recommendations amounted only to a call for ameliorative reform, rather than radical structural change, in the form of more effective career guidance, extended maternity leaves, retraining programmes for women over forty, and greater collective provision of laundries and meals in order to promote the rationalization of housework. In fact they made most of the idea that women themselves should demonstrate a greater commitment to individual planning for a two-phase career, the point Klein felt to be their most important.

Myrdal and Klein's concern to present their case for the reconciliation of home and work as a relatively unproblematic, rational and natural development was reflected in their prolonged search for an appropriate title for the book.[20] They began straightforwardly with 'Professional Women and their Opportunities for Family Life', but this was too revealing of their goal. 'The Surplus Energy of Women' was suggested by Myrdal late in 1952, emphasizing the way in which women's skills and effort were allowed to run to waste. In 1954 Klein favoured 'Motherhood and Career – Conflicting Roles or Double Opportunity?'. But Myrdal eschewed any title that might play up the possibility of a conflict they wanted to argue out of existence. She liked 'Two Lives for One', which played down both conflict and the fact that the subject matter was women. 'Women's Two Roles' must have proved just sufficiently neutral for her taste.

Myrdal and Klein's search for what was strategically the best form of presentation of their argument becomes more understandable when it is located in the context of the familialist ideology of the 1950s. Myrdal and Klein had to confront a postwar society in which concern about the level of the birth rate had not yet been overtaken by evidence of a baby boom (just as married women's work had not yet been legitimized by evidence of the increasing numbers of wives engaged in it); in which doctors, social workers, social scientists, magistrates and politicians all expressed their desire to see the family 'rebuilt' on traditional lines; and in which academics led the way in condemning the effect of married women's work on children's development.

On the first of these issues, Myrdal and Klein felt as obliged as any early feminist to address the question of whether married women's work (in the nineteenth century the variable would more likely have been women's higher education) resulted in lower levels of fertility. They admitted that work and family were difficult to combine – hence in part their idea of a two-phase career in adult life – but in line with their evolutionary optimism, pointed out that this was less the case than thirty years ago and with further technological progress would become less so in the future. More broadly, Myrdal certainly felt that concern about the birth rate, taken together with the shortage of labour, could be turned to women's advantage. *Women's Two Roles* repeated the observation made in *Nation and Family* that the contemporary problem was not so much married women's right to work as working women's right to marry.[21] In *Nation and Family* she declared that 'the remarkable thing is that in this crucial moment the population argument was wrenched out of the hands of the anti-feminists and instead used as a new and formidable weapon for the emancipatory ideal'.[22]

There is some evidence to support her idea that official arguments were being turned on their heads, although not to the extent that they supported feminist claims. In anticipation of the increased demand for married women's labour, the 1949 British Royal Commission on Population welcomed the idea of women doing two jobs and expressed the view that there was nothing inherently wrong in the use of contraceptives.[23] Similarly, fears of an adverse dependency ratio due to an ageing population caught the imagination of government departments and social researchers, and by 1952 the Ministry of Labour was arguing that employers should open the door to people able and willing to work no matter what their age, including older married women.[24] However, the postwar concern to rebuild the family ran counter to these concerns and in particular to Myrdal's and Klein's effort to argue in favour of women's work. As Denise Riley has shown, the Ministry of Health was closing day nurseries, opened during the Second World War, on the grounds that stable family life required full-time mothers at the very same time that the Ministry of Labour was urging more married women to enter the workforce.[25]

Myrdal and Klein were aware that in subtitling their book 'Home and Work' they might be accused of implying that home did not involve work and thus cause offence at a time when so much attention was being directed towards the importance of women's domestic role. This was true both in respect of the views of women themselves (although this was not Myrdal's and Klein's chief concern) and of policymakers. Beveridge, for example, was busy lauding the 'vital work' performed by wives and mothers in 'ensuring the adequate continuance of the British race and British ideals in the world'.[26] J. C. Spence, a leading paediatrician, wrote of the need to return to first principles in family life, stressing in particular the importance of full-time motherhood, and declaring his support for Beveridge's Plan for Social Security in so far as it would promote the traditional family form,[27] and John Newson produced a report in 1948 that advocated as separate a curriculum for girls – grounded in domestic subjects – as any advocated by early twentieth-century adherents of the eugenics movement.[28] Nor were Myrdal and Klein alone among feminists in feeling that they had to acknowledge the strength of such views. Juddith Hubback's book on college-educated women went considerably further in seeking accommodation with the majority view that women's first duty was to home and family. Hubback granted educated married women the right to a life of their own only if 'the husband, the children and the home are not neglected' and as long as they had their husbands' full support and approval.[29]

Myrdal and Klein were in many ways forthright in condemning those who glorified housework and, by telling housewives that they were performing a 'sacred duty', kept them employed in unpaid drudgery. They condemned the way in which housework 'like no other work', lent itself to the dissipation of time and energy, and cited studies which suggested that married women who went out to work managed to reduce their housework by ten hours a week if they were childless and thirty hours if they had children.[30] At no point did they argue that the work of the private sphere should be shared equally between husband and wife, suggesting only that the patriarchal model of family life give way more completely to one of partnership and, in general terms, that husbands accept more responsibility for 'building home life'. This meant that in the end Myrdal and Klein had to acknowledge that any married woman taking on paid work outside the home would inevitably shoulder a double burden, and certainly they suggested that women be praised rather than criticized for their double contribution. Yet their attitude towards the burden imposed by housework as opposed to child care was ambivalent. Women with no dependent children were as likely to be condemned for idleness if they did not go out to work as they were to be praised for working a double day. It is hard to avoid the conclusion that in the end Myrdal and Klein were not very sympathetic to the idea that housework constituted work. They believed housework to have lost any productive content, and thus while acknowledging that caring for children was both necessary and valuable, they tended to attach the label 'work' only to paid employment. This was because the main prop on their argument was that of the state's need for more workers to ensure economic and social progress, and women's obligation, as citizens, to step forward. Because of their national need-led argument, Myrdal and Klein put themselves in the position of exhorting women to do their duty as paid workers, rather than promoting their right to work outside the home.

Myrdal and Klein were much more consistently deferential to the view that mothers with young children should on no account go out to work, and it was this above all that resulted in their promotion of their idea of a two-phase career for married women. Almost the first piece of literature Klein asked Myrdal to send her in 1951 was Bowlby's *Maternal Care and Mental Health*, his classic text on the importance of full-time motherhood to normal child development.[31] Postwar literature generally attached most importance to the role of mothers within the family. Spence considered that women achieved 'mature motherhood' only with the sixth or seventh child, while in his radio broadcasts on motherhood, the psychologist Winnicott stressed the natural quality of the mother/child relationship and the natural place of married women in the home: 'Talk about women not wanting to be housewives seems to me just nonsense because nowhere else but in her own home is a woman in such command.'[32] Bowlby's connection between 'affectionless', or maternally deprived, and delinquent children was additionally picked up by social workers, guidance counsellors and magistrates. Basil Henriques, an East London magistrate, wrote:

> Quite simply it seems to me that by far the most far-reaching change in modern society is that the family is not considered to be so important as it used to be, and it is because of this that we have in our midst so many suffering, unhappy and delinquent children . . . legislation regulating the working hours of mothers of school age children is one of the most urgent reforms required for the creation of good homes.[33]

In 1952 Myrdal insisted on adding a further generalization about the current position of women to the four they had already developed: 'children need during their early years the undivided devotion of some one person, and most appropriately of their mothers. Mothers also as persons ought to be given the right to a break from other occupations for a period of creative, active motherhood.'[34] Myrdal and Klein devoted a whole chapter to the issue of child care and welfare, which accepted the need of young dependent children for full-time mothers, but sought to prepare the ground for older women to return to work by invoking the possibility of as destructive a behaviour to child welfare as maternal deprivation in the form of maternal over-protection.

When *Women's Two Roles* was written there were few thorough criticisms of Bowlby's ideas to draw on. Myrdal and Klein gratefully cited Margaret Mead, whose views on 'this new and subtle form of anti-feminism'[35] had impressed Klein earlier, and also made some preliminary observations that would later be subjected to testing by Bowlby's critics, for example the point that Bowlby's conclusions were based on a study of children totally deprived of maternal care as a result of traumatic wartime separation. Klein's later studies of married women's work, published in the early 1960s, were able to provide a much more robustly sceptical account of Bowlby's ideas.[36] In 1956 Myrdal and Klein were able only to alert their European audience to the mainly American literature on the dangers of 'Momism', the over-protective behaviour attributed to full-time housewives, who themselves received little by way of intellectual stimulation and who also stood accused of raising inadequate children.

On the whole, Myrdal and Klein were more moderate in their accommodation to postwar thinking on the family and women's role within it than were many other feminists. Typical were the views of the Conference on the Feminine Point of View (cited favourably by Judith Hubback in her study of college-educated wives), whose participants included the prominent inter-war feminists, Eva Hubback and Mary Stocks. In 1952 the Conference participants announced that they were less concerned with equality than with difference; that they believed women to be more compassionate, to have more intuitive sympathy and a greater commitment to selfless personal service than men; and that girls should expect their careers to be seriously interrupted by child-bearing and, further, should 'give this time joyfully, not grudgingly'.[37] Hubback reiterated in 1957 that 'reasonable modern feminism builds on the diversity of the sexes, it is not crudely equalitarian. It takes differences into account, not with the aim of over-emphasising them, but with the sole purpose of seeing what contribution each sex can make to the common good.'[38] In fact, both the Conference and Hubback were as anxious as Myrdal and Klein to advocate a larger role for educated women (working-class women did not feature in most postwar feminist literature) beyond home and family, but they were even more wary of asserting women's *right* to such a role. By 1956, the activities of the organized feminist movement were very limited. Two equalitarian feminist organizations, the Six Point Group and the Married Woman's Association, chose as the theme of their 1956 conference, 'Married Women out at Work', and delegates heard reports on Myrdal's and Klein's work by the treasurer of the British Federation of University Women and on Hubback's PEP survey by Betty Scharf, a lecturer in sociology at the London School of Economics. In her introductory remarks Mrs H. Hunkins Hallinan, president of the Six Point Group, stressed that women workers were now 'an indispensable factor in the nation's economic life' and that facilities had to be provided to help them perform their duties as wives and mothers and as workers.[39] More than anything else, Myrdal and Klein's language of 'two roles' slipped immediately and easily into use by feminist and non-feminist alike.

Like Myrdal and Klein, these women tried to base their case on the needs of nation and society rather than on women's rights. Myrdal and Klein made little mention of women's own needs, for example for self-fulfilment, stressing only the material need of the widow or the divorcee for means of self-support. But this again could as easily be interpreted as favourable to the interests of the state, which would not then be liable for their maintenance. Their argument relied on the marshalling of aggregate data in the manner of a government report and was designed to present a rational case for the consumption of policymakers. Unlike early twentieth-century women social investigators, neither Myrdal and Klein nor other feminist writers on the subject of women's work investigated the actual experience of women. Only Ferdinand Zweig relied on interview data in his self-styled voyage into the unknown country of women's work during the early 1950s.[40] Klein was thankful that he was at least honest enough to admit that instead of finding the downtrodden, over-burdened women workers of his imagination, the women he interviewed seemed to enjoy going out to work.[41]

Nevertheless, Myrdal's and Klein's analysis could be remarkably perceptive. For example, their analysis of women's behaviour as workers anticipated important, later feminist analysis of the family wage and of the relationship between paid and unpaid work:[42]

> Thus a vicious circle operates: the unequal remuneration of women reduces their sense of 'career' and contributes to the lack of continuity in their employment, and on the other hand, the lack of continuity in their work is one of the main reasons why they are paid at a lower rate and meet with difficulties in their promotions.[43]

However, the implications of such perceptions were never explored. After this passage, Myrdal and Klein turned back briskly to the 'social realities' – that women did 'waste' their training and were inflexible and unreliable from the employer's point of view – and to the practical ways of ameliorating the situation.

Myrdal and Klein wanted to promote greater choice for women but were not prepared to argue their case on the basis of a gender-based analysis, which would have involved confronting the privileges exercised by husbands and by male workers. They were at pains to stress that given the sexual segregation of the workforce, male workers need not fear female competition, and given their acceptance of the domestic division of labour, they were prepared to acknowledge that husbands might feel that wives were doing too much and advise against taking on a job. The logic of Myrdal's and Klein's position meant that women had to be the ones to change. Klein was correct in her judgement that their most striking recommendation was for individual women to plan for an interrupted work career. Women were urged to choose jobs that could be safely left for a number of years; teaching was the favourite example. Thus ironically, given Klein's early rejection of both 'equal but different' and 'fair field and no favour' feminist concepts of equality, and given the commitment of both Myrdal and Klein to making industrial organization adapt to women, in the end they left it to women to take the initiative in doing the adjusting, with some help in the form of retraining schemes and publicly provided services. In such formulation low-paid and sexually segregated work became a rational trade-off for the privilege of engaging in motherhood. Such a solution provided the semblance of neither formal nor substantive quality, amounting merely to making the best of the status quo.

After *Women's Two Roles*

Myrdal's later work focused more on peace and internationalism, but Klein continued to research married women's work, carrying out two studies for the Institute of Personnel Management in the early 1960s.[44] *Women's Two Roles* did in the end provide her with a passport out of the civil service: 1960 found her back as a research fellow at the LSE and 1965 in a teaching position at Reading University. Her two further studies of married women's work took the form of sample surveys and, while inherently descriptive, continued to carry the message that women's labour market participation was crucial for economic growth and social progress. Klein found no evidence from the surveys of young women planning to return to work after child rearing, but noted that the bimodal work pattern was only just beginning to be evident. Certainly, by the early 1960s the idea of women returning to work in later middle age was broadly accepted by other social scientists.[45] But so too was the idea of part-time work for women. In her 1963 study Klein stressed the numbers of married women working part time. *Women's Two Roles* had not recommended this option, believing that it would prove disadvantageous to employers. In practice, virtually all the increase in married women's work during the 1960s and 1970s came from the expansion of part-time employment. By 1972 a new generation of studies on the relationship of work and the family noted the beginnings of a movement towards continuous careers for married women,[46] but the vast majority of married women with children were (and are) working part time. Part-time work proved a cheaper and more flexible option for employers than Myrdal and Klein had envisaged, and in Britain where child care facilities were exceptionally limited proved the only feasible option for women.

In her later studies Klein tended to interpret her survey very conservatively: thus young women's lack of interest in returning to work indicated their overwhelming prior commitment to home and family. She recorded that there was no trace of feminist equalitarianism in the responses of her sample, only a growing sense that it might be lazy to stay at home and that they might have an obligation to engage in paid employment, seemingly a realization of Myrdal's and Klein's earlier prescriptions. In cataloguing the reluctance of employers to hire married women for anything but unskilled work, she remained reluctant to point the finger at discriminatory practices, preferring to emphasize the advantages to be reaped from drawing on the unused pool of female skills and suggesting, interestingly, that in the next decade employers would have to make a choice between employing married women and immigrant labour.

It is difficult to know why Klein continued the kind of work she had begun with Myrdal rather than returning to develop her earlier research. In 1951 she confessed to finding statistical analysis 'rather tedious'; certainly it was very different from her early work.[47] Yet her 1960s studies swung more determinedly still towards the survey method, eschewing both the development of gender-based analysis and any consideration of women's own experiences. In the first place, Klein was convinced of the power of social scientific data to persuade (she had recorded her faith in rational planning in *The Feminine Character*) and, second, she was also convinced that middle-class women were indebted to social science, both because of its capacity to undermine prejudice about the nature of femininity, and because of the opportunities it had afforded women for work in the caring professions. In the end, her Fabian-like faith in the efficiency of rational argument and planning was no different from that of many interested in social reconstruction during the postwar years. In many respect, Myrdal's and Klein's work set the tone for a whole generation of social scientific investigation into women's position in society.

Myrdal's and Klein's desire not to turn women into 'super-women' – mistresses of home, family and career simultaneously – and the emphasis they placed on the importance of family life for women have found echoes in the recent work of both Betty Friedan and Germaine Greer,[48] and in the overt celebration, particularly in the United States, of women's culture. But the fact remains that in Myrdal's and Klein's argument the chief beneficiary was to be not women but society at large. In their effort to construct a rational argument that would win over policymakers and employers, Myrdal and Klein failed to consider what would happen if and when it suited those same agents to behave differently. Attitudinal change without structural change was unlikely to prove lasting, especially when it was born of instrumentalism rather than, as Myrdal imagined, of a conversion to the feminist point of view. The demand for labour was such that married women's employment increased without any urging from social scientists or feminists.

The arguments of later 1960s and early 1970s feminism appear much more soundly based and much more radical than those of Myrdal and Klein. They also seem to have had greater practical result, in the form of equal opportunities legislation for example. However, from the perspective of the 1980s Myrdal and Klein may be worthy of rather more than passing historical interest. The energy they devoted to the strategic formulation of their case and the importance they attached to its presentation in what was a climate hostile to feminist aspirations must surely be something of an object lesson for feminists living in Thatcher's Britain.

Notes

1. Alva Myrdal and Viola Klein, *Women's Two Roles, Home and Work* (Routledge and Kegan Paul, London, 1956).
2. Talcott Parsons and Robert F. Bales, *Family Socialization and Interaction Process* (Free Press, Glencoe, Ill., 1955).
3. Catherine Hakim, *Occupational Segregation*, Research Paper No. 9 (Department of Employment, London, 1979), p. 4.
4. Alva Myrdal, *Nation and Family: The Swedish Experiment in Democratic Family and Population Policy* (Harper and Brothers, N. Y. and London, 1941).
5. Perhaps the most dramatic and pessimistic forecast by a social scientist was that of Enid Charles, *The Twilight of Parenthood* (Watts and Co., London, 1934); Report of the Royal Commission on Population, Cmd. 7695, (HMSO, London, 1949).
6. Myrdal, *op. cit.* note 4, p. 418.
7. *Idem*, p. 121.
8. Report by Sir William Beveridge on Social Insurance and Allied Services, Cmd. 6404 (HMSO, London, 1942).
9. Viola Klein, *The Feminine Character. The History of an Ideology*, 1st edn, 1946 (Routledge and Kegan Paul, London, 1971).
10. *Idem*, p. 67; Elizabeth Fee, 'The sexual politics of Victorian anthropology', in Lois Banner and Mary Hartman (eds), *Clio's Consciousness Raised* (Harper Torchbooks, New York, 1976).
11. The material for this section is drawn from the Papers of Viola Klein, University of Reading Archives, Acc. 1568.
12. Judith Hubback, *Wives who went to College* (Heinemann, London, 1957).
13. Klein to Myrdal, 27 May 1952.
14. Klein to Myrdal, 8 July 1952.
15. Myrdal to Ordway Tear (publisher), 28 May 1954.
16. Myrdal and Klein, *op. cit.* note 1, p. 7.
17. Alice Clark, *Working Life of Women in the Seventeenth Century* (Routledge and Kegan Paul, London, 1919); Ivy Pinchbeck, *Women Workers and the Industrial Revolution, 1750–1850* (Routledge and Kegan Paul, London, 1930).
18. Myrdal to Klein, 5 May 1955, and Klein to Myrdal, 10 Sept. 1955.
19. Klein to Myrdal, 11 Dec. 1951.
20. The lengthy discussion of this is to be found in Acc. 1568.
21. Myrdal, *op. cit.* note 4, p. 403; Myrdal and Klein, *op. cit.* note 1, p. 34.
22. Myrdal, *ibid.*
23. Cmd. 7695, pp. 159–60.
24. Ministry of Labour and National Services, *Employment of Older Men and Women. The Economic and Social Effects of the Increased Proportion of Older People in the Population* (HMSO, London, 1952).
25. Denise Riley, *War in the Nursery* (Virago, London, 1983).
26. Cmd. 6404, p. 53.
27. J. C. Spence, *The Purpose of the Family*, Convocation Lecture for the National Children's Home (1946).
28. John Newsom, *The Education of Girls* (Faber and Faber, London, 1948).
29. Hubback, *op. cit.* note 12, p. 155.
30. Myrdal and Klein, *op. cit.* note 1, p. 36.
31. John Bowlby, *Maternal Care and Mental Health* (WHO, Geneva, 1951).

32. Spence, *op. cit.* note 27, p. 49; D. Winniciott, *The Child and the Family: First Relationships* (Tavistock, London, 1957), p. 88.
33. Basil Henriques, *The Home Menders: The Prevention of Unhappiness in Children* (Harrap, London, 1955), p. 23.
34. Klein to Myrdal (commenting on an earlier letter of Myrdal's), 8 July 1952. This point was very similar to the position adopted by an earlier influential Swedish feminist, Ellen Key: see *Love and Marriage* (Putnam's, New York, 1912) and *The Renaissance of Motherhood* (Putnams, New York, 1914). See also Ruth Roach Pierson, 'Ellen Key: maternalism and pacifism', in K. Arnup, A. Levesque and R. R. Pierson (eds), *Delivering Motherhood: Maternal Ideologies and Practices in the Nineteenth and Twentieth Centuries* (Routledge and Kegan Paul, London, 1988).
35. Myrdal and Klein, *op. cit.* note 1, p. 129.
36. Viola Klein, *Britain's Married Women Workers* (Routledge and Kegan Paul, London, 1965) pp. 142–50.
37. Olwen W. Campbell, *Report of a Conference on the Feminine Point of View* (Williams and Norgate, London, 1952), p. 40.
38. Hubback, *op. cit.* note 12, p. 83.
39. Notes on the Conference 'Married Women out at Work' (1956), Records of the Six Point Group, G6, Box 533, Fawcett Library.
40. F. Zweig, *Women's Life and Labour* (Gollancz, London, 1952).
41. Klein to Myrdal, 5 May 1952.
42. See especially Hilary Land, 'The family wage', *Feminist Review*, no. 6 (1980); and Irene Bruegel, 'Women's employment legislation and the labour market', in Jane Lewis (ed), *Women's Welfare/Women's Rights* (Croom Helm, London, 1983).
43. Myrdal and Klein, *op. cit.* note 1, p. 108.
44. Viola Klein, *Working Wives*, Occasional Paper no. 15 (Institute of Personnel Management, London, 1960), and *Employing Married Women*, Occasional Paper no. 17 (Institute of Personnel Management, London, 1961). Both these were republished as *Britain's Married Women Workers*.
45. E.g. F. Le Gros Clark, *Women, Work and Age* (Nuffield Foundation, Oxford, 1962).
46. Michael P. Forgarty, Rhona Rapoport and Robert N. Rapoport, *Sex Career and Family* (PEP and Allen & Unwin, London, 1971).
47. Klein to Myrdal, 11 Dec. 1951.
48. Betty Friedan, *The Second Stage* (Summit Books, New York, 1981), and Germaine Greer, *Sex and Destiny: The Politics of Human Fertility* (Picador, London, 1984).

11 British Feminism from the 1960s to the 1980s

Elizabeth Meehan

Introduction

It is commonplace now to see feminism in Britain as rising in the 1960s, flourishing in the 1970s and achieving a clutch of legislative victories, then dying in the 1980s under the assault of the New Right. This underestimates what was going on before the 1960s and what still continues. To say that feminism is still alive is not to underestimate the more repressive forces with which it has to contend. But it does require us to acknowledge that feminism has several strands which operate in different spheres at different times. Taken as a whole, the movement has been more proactive or reactive, depending on different political configurations within feminism itself and in the polity at large.

This chapter outlines feminist ideas and mobilization during the three decades from 1960. It then describes the main policy areas associated with liberal, socialist and radical feminism. This is not to say that theoretical differences isolate one strand from another; merely that courses of action have varied according to which type of analysis was prevalent. Indeed, the campaigns reveal practical co-operation. The changing political environment – from the 'social-welfarism' of the first two decades to the 'market individualism' of the 1980s – necessarily forms part of a concluding section on the prospects for British feminism.

Feminist ideas and mobilization

If feminism is broadly defined as the quest for a sexually just society, many people share at least some of its goals, though they disavow the label.[1] Among self-defined feminists views differ about the sources of oppression, priorities for change and appropriate forms of organization and methods. What is unambiguous, however, is that women's activism, whether in avowedly feminist politics or not, has risen substantially over the last three decades.

Since the three main streams of feminist thought in Britain have already been thoroughly discussed, an extended re-examination of them is unnecessary.[2] Broadly speaking they may be described as liberal, socialist and radical. Although their priorities and strategies differ, feminists with different perspectives work together on specific issues.

Feminist ideas

Liberal feminism of the twentieth century grew from nineteenth-century intellectual roots. As Carter points out, liberalism was the first social theory that offered the possibility of sex equality, stressing as it did equal political rights for men who by nature differed from one another.[3] It invited the extension of this logic from males to all human beings. Liberals do not expect that all women will be the same as all men but they contend that differentiation in society need not, and should not, be based on gender. The elimination of arbitrary differentiation is at the heart of all liberal feminist objectives: not only in the legal and political spheres that early liberals concentrated upon but also now in employment and social fields. Liberal feminists believe that the elimination of gender-based differentiation is a sensible objective for society as a whole as well as for women; labour markets, for example, would be more rational as well as fairer to women and men would be freer to enjoy the pleasures of family life.

Liberal feminists have been criticized for placing too much hope on the capacity of legal reform to lead to the full emancipation of women. The removal of formal barriers to equal opportunities in the labour market or in education does little to grapple with problems of the stunting experiences of poverty, unemployment, the conditions of employment of working-class women and customs and policies that locate women's primary role in the family. So, for what might be termed 'welfare socialist' feminists, reforms such as equal pay are meaningless without adequate health and safety provisions, nursery facilities, social services, and so on. This may imply different, instead of the same, treatment for women in such areas as protective legislation, matters relating to pregnancy, child-care and income maintenance.

Marxist feminists explain the condition of women partly in terms of the capacity of employers to use them as the 'reserve army' of labour which can be engaged and disengaged as the situation demands. Marxist feminists also explain women's role in the family by the function the family fulfils in the maintenance of capitalist economic relations. The family is thought to sustain the emotional and physiological needs of the male primary labour force and to socialize each new generation into the norms of society. British Marxist women have enriched their theory by fusing it with neo-Marxist ideas about ideology and the social construction of identities, by psychoanalysis and by theories of patriarchy.[4]

Patriarchy literally means rule by the father. In feminist theory, it has come to mean domination by men, not only in the family but also collectively in public matters. The development of capitalism seemed at first to threaten the patriarchal family because of its separation of work and family and the transference of 'women's work' away from the home. Instead, Marxist feminists argue, capitalism incorporated patriarchy because it assumed women were supported financially by male relatives. This was used to justify lower wages for women. For Marxist feminists, then, a socialist critique of patriarchal capitalism must discuss its social constructs and also the material conditions that give rise to both male and class domination.

Radical feminism also grew out of dissatisfaction with the traditional socialist theory and practice. The concept of patriarchy is central to radical feminists. But, whereas Marxists see male domination as having been taken over by capitalism, radicals argue that men, not an economic system, are the primary source of oppression. While Marxist and radical feminists both use the concept of patriarchy, it is not historically specific for radicals as it is for Marxists. Even so, their analyses are similar with respect to matters such as the social construction of femininity and sexuality, women's rights of control over reproduction and problems of sexual violence.

Some radical feminists, however, pursue the logic of their analysis to a point where a united women's movement of the broad left becomes difficult to realize. In their view, women's physiological capacities for reproduction are analogous to the material production of the working class in traditional Marxism. Women, then, constitute a class in the same way that workers do. Just as the working class must become a class for itself by taking control of production, so, too, must women take control of their reproduction in order to become free. An absolute extension of the class analogy must lead to the idea of the destruction of the previous dominant class – men; or, at least, separation from it. Radicals demand that lesbianism be considered not merely a matter of freedom of choice but as essential political practice for feminists. Conversely, socialist feminists see separatism as helpful, for example in launching women's political activism, but not as a final goal. They share with liberals the idea that it is possible to redesign social institutions so as to realize freely chosen heterosexual or homosexual relations that are based upon a real equality of autonomous individuals.

The newest theoretical controversies are over the argument by ethnic minority women that feminism has been so preoccupied with the connection between sex and class inequality that it has failed to provide a coherent analysis of oppression which includes racial discrimination.[5]

Feminist mobilization

The growth of women's activism between the early 1960s and the mid-1980s disproves the thesis commonly held at the beginning of the period that women are not 'natural joiners'.[6] In 1964 three million women were active in 120 national groups but only fifteen of these were said to be feminist.[7] In 1983 Bouchier reported that there were about 300 feminist groups of about 20 000 activists.[8] He points out that this is low in comparison to the Women's Institute (WI), which, of course, was not set up in order to promote sex equality. But organizations such as the WI and trade unions have sometimes lobbied for reforms that are advocated by feminists. There have been large demonstrations on equal pay, nuclear bases and abortion, the last drawing 100 000 supporters of which 60 000 were women.[9]

In 1964 most feminist groups were old suffrage societies which remained in existence to promote further steps towards equality; for example, the Fawcett Society, the Six Point Group, the Women's Freedom League, the Suffrage Fellowship. The Status of Women Group, founded in the 1930s, was also active in the 1960s. From 1966 onwards the Six Point Group and the Fawcett

Society initiated alliances between the women's rights groups and others such as the National Council of Married Women, the National Council for Civil Liberties (NCCL) and women's professional and employment associations (for example, the British Federation of Business and Professional Women, the Association of Headmistresses, the Women's Employment Federation and the Trades Union Congress (TUC) Women's Advisory Committee). The main aims were equal opportunities, equal pay, equal taxation and better treatment for unmarried mothers. Recognizing the need for a broad base of support, traditional feminist societies encouraged women to join trade unions and supported strikes for equal pay such as the one by women machinists at the Ford Motor Company in Dagenham. Liberal feminists joined with the Labour movement in the 1969 rally at Trafalgar Square, London, organized by the National Joint Action Committee for Women's Rights. The then conventional wisdom about women's lack of aptitude for pressure group politics seemed vindicated when, despite the efforts at mass mobilization, no unified, integrated reformist women's rights organization developed. But to have expected this would have been to have overlooked the strength of established party loyalties and to have ignored the deliberately unconventional methods of organization espoused by the new wave of feminism which was also emerging at this time.

The political origins of the new movement are located by Randall in the Campaign for Nuclear Disarmament, the Vietnam Solidarity Campaign and among the women of International Socialists and the International Marxist Group (IMG).[10] The commemoration by women's peace groups of the fiftieth anniversary of women's suffrage in 1968 was a catalyst for the emergence of women's liberation.[11] But, whereas the politics of race was a factor in the birth of American women's liberation, class politics was more significant in Britain. In addition to the equal pay strikes of the late 1960s, a militant campaign by Hull women for better safety standards for men on fishing trawlers attracted considerable attention. This led to the formation of equal rights groups in Hull and elsewhere. The politicization of women as a result of other working-class campaigns has continued, most recently during the miners' strike of 1983.[12]

By 1969 there were seventy local women's liberation groups in London. Together they initiated the newsletter, *Shrew*. The IMG and other new left groups also published journals which drew attention to connections between class and sex inequality in capitalist societies. Bouchier points out that the success of London Women's Liberation Workshop spread quickly to other large cities in England, to Scotland and to Wales (and the Republic of Ireland).[13] The first national Women's Liberation Workshop was held in Oxford in 1970. It drew 600 delegates – twice the expected number.[14] British women's liberation moved quickly into specific campaigns. Action by, and on behalf of, night-time office cleaners, often poor and immigrant women, took place throughout the 1970s. Demands by other women workers were supported and co-operation with the TUC led to an extension of its 1963 Charter for Women at Work.

A shift of emphasis towards radical feminist issues became discernible by the mid-1970s. Bouchier argues that this began with the 1975 Wages for Housework demonstration in London.[15] The question of domestic labour is, of course, an important feature of socialist analyses of capitalism and sexism. But, as Bouchier points out, the Wages for Housework Campaign, being linked to the radical strand of feminism, focused on those manifestations of power exercised by men because they are men; control over reproduction, sexuality and violence against women. This is not to say that liberal and socialist feminists were against these campaigns; on the contrary, defence of freedom of sexual preference, of the rights of women to be free from molestation and the protection of the 1967 Abortion Act were widely supported. These issues have assumed a high priority in feminist politics among all three strands since the late 1970s.

Earlier it was noted that organization in the women's movement does not conform to the conventions of pressure group politics. The movement has challenged male methods of leadership and their structures of relatively permanent office-holders and committees, and so on. It is true that structurelessness and informality have drawbacks.[16] But these features also seem to have facilitated the upsurge of activism by women, hitherto impatient with more conventional forms of politics. Women with experience in the feminist movement, often in women-only groups, were able to use this as a base for fuller participation in other organizations such as political parties, trade unions and professional associations. But because of the 'decentralism' of feminist organization, much of women's political activity is not visible at the national level.

As in England, Scottish women's liberation is also, according to Bouchier, primarily urban but has more working-class participation and more emphasis on male violence.[17] It is also tinged with concern about English domination of feminism. Women's liberation groups are also active in Wales and Northern Ireland. Although there is pessimism about the current size and strength of organized feminism, if we include all the local or regional branches of 'old' organizations and the women's caucuses of local political parties, trade unions and professional associations, it seems clear that feminist politics was well established by the early 1980s.

Feminism and public policy

At the first Women's Liberation Conference in 1970 the following demands were adopted: equal pay, equal opportunities and education, twenty-four-hour nurseries, free contraception and abortion on demand. Later these were expanded to include legal and financial independence, an end to discrimination against lesbians, and freedom from intimidation by violence or sexual coercion. In addition to these and other issues referred to in the previous section, women have campaigned for greater control over the processes of childbirth, against cuts in the health and social services, against pornography and for increased representation of women in public life. This chapter concentrates on those which epitomize the three strands of feminist thought. Equal pay and opportunities spring from the liberal analysis but have been redefined as a result of the socialist perspective. Taxation and social security, of some interest to early liberals, have become prominent as a result of the socialist identification of the 'feminization of poverty'. Freer abortion has always been a concern but abortion on demand stems from the radical feminist view that women must be able to control reproduction.

Equal pay and opportunities
There is now a considerable literature about employment rights.[18] The main landmarks during the period under review are the Equal Pay Act 1970 (compliance with which was voluntary until 1975),

the Sex Discrimination Act (SDA) 1975 and the amendments to both Acts in the 1980s. The SDA was preceded by several private members' bills in both Houses of Parliament which, like the eventual legislation, also dealt with equal treatment in other spheres such as education and training.

During the 1960s liberal feminist groups, supported by socialist women and representatives of the Labour movement, called for action on equal education and employment opportunities. In 1967 the Fawcett Society took the lead in co-ordinating what seemed a disparate lobby. Although socialists were less convinced than liberals of the value of legal reforms, all co-operated in bringing about the changes of the 1970s. The women's lobby provided a bridge between the liberals and women's liberation; Women in the Media was created to improve the way in which the public were informed about the position of women.

The Equal Pay Act did not originate solely from feminist pressure. But the women's movement played a part. It has already been noted that the liberal wing of feminism supported equal pay strikes. Reform was accelerated when Barbara Castle took over as Secretary of State for Employment in the Labour government. She thought equal pay would appeal to working-class women voters. And she was able to find a compromise between the Confederation of British Industry and the TUC over how equal pay should be defined in law. The result was equal pay for the same or similar work or for work that had been rated as equivalent under an evaluation scheme.

Between 1970 and 1972 women's groups co-operated in drawing attention to the wider private members' anti-discrimination bills and in influencing their substantive content by giving evidence to the House of Lords Select Committee that was considering Lady Seear's proposals.[19] This activity intensified when the government announced that it would bring in its own legislation. Three hundred groups and individuals responded to its consultative document. In 1974, when Labour replaced the Conservatives in office, feminists, trade unionists and the NCCL co-operated to strengthen the Labour government's proposals. Views diverged over the question of protective legislation but joint lobbying contributed to at least two key improvements in the proposals: indirect discrimination and a limited version of positive action.

The SDA 1975 established the Equal Opportunities Commission (EOC) but, although it has been criticized for being too distant from the feminist lobby, its neutrality does not seem to have increased its legitimacy in the eyes of subsequent governments; rarely have its recommendations for legal improvements been followed directly. Nevertheless, the EOC (and other groups) played a significant part in obtaining the 1980s amendments by supporting cases that went to the European Court of Justice. The main change, the 1983 extension of the Equal Pay Act to cover work of equal value, was brought about as a result of action by the European Commission against the United Kingdom government. The impact of this change is difficult to assess since, at the time of writing, all but one of the first cases are still proceeding through the domestic judicial appeal system.[20] But potential improvements in the wages of low-paid women are great. This new provision challenges relations between feminism and the Labour movement. Since it threatens traditional differentials, it tests the depth of the male union organizers' commitment to equal treatment. But unions increasingly need to find issues that attract women members and equal value can provide a lever of influence over pay and gradings that might benefit all workers.

The impact of the equal treatment at work laws has been mixed. Women's pay, compared to men's, rose rapidly at first then settled at about 73 per cent; it now depends on the effectiveness of the equal value law. There are still high degrees of horizontal and vertical occupational segregation. Though the EOC reports that some employers are co-operating with it over positive action schemes, it is difficult to use the positive action provisions. Other legislation has complicated access to maternity pay and allowances and has weakened employment protection for pregnant women. The rights of part-time workers have also been undermined and further deregulation is expected.[21]

Child-care provision, especially facilities run on egalitarian lines, is inadequate. A new tax disincentive discourages women from using facilities subsidized by employers. Cuts in expenditure and privatization of health and social services reduce traditional sources of work for women and reinforce the idea that women should be at home to care for the sick and elderly relatives. These are the adverse effects that socialists warned would be the consequence of merely removing formal barriers to equal treatment at work. However, the feminist movement may find unlikely allies among some employers who recognize the twin problems of social injustice and labour market irrationalities. The Chief Economic Adviser to Lloyds Bank has recently outlined a set of recommendations, including child-care facilities, funded by government and employers with changes in social services and tax policies that would not be out of place on the agenda of a liberal-socialist women's meeting.[22]

Financial independence; social security and taxation
Financial independence through means other than employment, a long-standing goal of liberal feminists, has been given a new lease of life by socialists with their special concern about poverty. Rising divorce rates since the 1960s and defaults in maintenance payments mean that there are many single-parent families, usually headed by women, living in poverty. Even among two-parent families, high unemployment or low wages mean that one in five of them lives at or below the level at which they become eligible for means-tested benefits.[23] Poverty, and particularly the 'feminization' of poverty, is now a major concern of the European Network of Women.

In the 1930s socialists debated whether family allowances for mothers would reinforce the sexual division of labour or give a little real independence to women with children. In the event, an allowance payable to mothers was introduced and married men were given tax relief for wives and children. Many writers have noted that women rarely benefited directly from their husbands' tax concessions.[24] In 1979 the allowance paid to mothers and the tax relief for children were replaced by Child Benefit, payable directly to the person with day-to-day responsibility for children. Direct payment was welcomed by feminists and the anti-poverty lobby. But money saved from abolishing the tax concession did not continue to supplement the direct payment. The real value of the Child Benefit has been allowed to dwindle and has now been 'frozen' until at least 1990. It is also possible that entitlement to it may become means-tested instead of universal. The government has also considered eliminating the directness of payment to the person with routine parental responsibilities by proposing that it be administered, like taxation, by employers through wage packets. This idea was halted by the combined opposition of small employers, the anti-poverty lobby and feminists. Since the end of

1987 over seventy organizations, under the banner of Save Child Benefit, have been campaigning to resist impending risks to the scheme.[25]

Married women workers are also disadvantaged in respect of benefits relating to employment. Part-time employment and even short breaks in employment reduce eligibility for unemployment benefit and social assistance. Family and unemployment benefit policies mean that women who form families lose a vast amount of financial independence over their lifetimes.[26]

On the other hand, allowances for caring for sick or disabled relatives, previously available to all men and single women, are now available to married women who may also have to give up work or employ help. This is the result of European policy on equal treatment in social security and of a ruling in the European Court of Justice. The case was backed by the Child Poverty Action Group and welcomed by feminists. But Hoskyns notes that equalization steps sometimes reduce eligibility for all claimants.[27]

Feminists have always challenged the gender assumptions of the tax system. The married men's allowance is available to men irrespective of their wives' employment status, resulting in anomalous treatment of families with one or two earners without directly benefiting women who do not take paid employment. Hitherto, neither the earned nor the unearned income of married women was assessed separately from that of their husbands, leaving them with no privacy in their financial affairs. Until the early 1980s women who, exceptionally, *were* able to establish that they, not their husbands, were heads of household, had all matters adjusted via their husbands. Under continuous pressure from liberals, the newer Campaign for Financial and Legal Independence, Rights of Women, the NCCL and the EOC, some changes have been made. In 1988 separate tax assessment was made possible and, from 1990, the married man's allowance will be replaced by a married couple's allowance. The EOC sees the changes as fundamental though, according to the Fawcett Society, the difference between the two allowances is little more than the name. The latter supports the socialist feminist campaign for the replacement of this form of tax relief by a major supplementation of the Child Benefit scheme.[28]

Abortion

Abortion politics have been important to feminism since the 1960s, even before radical feminism emerged. Though not all feminists agree with the radical view that women have an absolute right to control reproduction through 'abortion on demand', all strands have co-operated to defend the 1967 Abortion Reform Act.

This Act legalized abortion up to twenty-eight weeks on grounds of the mental and physical health of the mother, the welfare of other children and when there was a risk of serious abnormality. The Act was introduced as a private member's bill by a Liberal MP, David Steel. Lovenduski identifies several features which contributed to his success: his own skill, the benevolently neutral attitude of the government, social concern about the public health problems of illegal abortions and about the thalidomide tragedy and, perhaps most important, the skilful assistance of the Abortion Law Reform Association (ALRA).[29] The ALRA was formed in the 1930s solely for the purpose of abortion reform. In the 1960s twenty-five national groups supported it and these included traditional women's groups and the NCCL. Its wide range of support from traditional groups of all types was important in demonstrating the legitimacy of the ALRA's concerns but it was the ALRA itself which provided David Steel with detailed assistance over the content of the bill. During the passage of the bill the Society for the Protection of Unborn Children (SPUC) was formed to try to defeat it. SPUC and the younger group, LIFE, have tried ever since to have the Act repealed or modified.

The National Abortion Campaign (NAC) was created to defend the Act. It has been argued that the NAC was able to activate a feminist network in the British Labour movement which drew attention to difficulties in securing abortions under the new law and organized resistance to the various attempts to undermine it.[30] To do so, it operated at both local and national levels; it picketed health authorities where abortions were difficult to obtain, held conferences, gained 350 affiliates from other organizations and drew the support of the TUC, which included the reform in its Charter for Women at Work. The NAC joined the Co-ordinating Committee in Defence of the 1967 Act, which was founded in 1976 and which, by 1983, had fifty-eight affiliated organizations, including groups from the Conservative, Liberal and Labour parties and professional medical associations. One of the most public achievements of the NAC was a march, on 31 October 1979, of 100 000 people, including TUC delegates, to oppose John Corrie's private member's bill to alter the law.

His bill was one of a series (James White, 1975; William Benyon, 1977; David Alton, 1988 and various others) that aimed to restrict the activities of charitable agencies which provided abortion advice and facilities, to reduce the time limits, to increase the scope for conscientious objection on the part of nurses and doctors and to stop facilities for foreign women. In 1981 the Health Secretary tried to reduce the law's scope by administrative action by confining the meaning of a mother's health to its strictly physical manifestations.

David Alton, a Liberal MP opposed to any abortion, introduced a bill in 1988 that would ban abortion after eighteen weeks, except in cases of young rape, incest or the severest handicap. A hugh campaign against it, under the umbrella group, Fight the Alton Bill (FAB), linked feminists with other groups drawn from the leading political parties, the trade unions and leading medical organizations. An opinion poll, carried out by the ALRA with Dr C. Francome, revealed that 79 per cent of the public supported the idea that women should be able to choose, in consultation with their doctors, whether to have late abortions. During the bill's parliamentary stages in May 1988, a concerted effort by feminists and their allies blocked the bill and preserved the terms laid down by the 1967 Act.[31]

Conclusions: assessment and prospects

These brief accounts of some feminist campaigns reveal that, as with any other social movement, the impact of feminism is mixed. At the level of the diffusion of ideas, there are some signs of success. 'Quality' newspapers and traditional women's magazines have extended or introduced coverage of women's rights and new magazines have been launched. There is a flourishing academic literature in many disciplines on previously undiscussed issues relating to women. Local authorities and political parties are more conscious about the impact of their organization and policies on women's needs. In Parliament there are elements of a cross-party feminist perspective on matters of special interest to women. This is perhaps more obvious in the European Parliament where efforts have been made to extend women's rights policies from those rooted in their status as worker to ones which relate to reproduction and sexual violence. Most important, perhaps, has been the politicization of working-class and ethnic minority women.[32]

Nevertheless, these advances, too, are fragile. The organs of popular culture are often criticized for not giving up the old images but simply advising on how to combine old duties with new opportunities. Awareness of feminist consumers is not matched by better representation of women at the higher levels of media and academic occupations. In political parties, government departments and public bodies women are rarely allocated safe seats or appointed to senior positions. At the European level, women's rights are salient because of the dedication of a few MEPs, usually female, and, while this is welcomed by the Commission, parliamentary committees that deal with 'male' issues such as monetary policy and industrial development seem unaffected.

When Mrs Thatcher became the first woman party leader and then Prime Minister in British history, much discussion ensued as to whether her success was good for women. For some, even a symbolic victory for feminism was a victory. Others agreed with the anecdotes that she 'owed nothing to feminism' and was the 'best man' to lead the Conservative government. Numerous policy studies have shown that the social policies of the Thatcher administration, not explicitly or necessarily about women, have particularly adversely affected women.[33] Decisions about staffing levels and service provision in the health and social services have affected women's employment opportunities, their own well-being and have increased their responsibilities for dependants. Education and training policies have also had direct and indirect adverse consequences for women. New Right policies link ideas about economic libertarianism and social conservatism, a combination which makes many people pessimistic about the prospects for women's liberation. This outlook seems to be corroborated by the fact that some Conservatives seem to feel again that it is respectable to make anti-feminist remarks. One minister in Thatcher's first cabinet observed in 1979 that, 'if the Good Lord had intended us to have equal rights to go out to work, He wouldn't have created man and women'.[34] On the other hand, David Alton accused the economic libertarian, Teresa Gorman MP, of being one of the main wreckers of his 1988 Abortion Bill.

Policy fields where there is a European Community dimension may provide opportunities for maintaining improvements. The Conservative government makes it plain that it does not like European encroachments into social, as distinct from economic, policy. Feminists often note that women's rights policies of the EC are limited because they focus so exclusively on women as employees. Nevertheless, proponents of women's equality believe Europe offers better prospects for improvement than the domestic political system. The EC may enable feminists to 'keep things on the boil' until Conservative promises of universal improvements become a reality or until the election of a government that is more unequivocally in favour of women's liberation.

Notes

1. Janet Radcliffe Richards, *The Sceptical Feminist* (Routledge and Kegan Paul, London, 1980). See also Pippa Norris, *Politics and Sexual Equality* (Wheatsheaf and Riener, London and Boulder, Colorado, 1987), and April Carter, *The Politics of Women's Rights* (Longman, London and New York, 1988), especially chap. 4.
2. E.g. David Bouchier, *The Feminist Challenge* (Macmillan, London, 1983); Carter, *ibid*; Anna Coote and Bea Campbell, *Sweet Freedom* (Picador/Pan, London, 1982). Vicky Randall, *Women and Politics* (Macmillan Education, Basingstoke, 1987). Sheila Rowbotham, Lynne Segal, Hilary Wainwright, *Beyond the Fragments* (Merlin, London, 1979). Chris Weedon 'Radical and revolutionary feminism' and 'Socialist feminism', in Frankie Ashton and Gill Whitting (eds), *Feminist Theories and Practical Policies* (School for Advanced Urban Studies, Bristol, 1987).
3. Carter, *idem*, p. 167.
4. Weedon ('Socialist feminism', *op. cit.* note 2) points out that Marxist feminists draw on Gramsci, Althusser and Poulantzas. Foucault's work on the 'deconstruction' of the language of socio-political arrangements to reveal the social construction of roles has also inspired socialist and radical feminists. See also Coote and Campbell, *op. cit.* note 2.
5. Randall, *op. cit.* note 2, pp. 9, 46–8, 250. Reena Bhavani, 'Race, women and class', in Ashton and Whitting, *op. cit.* note 2, pp. 30–1.
6. Lionel Tiger, *Men in Groups* (Thomas Nelson, London, 1969).
7. J. Barr, *New Society*, 17 Dec. 1964; *Sunday Times*, 11 June 1967. Central Office of Information, *Women in Britain* (HMSO, London, 1972).
8. Bouchier, *op. cit.* note 2, pp. 177–8.
9. Bouchier, *ibid*. Joni Lovenduski, 'Parliament, pressure groups, networks and the women's movement: the politics of abortion law reform in Britain', in Joni Lovenduski and Joyce Outshoorn (eds), *The New Politics of Abortion* (Sage, London and Beverly Hills, 1986), p. 61.
10. Randall, *op. cit.* note 2, p. 230.

11. Elizabeth Wilson, *Only Halfway to Paradise: Women in Postward Britain 1945–1968* (Tavistock, London, 1980), cited by Randall, *ibid*.
12. Norma Dolby, *Norma Dolby's Diary, An Account of the Great Miners' Strike*, (Verso, London, 1987).
13. Bouchier, *op. cit.* note 2, pp. 58–9, 118, 177–9.
14. Coote and Campbell, *op. cit.* note 2, pp. 20–4. Bouchier, *idem*, p. 93.
15. Bouchier, *idem*, pp. 111, 142.
16. *Idem*, pp. 217–23; Coote and Campbell, *op. cit.* note 2, p. 36; Randall, *op. cit.* note 2, pp. 254–7.
17. Bouchier, *idem*, pp. 178–9. See also Gill Whitting, 'The development of women's self-help groups', in Ashton and Whitting, *op. cit.* note 2, pp. 104–6, 107–14.
18. See Elizabeth Meehan, *Women's Rights at Work* (Macmillan, Basingstoke, 1985); Carter, *op. cit.* note 2; Jeanne Gregory, *Sex, Race and the Law* (Sage, London and Beverly Hills, 1987); Randall, *op. cit.* note 2.
19. Claire Callender estimates that over half the evidence submitted in the House of Lords came from women's groups: 'The development of the Sex Discrimination Act 1971–1975', unpublished dissertation submitted at Bristol University (1978).
20. Gregory, *op. cit.* note 18. See also Peggy Kahn and Elizabeth Meehan (eds), *Comparable Worth/Equal Value* (Macmillan, London, forthcoming); Leah Warwick, '1888 to 1988. From equal pay for equal work to equal pay for work of equal value. The changing role of the British trade union movement', unpublished dissertation submitted at Bath University (1988).
21. On maternity pay and allowances, see EOC, *12th Annual Report, 1987*. (HMSO, London, 1988). On part-time workers see the *Independent*, 2 Nov. 1987.
22. Christopher Johnson, *Lloyds Bank Economic Bulletin*, no. 115 (July 1988).
23. House of Commons, *Report of Select Committee on Social Services* (HMSO, London, 1988); reported in the *Observer*, 10 July 1988.
24. E.g. Hilary Land, 'Social policies and women in the labour market', in Ashton and Whitting, *op. cit.* note 2.
25. Information about this group is circulated by the Fawcett Society. Perhaps it should also be noted that the maternity grant, payable at birth, has become means-tested instead of universal: EOC, *op. cit.* note 21.
26. Heather Joshi, quoted by Land, *op. cit.* note 24, p. 87.
27. Catherine Hoskyns, 'Women, European law and transnational politics', *International Journal of Sociology of Law* (special issue, 1986).
28. Fawcett Society, *Annual Report for 1987–1988*; EOC, *op. cit.* note 21, chap. 4; A. Phillips, the *Independent*, 22 August 1988; P. Toynbee, the *Guardian*, 14 July 1988.
29. Lovenduski, *op. cit.* note 9, also provides good references to the range of abortion literature.
30. *Ibid*.
31. *Breaking Chains*, the newspaper of the ALRA; P. Toynbee, the *Guardian*, 5 May 1988; T. Lynch, the *Financial Times*, 6 May 1988; P. Wintour, P. Carvel, M. Linton and S. Tirbutt, the *Guardian*, 7 May 1988; M. Linton, the *Guardian*, 9 July 1988.
32. Coote and Campbell, *op. cit.* note 2, Elizabeth Vallance and Elizabeth Davies, *Women of Europe* (Cambridge University Press, 1986); Whitting, *op. cit.* note 17; Randall, *op. cit.* note 2; Carter, *op. cit.* note 1.
33. Clare Ungerson (ed), *Women and Social Policy : A Reader* (Macmillan Education, Basingstoke, 1985); Whitting, *ibid*; Land, *op. cit.* note 24.
34. Patrick Jenkin MP, quoted in Land, *idem*, p. 98.

Select Bibliography

Books

Banks, Olive (1981) *Faces of Feminism*, Blackwell, Oxford.

Banks, Olive (1985) *Biographical Dictionary of British Feminists, 1800–1930*, Wheatsheaf Books, Brighton.

Banks, Olive (1986) *Becoming a Feminist*, Wheatsheaf Books, Brighton.

Berkman, Joyce (1989) *The Healing Imagination of Olive Schreiner*, University of Massachusetts Press, Boston.

Berry, Paul and A. Bishop (1985) *Testament of a Generation: The Journalism of Vera Brittain and Winifred Holtby*, Virago, London.

Black, Naomi (1983) 'Virginia Woolf and the women's movement', in Jane Marcus (ed), *Virginia Woolf*, University of Nebraska Press, Lincoln, Nebraska.

Bouchier, David (1983) *The Feminist Challenge. The Movement for Women's Liberation in Britain and the United States*, Macmillan, London.

Brittain, Vera (1940) *Testament of Friendship: The Story of Winifred Holtby*, Macmillan, London (Virago, 1981).

Carter, April (1988) *The Politics of Women's Rights*, Longman, London.

Coote, Anna and Beatrix Campbell (1982) *Sweet Freedom: The Struggle for Women's Liberation*, Picador/Pan, London (2nd edn, 1987).

Doughan, David (1980) *Lobbying for Liberation: British Feminism 1918–1968*, City of London Polytechnic, London.

Eglin, Josephine (1987) 'Women and peace: from the suffragists to the Greenham women', in Richard Taylor and N. Young (eds), *Campaigns for Peace*, Manchester University Press.

First, Ruth and Ann Scott (1980) *Olive Schreiner*, Schocken, New York.

Fleming, Suzie (1986) 'Introduction', in Eleanor Rathbone, *The Disinherited Family*, Falling Wall Press, London (originally published 1924).

Garner, Les (1984) *Stepping Stones to Women's Liberty: Feminist Ideas in the Women's Suffrage Movement 1900–1918*, Hutchinson, London.

Hall, Ruth (1977) *Marie Stopes*, Virago, London.

Harrison, Brian (1981) 'Women's health and the women's movement', in Charles Webster (ed), *Biology, Medicine and Society, 1840–1940*, Cambridge Univerity Press.

Harrison, Brian (1983) 'Women's suffrage at Westminster, 1866–1928', in Michael Bentley and J. Stevenson (eds), *High and Low Politics in Modern Britain*, Clarendon, Oxford.

Harrison, Brian (1987) *Prudent Revolutionaries: Portraits of British Feminists Between the Wars*, Clarendon, Oxford.

Holton, Sandra Stanley (1986) *Feminism and Democracy. Women's Suffrage and Reform Politics in Britian 1900–1918*, Cambridge University Press.

Hopkinson, Diana (1954) *Family Inheritance. A Life of Eva Hubback*, Staples Press, London.

Jeffreys, Sheila (1985) *The Spinster and Her Enemies: Feminism and Sexuality 1880–1930*, Pandora, London.

Kent, Susan Kingsley (1987) *Sex and Suffrage in Britain 1860–1914*, Princeton University Press.

Leathard, Audrey (1980) *The Fight for Family Planning*, Macmillan, London.

Levine, Philippa (1987) *Victorian Feminism 1850–1900*, Hutchinson, London.

Lewis, Jane (1980) *The Politics of Motherhood*, Croom Helm, London.

Lewis, Jane (1984) *Women in England 1870–1950*, Wheatsheaf Books, Brighton.

Lewis, Jane (ed) (1983) *Women's Welfare/Women's Rights*, Croom Helm, London.

Liddington, Jill (1984) *The Life and Times of a Respectable Rebel: Selina Cooper 1864–1946*, Virago, London.

Liddington, Jill and Jill Norris (1978) *One Hand Tied Behind Us. The Rise of the Women's Suffrage Movement*, Virago, London.

Linklater, Andro (1980) *An Unhusbanded Life. Charlotte Despard, Suffragette, Socialist and Sinn Feiner*, Hutchinson, London.

Lovenduski, Joni (1986) 'Parliament, pressure groups, networks and the women's movement: the politics of abortion law reform in Britain', in Joni Lovenduski and Joyce Outshoorn (eds), *The New Politics of Abortion*, Sage, London.

Macnicol, John (1980) *The Movement for Family Allowances 1918–45: A Study in Social Policy Development*, Hutchinson, London.

Meehan, Elizabeth (1985) *Women's Rights at Work. Campaigns and Policy in Britain and the United States*, Macmillan, Basingstoke.

Mitchell, Juliet and Ann Oakley (eds) (1986) *What is Feminism?* Pantheon, New York.

Newsome, Stella (1957) *The Women's Freedom League 1907–1957*, Women's Freedom League, London

Randall, Vicky (1987) *Women and Politics*, Macmillan Education, Basingstoke.

Rathbone, Eleanor (1929) *Milestones: Presidential Addresses at the Annual Council Meetings of the NUSEC*, Lee and Nightingale, Liverpool.

Rendall, Jane (ed) (1987) *Equal or Different: Women's Politics 1800–1914*, Blackwell, Oxford.

Riley, Denise (1983) *War in the Nursery*, Virago, London.

Romero, Patricia (1987) *E. Sylvia Pankhurst. Portrait of a Radical*, Yale University Press, New Haven, Conn.

Rowbotham, Sheila (1977) *A New World for Women: Stella Browne – Socialist Feminist*, Pluto Press, London.

Smith, Harold L. (1986) 'The effect of the war on the status of women', in Harold L. Smith (ed), *War and Social Change: British Society in the Second World War*, Manchester University Press.

Soloway, Richard (1982) *Birth Control and the Population Question in England, 1877–1930*, University of North Carolina Press, Chapel Hill, North Carolina.

Spender, Dale (1982) *Women of Ideas*, Routledge & Kegan Paul, London.

Spender, Dale (1984) *Time and Tide Wait for No Man*, Pandora, London.

Spender, Dale (ed) (1983) *Feminist Theorists*, Women's Press, London.

Stetson, Dorothy (1982) *A Woman's Issue: The Politics of Family Law Reform in England*, Greenwood Press, Westport, Conn.

Stocks, Mary (1949) *Eleanor Rathbone*, Gollancz, London.

Strachey, Ray (ed) (1936) *Our Freedom and Its Results*, Hogarth Press, London.

Vellacott, Jo (1987) 'Feminist consciousness and the First World War', in Ruth R. Pearson (ed), *Women and Peace*, Croom Helm, London.

Vernon, Betty (1982) *Ellen Wilkinson*, Croom Helm, London.

Vicinus, Martha (1985) *Independent Women: Work and Community for Single Women 1850–1920*, Chicago University Press.

Weedon, C. (1987) 'Radical and revolutionary feminism', in F. Ashton and G.

Whitting (eds), *Feminist Theories and Practical Policies: Shifting the Agenda in the 1980s*, School for Advanced Urban Studies, Bristol.

Weedon, C. (1987) 'Socialist feminism', in *ibid*.

Wilson, Elizabeth (1980) *Only Halfway to Paradise: Women in Postwar Britain 1945–1968*, Tavistock, London.

Wiltsher, Anne (1985) *Most Dangerous Women: Feminist Peace Campaigners of the Great War*, Pandora, London.

Articles

Davin, Anna (1978) 'Imperialism and motherhood', *History Workshop*, vol. 5, pp. 9–65.

Harrison, Brian (1986) 'Women in a men's house: the women MPs, 1919–1945', *Historical Journal*, vol. 29, no. 3, pp. 623–54.

Kent, Susan (1988) 'The politics of sexual difference: World War I and the demise of British feminism', *Journal of British Studies*, vol. 27 (July), pp. 232–53.

Lewis, Jane (1975) 'Beyond suffrage: English feminism in the 1920s', *The Maryland Historian*, vol. 7 (Spring), pp. 1–17.

Lewis, Jane (1978) 'The English movement for family allowances, 1917–1945', *Histoire Sociale*, vol. 11 (November), pp. 441–59.

Lewis, Jane (1979) 'The ideology and politics of birth control in interwar England', *Women's Studies International Quarterly*, vol. 2, no. 1, pp. 33–48.

Mellown, Muriel (1987) 'Lady Rhondda and the changing faces of British feminism', *Frontiers*, vol. 9, no. 2, pp. 7–13.

Offen, Karen (1988) 'Defining feminism: a comparative historical approach', *Signs*, vol. 14 (Autumn), pp. 119–57.

Rowan, Caroline (1982) 'Women in the Labour Party, 1906–1920', *Feminist Review*, vol. 12 (October), pp. 74–91.

Smith, Harold L. (1978) 'The issue of "equal pay for equal work" in Great Britain', *Societas*, vol. 8 (Winter), pp. 39–52.

Smith, Harold L. (1981) 'The problem of "equal pay for equal work" in Great Britain during World War II', *The Journal of Modern History*, vol. 53 (December), pp. 652–72.

Smith, Harold L. (1984) 'Sex vs. class: British feminists and the Labour movement', *The Historian*, vol. 47 (November), pp. 19–37.

Smith, Harold L. (1984) 'The womanpower problem in Great Britain during the Second World War', *The Historical Journal*, vol. 27 (December), pp. 925–45.

Index